Thomson Round Hall

PRE-NUPTIAL AGREEMENTS

UNITED KINGDOM

Sweet & Maxwell Ltd
London

AUSTRALIA

Law Book Co. Ltd
Sydney

CANADA AND THE USA

Carswell
Toronto

NEW ZEALAND

Brookers
Wellington

SINGAPORE AND MALAYSIA

Sweet and Maxwell
Singapore and Kuala Lumpur

Thomson Round Hall

Pre-Nuptial Agreements

Ross Aylward

DUBLIN
THOMSON ROUND HALL
2006

Published in 2006 by
Thomson Round Hall Ltd
43 Fitzwilliam Place
Dublin 2
Ireland

Typeset by
Siobhán Mulholland

Printed by
ColourBooks, Dublin

10 Digit ISBN: 1-85800-464-0
13 Digit ISBN: 978-1-85800-464-8

A catalogue record for this book
is available from the British Library.

Table of Contents

Preface

The origins of this book can be traced back to an M.Litt research thesis I undertook at Trinity College Dublin in 2006. Having never even contemplated publishing my work, I am both surprised and humbled by the fact that I now sit here writing a preface. Family law has always been of interest to me due to the human element involved. It represents perhaps the most vibrant and dynamic area of law in Ireland today. Despite this, there are serious shortcomings evident throughout this field of law, none more so than in the law concerning marriage.

Marriage in Ireland has undergone significant reform in recent years, both socially and legally. Traditionally, marriage has been deemed the life-long union of one man and one woman. The introduction of divorce, however, has removed the very element perceived to render marriage unique; its perpetualness. On this basis, it is evident that marriage as a concept is amenable to change. Unfortunately, reform in this area seems to be focussed on the termination of marriage, with little attention being paid to the formation stage. Historically, marriage has been subject to state regulation, however, for reasons postulated in this book this should no longer be the case. As marriage represents one of the most intimate moments in an individual's life, it ought to be formulated to cater for each individual's needs.

At present, pre-nuptial agreements are an unknown concept within the Irish legal system. There is evidence of their availability through various solicitors, but their standing in Irish law has yet to be determined. With this in mind, this book attempts to foresee possible grounds upon which pre-nuptial agreements may be deemed enforceable, and also certain factors that ought to be borne in mind when constructing such a contract. In order to do this, an analysis is conducted as to the approach taken in other jurisdictions where such agreements are enforceable. Furthermore, several grounds are submitted for the enforceability of such agreements based on the law as it stands at present in Ireland.

I would like to take this opportunity to thank a number of people who have assisted me in various ways in the writing of this book.

First, and foremost, I would like to thank Professor William Binchy who acted as my supervisor at Trinity College Dublin whilst I was completing my M.Litt thesis. His support, advice, encouragement, generosity of time and unparalleled knowledge was much appreciated throughout the year. Also, a debt of gratitude is owed to Dr Oran Doyle whose lectures in Jurisprudence at undergraduate level provided much of the impetus for the moral debate contained throughout this book. Furthermore, his comments and thoughts at the beginning of the year were of great assistance in providing a sense of clarity to some of the topics dealt with in the early chapters of this book. I would also like to thank the staff of the Berkeley Library, University of Dublin, for their assistance.

Of special note, I would like to thank the staff at Thomson Round Hall, in particular Catherine Dolan and Una McCann, for their assistance and expertise in bringing this book to publication.

I also thank my friends and colleagues who have supported and encouraged me throughout my studies, and in the completion of this book. I would like to thank my family who have provided me with great love, support and encouragement throughout my life, without which I would not have been in a position to undertake this book. Finally, I would like to thank Lynne for her unwavering love, support and patience; long may it last!

I have endeavoured to state the law as it stands on August 23, 2006. Whilst this book is designed to analyse and comment on the possible enforceability of pre-nuptial agreements in Ireland, it is not intended to form the basis for the construction of a pre-nuptial agreement and, as such, no liability is accepted by the author for any agreements so constructed. The author welcomes any comments in relation to this work, and is contactable at rossaylward@gmail.com.

Ross Aylward
Dublin
August 23, 2006.

Table of Legislation

TABLE OF CASES

1. The Family in Ireland

A pre-nuptial agreement is designed to regulate the course and, if necessary, the termination of a marriage. Such a contract causes the parties to predetermine the structure of their marriage. Consequently, pre-nuptial agreements may seek to regulate an infinite variety of related matters ranging from the form a marriage might take, to the division of assets upon its termination. It is clear that such contracts can touch upon various aspects of social life. In turn, there is a need to regulate these agreements. Notwithstanding the typical implications associated with pre-nuptial agreements, there are added complications concerning their enforcement in an Irish context.

The concept of a pre-nuptial agreement has constitutional implications in Ireland as marriage is the cornerstone of family life and, consequently, any interference with marriage has possible ramifications for the constitutionally protected entity that is the family. Therefore, one must first understand the role the "family" plays in Irish constitutional law before assessing the validity of pre-nuptial agreements. Within such an analysis it is necessary to consider the importance of the institution of marriage in Irish society, and whether it should be the fundamental building-block upon which a family is based.

This first chapter illustrates the need to reassess marriage and the "family" in Irish law. Recent developments in Irish society demonstrate a divergence between the legal definition of the "family" and the sociological definition. Furthermore, the interpretation and significance of marriage has developed beyond traditional Roman Catholic viewpoints, thereby generating a need for reform.

THE FAMILY IN IRELAND

The main constitutional provision dealing with the "family" is Art.41, within which the family is deemed to be the "natural primary and fundamental unit group of Society".[1] Furthermore, the courts have deemed that the "family referred to in [Art.41] is the family which is founded on the institution of marriage".[2] As such, the State is required to "guard with special care the institution of Marriage ... and to protect it against attack".[3]

---

[1] Art.41.1.1°.
[2] *State (Nicolau) v An Bord Uchtála* [1966] I.R. 567 at 643.
[3] Art.41.3.1°.

The concept of the "family" being the cornerstone of society is not unique to Ireland.[4]

At the time of drafting of the Constitution the "family" was an important entity in Irish society and as such received significant constitutional protection. At the heart of this mindset was Roman Catholic teaching, in particular the Papal Encyclical *"Quadragesimo Anno"* which promoted the concept of "subsidiarity". This mandate states to protect and support small groups in society, including the family, and to protect the position of the family in society so as to prevent it from being undermined. This philosophy was adhered to in Art.41.1.1° of the Constitution where the rights of the "family" are described as being "inalienable and imprescriptible rights, antecedent and superior to all positive law".

In *Ryan v Attorney-General*[5] Kenny J. shed some light on the meaning of "inalienable and imprescriptible" when he said:

"'Inalienable' means that which cannot be transferred or given away while 'imprescriptible' means that which cannot be lost by the passage of time or abandoned by non-exercise".[6]

As is clear from the dicta of Kenny J., the protection of the rights of the family are substantial; however, it is important to note that these rights are not absolute.[7]

The rights set out in Arts 41 and 42 of the Constitution were designed to protect the family unit from unnecessary interference from the State and did not grant any rights to individual members of the family.[8] In its Report in 1996 the Constitution Review Group was of the opinion that the inclusion and judicial interpretation of the adjectives "inalienable and imprescriptible" have resulted in the rights of the "family" being overly

---

[4]   See Art.16 of the Social Charter of Europe (1961); Art.23 International Treaty on Civil Rights; Art.10 of the International Charter on Economic, Social, and Cultural Rights; Art.16 of the Universal Declaration of Human Rights. Also Art.21(1) of the Greek Constitution describes the family as "the cornerstone of the preservation and the advancement of the Nation". Indeed the sentiments expressed in Art.41 are remarkably similar to those in Art.119 of the Weimar Constitution of 1919, which stated:

"… It is the task of both the state and the communities to strengthen and socially promote the family …" Also the preamble of the Doha Declaration, adopted by the UN as a Resolution in 2004 states:

"the family is not only the fundamental group unit of society but it is also the fundamental agent for sustainable social, economic and cultural development." See UN Resolution A/Res/59/111, adopted December 6, 2005.

[5]   [1965] 2 I.R. 294.

[6]   *ibid.* at 308.

[7]   *Murray v Ireland* [1985] I.R. 532.

[8]   *L v L* [1992] 2 I.R. 77 at 108.

protected in comparison to the rights of the individual family members.[9] The Group recommended that "inalienable and imprescriptible" be deleted from constitutional provisions relating to the family so as to realign the balance of rights between the family unit and individual members of the family.[10]

However, at present there is no sign of any such constitutional amendment. Therefore, it is evident that, upon marriage, husband and wife form a formidable legal entity in Ireland. As such it is fair to comment that marriage in Ireland is the gateway to a plethora of rights and privileges under the guise of the "family". The question to be asked, however, is whether this concept of the family based on marriage accords with the modern realities of Irish society.

The marital family—an extinct ideal?

As is clear from the Constitution, the definition of "family" is one based on marriage. Yet the definition of marriage itself is up for debate, and the following chapter analyses in detail the definition of marriage. Suffice it to say for present purposes that marriage is traditionally defined as a:

"voluntary union for life of one man and one woman to the exclusion of all others".[11]

As noted by the Constitution Review Group, "Articles 41 and 42 were heavily influenced by Roman Catholic teaching and Papal encyclicals. They were clearly drafted with only one family in mind, namely, the family based on marriage."[12]

Indeed the present-day view of the Catholic Church is that the family should still be based on the institution of marriage.[13] As a result, the

---

9   Constitution Review Group, *Report of the Constitution Review Group* (Government Publications, 1996), p.323.
10   *ibid.* at 336.
11   *Hyde v Hyde and Woodmansee* [1861–1873] All E.R. Rep. 175.
12   Constitution Review Group, *Report of the Constitution Review Group* (Government Publications, 1996), p.319. Sheehy, however, argues that the constitutional framework for marriage was not influenced by Catholic teachings at the time of drafting, but instead was a consolidation of the law in that area which had remained undisturbed for decades beforehand. See Sheehy, "The Right to Marry in the Irish Tradition of the Common Law" in O'Reilly (ed.), *Human Rights & Constitutional Law: Essays in Honour of Brian Walsh* (Round Hall Press, 1992), p.13.
13   See the various submissions from Roman Catholic lobbying groups in All Party Oireachtas Committee, "10th Progress Report: The Family" (Government Publications, 2006), Appendix 3.

institution of marriage, from which a "family" is established, has been strongly protected by the Irish courts.

The seminal case illustrating this is that of *Murphy v Attorney-General*[14] where the plaintiffs, a married couple, argued that certain provisions in the Income Tax Act 1967 discriminated against married couples in favour of non-marital couples. It was claimed that the taxation scheme, which regarded a married couple's income as constituting one income, subjected married couples to greater taxation than non-marital couples whose incomes were assessed separately for taxation purposes. The Supreme Court found for the plaintiffs on the basis that such a tax provision breached the State's obligation to protect the institution of marriage against attack as it acted as a disincentive to enter into marriage. The principle enunciated in *Murphy* has been expanded and applied in other fields such as social welfare[15] and administrative law.[16] Central to the reasoning of the courts is that the institution of marriage should not be undermined by other family forms.

In the past 20 years there have been several attempts, mainly in the area of guardianship claims by natural fathers, to have the rights and duties enjoyed by the marital family extended to other family forms, most commonly the *de facto* family. Nevertheless, the courts have repeatedly adopted a narrow approach, only recognising the traditional nuclear family.

It was originally stated in the case of *State (Nicolau) v An Bord Uchtála*[17] that the only family recognised in Irish law was that based on marriage; therefore, the natural father has no constitutional right to guardianship of his child. Henchy J. was of the view that:

> "For the State to award equal constitutional protection to the family founded on marriage and the 'family' founded on an extra-marital union would in effect be a disregard of the pledge which the State gives in Article 41, s.3, sub-s.1 to guard with special care the institution of marriage."[18]

This decision was upheld in *K v W*[19] and more recently in *WO'R v EH*.[20] In *Nicolau* and *K v W* the courts were reluctant to expand the scope of fam-

---

[14]   [1982] I.R. 241.
[15]   *Hyland v Minister for Social Welfare* [1989] I.R. 624; [1990] I.L.R.M. 213.
[16]   *Greene v Minister for Agriculture* [1990] 2 I.R. 17; [1990] I.L.R.M. 364.
[17]   [1966] I.R. 567.
[18]   *ibid.* at 622.
[19]   [1990] 2 I.R. 437.
[20]   [1996] 2 I.R. 248.

ily rights to encompass natural fathers on the basis that it could give the appearance that the courts were equating a relationship potentially borne out of an act of "casual commerce"[21] with a relationship based on the institution of marriage. To do so, the courts felt, would be to undermine the institution of marriage.

Such reasoning is palatable. Nonetheless, the facts in *WO'R* were quite the opposite. In this case the father and mother were not married, but were in a relationship for 11 years during which they had two children, the second of which was planned. The father and mother split when the children were aged 11 and six. Two years later the mother married and then sought to have her husband made guardian of the two children; the natural father objected and sought guardianship himself. It was argued on behalf of the applicant father that the relationship between the natural father and his children bore all the hallmarks of family life that one would expect, except that the father and mother had never been married. On these facts it was claimed that there was a de facto family and that therefore the natural father should have constitutional rights.

Despite these facts the Supreme Court was not prepared to extend the rights enunciated under Arts 41 and 42 to such a relationship due to the absence of marriage. It was noted by the court that the relationship between the father and mother in which the children had been brought up had been a stable, loving and caring one but that this could only be a factor taken into account by the court and no more. The court held that "the concept of a '*de facto*' family is unknown to the Irish Constitution"[22] and as such marriage was still the requirement for there to be a family.

This issue came before the courts again in *Ennis v Butterly*.[23] Here, the plaintiff and defendant cohabited, but they were both married to other parties. Upon the breakdown of their relationship the plaintiff sought to enforce an agreement entered into by herself and the defendant. The alleged contract effectively stated that they would cohabit as man and wife until divorce became legal so that they could then marry each other. Essentially the court had to determine if such a cohabitation contract could be enforced in Ireland or whether it would be contrary to public policy. Following the reasoning of the Supreme Court in *Nicolau*, Kelly J. held that "the public policy of this State ordains that non-marital cohabitation does not and cannot have the same constitutional status as marriage".[24] To

---

21   *State (Nicolau) v An Bord Uchtála* [1966] I.R. 567 at 641.
22   *WO'R v EH* [1996] 2 I.R. 248 at 270.
23   [1996] 1 I.R. 426.
24   *ibid.* at 438.

recognise extra-marital family forms would be to dilute the institution of marriage which the State pledged to protect.

Therefore, as is clear from the above case law, the concept of a "family" for the purposes of Irish law is firmly based on the requirement of marriage; no other forms of family are recognised. It is now necessary to determine whether the attitude of the Irish courts fairly reflects the reality of Irish society and to question whether a broader definition ought to be given to the "family". In doing so, the relevant European Court of Human Rights decisions will be examined in order to provide alternative views to the problems based on the definition of the family which the Irish courts have tackled as of late. It will then be necessary to decide whether the "family" ought to be redefined in Irish law and, if so, in what manner. If such is the case then marriage, as it is currently interpreted in legal discourse, needs to be reassessed so as to become more inclusive. As shall be seen, a corollary of such an assessment is the possibility of pre-nuptial agreements becoming enforceable under Irish law.

Developments in Irish society

As is evident from the case law, the "family", as recognised under the Constitution, is one based solely on marriage. Irish society, however, has changed dramatically over the last 20 years, and as such it is now questionable whether the constitutional definition of the family fairly reflects society's perception of the family. These changes are not merely legal, but also cultural and economic.

The main legal change has been the introduction of divorce following a referendum in 1995, resulting in the Family Law (Divorce) Act 1996. The effect of the divorce amendment was to alter the entire reasoning behind Arts 41 and 42. Gone is the lifelong commitment and the unique nature of marriage, thereby raising the question of whether it is deserving of the sole entitlement to the constitutional rights and protections it receives.

In 2005 there were 4,096 applications for divorce in the Circuit Court, and 30 in the High Court, representing a slight increase on the previous year.[25] Notwithstanding this, one cannot calculate the true extent of marital breakdown solely from divorce figures. Cliquet states that one must combine the number of divorces with the separation figures of cohabiting couples in order to obtain a true picture of the extent of mari-

---

[25]   Courts Service, *Annual Report 2005* (Government Publications, 2006), p.26.

tal breakdown in a society.[26] In its report, titled "10th Progress Report: The Family", the All Party Oireachtas Committee noted that the number of separated or divorced people has risen dramatically over the last two decades. In 1986 there were 37,000 separated persons; in 1996 this had risen to 88,000; and in 2002 the number stood at 134,000.[27] As there are approximately 692,000 married couples in Ireland, this means that on average one in five marriages have broken down.

Perhaps the biggest change in relation to marriage and the "family" in Ireland has been social in character. Society's perception of family life and marriage has altered dramatically in the last 20 years. This was noted by the Constitution Review Group in 1996 when it reported that "an exclusively marriage based definition of the family ... no longer accords with the social structure in Ireland".[28] A number of social factors have contributed to this, including the increase in the number of cohabiting couples and the increase in extra-marital births.

According to the 2002 census 77,600 couples were cohabiting, representing 8.4 per cent of all family units, compared to 3.9 per cent in 1996. The number of same-sex couples cohabiting also rose dramatically in this period from 150 to 1,300. Also, the number of extra-marital births had increased from 14.5 per cent in 1990 to 31.2 per cent in 2001.[29] Coinciding with these changes is the increase in the average age of those getting married. It is thought that this is due to prevailing economic pressures forcing people to accumulate wealth first, to enter the property market and to achieve stability and security in their lives before making the commitment of marriage.

A further economic development illustrating the changing views toward married life was introduced in the 2000 Budget by the then Minister for Finance, Charlie McCreevy. He introduced an amendment to the tax code so as to favour couples with two incomes, thereby encouraging married women to enter the workforce. Such an attitude reflects the modern shift toward recognising a married couple as in fact being two indi-

---

[26] Cliquet, "Major Trends Affecting Families in the New Millennium—Western Europe and North America" Report for United Nations, Department of Economic and Social Affairs, Division for Social Policy and Development, Program on the Family (2003), available online at http://www.un.org/esa/socdev/family/Publications/mtcliquet.pdf

[27] All Party Oireachtas Committee, "10th Progress Report: The Family" (Government Publications, 2006), p.26.

[28] Constitution Review Group, *Report of the Constitution Review Group* (Government Publications, 1996), p.332.

[29] Treoir, *Births Outside Marriage 1990–2001* (October 2002), p.1.

viduals forming a unit and not simply a unit, thereby reducing the conceptual divide between married couples and cohabiting couples as interpreted by the courts thus far.

As is evident, Irish society has become more accepting of various forms of family units beyond that based on marriage. The concept of the nuclear family has become outmoded and no longer accurately reflects Irish society. The growth in family diversity has also been accompanied by the increase of inter-generational reliance within the traditional nuclear family. This has been caused mainly by economic pressures whereby mothers are being forced into the workplace in order to contribute to the family income in today's economy. This has resulted in a dramatic increase in the number of children being cared for in crèches, which has subsequently increased the cost of childcare to astronomical levels. As a result, many working parents are relying on their own parents to mind their children, thereby extending the nuclear family which, it is predicted, will lead to closer ties between grandparents and grandchildren in the future.[30]

The change in society's perception of the "family" has been implicitly recognised by the Government in its establishment of the Family Support Agency (FSA) pursuant to the Family Support Agency Act 2001. In its strategic plan the FSA did not limit its scope to the family based on marriage, but rather acknowledged the diversity of family life in modern Ireland.

Irish society is not alone in its changing views of the "family"; Daly and Clavero remark that throughout Europe the "family" is being redefined in a manner that "focus[es] on the obligations of parenthood as distinct from conjugal ties … Family solidarity is being reinterpreted and redefined to refer to parental responsibility rather than spouses or partners' solidarity towards each other."[31]

As is evident, the Irish constitutional definition of the family no longer accords with society's perception. This has resulted in a distinct lack of constitutional protection to those who form a family in the eyes of society, but not in the eyes of the Constitution. This problem was noted by Archbold a number of years ago in relation to the law in Northern Ireland when she stated:

---

[30] Daly and O'Leary, "Family Life in Ireland—Challenges for the Future", Report of Public Consultation Fora (Department of Social & Family Affairs, 2004), p.23.

[31] Daly and Clavero, *Contemporary Family Policy in Ireland & Europe* (School of Sociology & Social Policy, Queen's University, Belfast, 2002), p.107.

"Marriage is no longer the only, or even the preferred life choice
for enormous numbers of people ... and if our legal system
ignores these trends, it risks becoming irrelevant, and worse,
providing no legal protection to people who may be in great
need of it."[32]

Following a Hartian[33] approach, the current "rule of recognition" in Irish
law is that of popular sovereignty[34]; therefore, it is argued that the Constitution ought to accord with what the people of Ireland deem to be a
"family". Similar sentiments were expressed by the Australian Law Reform Commission which stated:

"... generally speaking the law should not inhibit the formation
of family relationships and should recognise as valid the relationships people choose for themselves. Further, the law should
support and protect those relationships."[35]

As is clear from the facts as presented, the narrow prescriptive approach
adopted by the Irish courts thus far to defining the "family" is at odds with
social reality. It is therefore now necessary to analyse the broader approach adopted by other courts, most notably the European Court of Human Rights (hereinafter referred to as the ECtHR), where one is directly
able to compare and contrast the narrow and broad approaches in relation
to the Irish cases that were appealed to the ECtHR.

BROAD "FUNCTIONAL" APPROACH

Under this approach one is not concerned with the form a family takes,
but rather with the nature of the relationship between those claiming to
be family members. Such an approach has been adopted by the ECtHR
over the past two decades and, following the incorporation of the European Convention on Human Rights (ECHR) into Irish law,[36] one must now
consider this approach, that to date has eluded the Irish courts.

---

[32] Archbold, "Divorce—The View From the North" in Shannon (ed.), *The Divorce Act in Practice* (Round Hall, Dublin, 1999), p.50.

[33] Hart, *The Concept of Law* (2nd ed., Oxford Clarendon Press, 1994), Chap.6.

[34] *Re Article 26 of the Constitution and the Regulation of Information (Services outside the State for the Termination of Pregnancies) Bill 1995* [1995] 1 I.R. 1; [1995] 2 I.L.R.M. 81. See Doyle, "Legal Validity: Reflections on the Irish Constitution" (2003) 25 D.U.L.J. 56

[35] Australian Law Reform Commission Paper No. 47, *Multiculturalism and Family Law* (1991), para.24.

[36] European Convention of Human Rights Act 2003.

Article 8(1) of the ECHR states:

"Everyone has the right to respect for his private and family life, his home and his correspondence."

In its interpretation of this Article the ECtHR has taken an expansive view of what constitutes "family life" which has kept pace with the evolving nature of society throughout Europe. Not only does it include the traditional family based on marriage but also the relationships of a non-marital cohabiting couple with a child,[37] one-parent families,[38] an estranged father and his child,[39] children and their grandparents,[40] siblings,[41] and an uncle and his nephew.[42] As is evident, under this approach "family life" is determined on a case-by-case basis, focusing on the relationship and ties between the parties.

In 1979 the ECtHR was faced with the then prevalent practice of distinguishing between "legitimate" and "illegitimate" children.[43] Belgian law at the time denied "illegitimate" children many of the rights conferred on "legitimate" children, especially in the area of succession law. The court held that Art.8 draws no distinction between "legitimate" and "illegitimate" children and that a single woman and her child form a family under Art.8.[44] Such protection does not merely prohibit unnecessary state interference with "family life", but also requires the state to take positive action in order to respect family life. The court was of the opinion that from the moment of a child's birth a family is created.

A similar case from Ireland came before the ECtHR in 1986. The applicant in *Johnston v Ireland*[45] had been married but was now separated and living with his partner and their daughter. Due to the non-availability of divorce at that time in Ireland, the applicant was unable to marry his partner and as a result their daughter was deemed "illegitimate". The ECtHR held that the applicant and his cohabiting partner of 15 years, with their child, did form a family for the purposes of Art.8 notwithstanding the non-marital status of their relationship.[46] Nevertheless, the court held

---

[37] *Johnston v Ireland* (1987) 9 E.H.R.R. 203.
[38] *Marckx v Belgium* (1980) 2 E.H.R.R. 330.
[39] *Keegan v Ireland* (1994) 18 E.H.R.R. 342.
[40] *ibid.* at para.45.
[41] *Olsson v Sweden* (1989) 11 E.H.R.R. 259.
[42] *Boyle v UK*, No. *16580/90*, Comm Rep. 9.2.93.
[43] *Marckx v Belgium* (1980) 2 E.H.R.R. 330.
[44] *ibid.* at para.31.
[45] *Johnston v Ireland* (1987) 9 E.H.R.R. 203.
[46] *ibid.* at para.56.

that Ireland's failure to introduce a scheme of divorce was not an unjust interference with the applicant's family life under Art.8. Importantly, however, the court reiterated the point that it had made in the *Marckx* case that respect for "family life" under Art.8 requires that the ties that exist between near relatives impose an obligation on the state to act in a manner so as to allow these ties to develop normally.[47]

This is illustrative of the broad functional approach adopted by the ECtHR in its recognition of what constitutes a family. By concentrating on the ties between near relatives the court focuses on the nature of the relationship, and not its form.

In relation to the narrow prescriptive approach of the Irish courts in recognising what constitutes a family, the case of *K v W*[48] was referred to. The applicant in that case was an estranged father of a child who sought guardianship of his child so as to prevent the mother from putting the child up for adoption. Having exhausted the legal process in Ireland to no avail, he brought his case to the ECtHR where it was alleged that his lack of guardianship rights violated his Art.8 right to family life.[49] This case clearly illustrates the difference between the narrow prescriptive approach and the broad functional approach. Essentially the argument put forward by the Government was based on the jurisprudence of the Irish courts to date, that a relationship outside of marriage cannot be capable of forming a family as it is too unstable and lacks the commitment inherent in marriage. In contrast, the applicant's argument, which ultimately prevailed, was based on previous decisions of the ECtHR invoking the broad functional approach. The ECtHR firmly demonstrated its opinion that the broad functional approach was superior to the narrow prescriptive approach when it stated:

> "… the notion of the 'family' in [Article 8] is not confined solely to marriage-based relationships and may encompass other *de facto* 'family' ties where the parties are living together outside of marriage."[50]

In relation to the specific facts of the case before it, the court held that the two-year relationship between the applicant and the mother of his

---

[47] *ibid.* at para.74.
[48] [1990] 2 I.R. 437.
[49] *Keegan v Ireland* (1994) 18 E.H.R.R. 342.
[50] *ibid.* at para.44.

child, the plan to get married and the deliberate decision to bear a child bore all the hallmarks of "family life" for the purposes of Art.8.[51]

It is submitted that by adopting this broad functional approach to recognising a family, the ECtHR has been able to develop its case law in accordance with the developments that it has witnessed in society throughout the years. The *Keegan* decision is illustrative of this as, in an age where marriage rates are declining[52] and cohabitation of non-marital couples is increasing, the court was prepared to expand the definition of "family life" to encompass these new family units so as to protect them and to foster respect for them.

There have been significant academic[53] and social[54] calls for the introduction of a functional approach into Irish law. It has been noted that:

> "[Ireland] is seen to be undergoing a process of transition from
> the type of family norm envisaged in the Constitution to a soci-
> ety where more mothers are employed, families are smaller,
> marital breakdown is more frequent and ethnic diversity more
> widespread."[55]

This debate has been particularly active in the past year as the All Party Oireachtas Committee heard submissions and prepared its "10th Progress Report: The Family". From the submissions received it is clear that there is a divide as to how best to approach the task of redefining the family. Those in favour of retaining the traditional approach largely based their arguments on the reasoning that the traditional approach has stood the test of time and has resulted in many happy families throughout the country and therefore should not be disturbed. However, it is submitted that such reasoning is fundamentally flawed for two reasons:

---

[51] *ibid.* at para.45.

[52] See Cliquet, "Major Trends Affecting Families in the New Millennium—Western Europe and North America" Report for United Nations, Department of Economic and Social Affairs, Division for Social Policy and Development, Program on the Family (2003), available online at http://www.un.org/esa/socdev/family/Publications/mtcliquet.pdf.

[53] See Ryan, "Family Diversity and Partnership Rights—Towards New Models of Recognition", presented to the Irish Council of Civil Liberties Partnership Rights and Family Diversity Consultation 2004. See also Ryan, "Recognising Family Diversity: Children, One-Parent Families and the Law" [2006] 1 I.J.F.L. 3.

[54] Daly and O'Leary, "Family Life in Ireland—Challenges for the Future", Report of Public Consultation Fora (Department of Social & Family Affairs, 2004), p.24.

[55] *ibid.*, p.57.

1) It is based on how the family has performed in Irish society in the past. But as can be seen from the demographic statistics, Irish society has changed dramatically in the last decade and continues to do so and everything seems to point to the conclusion that the current definition of the family cannot cope with such change.

2) The problem is not that families are failing or dysfunctional, but rather that an increasing portion of society is being excluded from the "family" category because of the current definition. The problem before us is not one of marital breakdown but is one of under-inclusiveness in the Constitution due to the current definition.

It is further submitted that the approach adopted by the Church of Ireland General Synod is favourable, in that:

> "[a] clear distinction needs to be made between the definition of marriage and the definition of the family. We favour the inclusion in the Constitution of a broad definition of the family which will not only continue to protect the institution of marriage but will also allow the State to recognise the numerous units which are generally regarded as family units but which are not marriage based."[56]

To achieve this it is argued that the broad functional approach is a superior method of judicial reasoning than that currently adopted by the Irish courts and is capable of coping with the changes that have occurred and indeed will continue to occur in Irish society. There are indications that Ireland is on the verge of adopting the broad functional approach. It seems the Oireachtas is becoming more aware of the need to recognise de facto families.[57] Nevertheless, this piecemeal change is not enough and the Equality Authority recommends that:

> "legal policy and codes should be systematically reformed to ensure that references to the family recognise the diversity of family forms, households and couple relationships."[58]

---

[56] All Party Oireachtas Committee, "10th Progress Report: The Family" (Government Publications, 2006), p.58.

[57] See Non-Fatal Offences Against the Person Act 1997; Domestic Violence Act 1996; Parental Leave Act 1998; Employment Equality Act 1998; Mental Health Act 2001 and the Residential Tenancies Act 2004.

[58] The Equality Authority, *Implementing Equality for Lesbians, Gays and Bisexuals* (Dublin, 2002), p.29.

Ireland's continuing perception of marriage as the bedrock of family life is no longer sustainable as more and more people choose to form different bases for their families. If the Constitution is indeed a "living"[59] document then it ought to develop with society. It is clear from the debate in this chapter that marriage ought not to be the basis for family life under the Constitution; as such, the institution of marriage is being overly protected under its current constitutional guise. Nevertheless, it is conceded that to attempt to redefine the "family" for the purposes of Art.41 is indeed an unenviable task, as noted by the Constitution Review Group.[60] Also, it is conceded that, if the "family" is to be redefined beyond the scope of marriage, the institution of marriage ought still to be accorded some level of protection under the Constitution, but such protection ought to be reduced from its current level.

It will be argued, however, that marriage itself ought to be redefined so as to reflect what the institution of marriage was intended to represent and not to discriminate against those who do not fall within the current definition. Marriage, although recognised as a public commitment, is better understood as a private commitment and therefore the element of choice ought to be accorded proper scope. Under such a redefinition it will become clear that there are indeed grounds for permitting pre-nuptial agreements in Irish law. The argument for choice and availability when it comes to marriage is pertinent in the current international debate in relation to same-sex marriage. In the next chapter I shall engage in this debate and use a degree of jurisprudential analysis in order to determine why the institution of marriage ought to be available to same-sex couples and in doing so will illustrate why people ought to be allowed to choose the form of marriage they wish to enter.

---

[59]   *Sinnott v Minister for Education* [2001] 2 I.R. 545 at 680. It is accepted that the Constitution is a dynamic document capable of representing contemporary mores. No one interpretation of the Constitution is intended to be final and determinative. This was alluded to by Walsh J. in *McGee v Attorney-General* [1974] I.R. 284 at 319 where he stated:

"The judges must, therefore, as best they can from their training and their experience interpret these rights in accordance with their ideas of prudence, justice and charity. It is but natural that from time to time the prevailing ideas of these virtues may be conditioned by the passage of time; no interpretation of the Constitution is intended to be final for all time."

Similarly, O'Higgins J. in *State (Healy) v Donoghue* [1976] I.R. 325 at 347 stated:

"[T]he Constitution did not seek to impose for all time the ideas prevalent or accepted with regard to these virtues at the time of its enactment."

[60]   Constitution Review Group, *Report of the Constitution Review Group* (Government Publications, 1996), p.321.

2. The Definition of Marriage

Marriage, in Irish law, has not been defined by the Constitution or the Oireachtas. Instead it has been judicially determined. The traditional definition provided by Lord Penzance in *Hyde v Hyde*[1] has been readily accepted by the courts in this jurisdiction throughout the years. The Supreme Court[2] affirmed the following definition enunciated by Costello J. in *Murray v Ireland*:

> "the Constitution makes clear that the concept and nature of marriage, which it enshrines, are derived from the Christian notion of a partnership based on an irrevocable personal consent, given by both spouses which establishes a unique and very special life-long relationship".[3]

However, marriage can no longer be defined in these terms as divorce has since been introduced into Irish law and, consequently, marriage ceases to be automatically classified as a "life-long relationship".

The definition of marriage is in a state of flux throughout the world at present, mainly due to the increasing calls to have it expanded so as to include same-sex couples. Traditionally, marriage has always been between a man and a woman, but an increasing number of jurisdictions are dispensing with the mixed-gender requirement and defining marriage in gender-neutral terms. An illustration of this development can be found in the *Oxford English Dictionary* where same-sex partnerships are acknowledged within the definition of "marriage".[4]

As noted in the previous chapter, Irish society is moving in a similar direction, albeit at a slower pace than our European counterparts and other common law jurisdictions. In the 2002 census it was noted that there were 1,300 same-sex couples cohabiting, compared to 150 in the 1996 census. This is indicative of the deterioration of the taboo surrounding homosexuality.[5]

---

[1] *Hyde v Hyde and Woodmansee* [1861–1873] All E.R. Rep. 175.

[2] *TF v Ireland* [1995] I.R. 321.

[3] *Murray v Ireland* [1985] I.R. 532 at 535.

[4] www.oed.com, accessed on March 13, 2006.

[5] It must be noted that there is general consensus that there are many more same-sex couples cohabiting, but who were not prepared to state this in the last census, mainly, it is thought, out of fear. See All Party Oireachtas Committee, "10th Progress Report: The Family" (Government Publications, 2006), at A89; submissions presented by The Gay Catholic Caucus.

We are living in an age where the institution of marriage as we know it is on the verge of great change. To date, this change has been piecemeal; however, there is strong argument to suggest that a radical overhaul of this institution is long overdue. It is time to question the State's role in marriage and determine if it is justified. Before doing so, it is worthwhile to analyse developments in other European countries so as to determine potential routes that Irish law may embark on.

THE OPENING UP OF MARRIAGE IN EUROPE

> "The right to marry is a right for everyone, without distinction. It cannot be understood as a privilege."[6]

> Maria Teresa Fernandez de la Vega,
> Deputy Prime Minister of Spain.

This statement was made in the run up to the introduction of same-sex marriage in Spain and it represents the changing view of marriage throughout Europe.[7] The origins of this revolution can be traced to Denmark, where in 1989 same-sex partnerships were legalised. However, it was the Netherlands that was the first country to allow same-sex couples to enter into civil marriage. In 2001 the Dutch legislature introduced the "Wet Openstelling Huwelijk" (Act of Opening Up of Marriage). The law as it now stands in the Netherlands states:

> "A marriage can be contracted by two persons of different sex or of the same sex".[8]

Two years later Belgium also amended its marriage law so as to allow same-sex couples to marry. The "Loi Ouvrant le Mariage a des Personnes de Même Sexe et Modificant Certaines Dispositions du Code Civil" (Law Opening up Marriage to Persons of the Same Sex and Amending Certain Provisions of the Civil Code) amended Art.143 of the Belgian Civil Code so as to read:

---

[6] Breaking News Top Stories Website, "Spain's Government approves gay marriage bill" issued December 30, 2004, www.breakingnews.ie/2004/12/30story182559.html.

[7] In general see Merin, *Equality for Same-Sex Couples: The Legal Recognition of Gay Partnerships in Europe and the United States* (University of Chicago Press, 2002); Waaldijk, "Others May Follow: The Introduction of Marriage, Quasi-Marriage and Semi-Marriage for Same-Sex Couples in European Countries" (2003–2004) 38 *New. Eng. L. Rev.* 569.

[8] s.1 of Art.30 of Book 1 of the Netherlands Code.

> "Two persons of different sex or of the same sex may contract
> into a marriage".

The Nordic countries[9] have not gone as far as the Netherlands and Belgium, but instead have introduced what has been described as *quasi-marriages*[10] in that they are based on marriage but do not grant all the rights and privileges attached to marriage. France, however, has introduced a scheme of registered partnerships[11] whereby non-marital heterosexual and same-sex couples can register their relationship and receive legal protection in various fields, *e.g.* property and taxation. Such a scheme as is operating in France is termed a "presumptive scheme" and the Law Reform Commission has recommended that this approach be adopted in Ireland in relation to cohabitees.[12] Same-sex partnerships also became legal in Germany in August 2001.

The most recent European country to allow same-sex marriage was Spain, when on June 30, 2005 its Parliament eventually approved the amending legislation. It officially became law on July 2, 2005 following royal assent. It is remarkable that Spain was to follow in the footsteps of some of the more liberal countries in Europe, especially when one has regard to the fact that the population of Spain is predominantly Catholic; nevertheless, this gives cause to question other conservative countries' refusal to follow suit.

It is clear that the tide is turning in Europe in relation to the form marriage ought to take, and such developments are not merely a European phenomenon. Other common law countries, most notably Canada[13] and South Africa,[14] have opened up marriage to same-sex couples, as has the US state of Massachusetts.[15] In light of this obvious wave of change one must ask why marriage should be opened up to same-sex couples. Implicit in such an analysis is the issue of the ability to choose the form of marriage that one wishes to enter. To tackle this question in a satisfac-

---

9   Denmark (1989), Norway (1993), Sweden (1994), Iceland (1996) and Finland (2001).
10 Waaldijk, "Others May Follow: The Introduction of Marriage, Quasi-Marriage and Semi-Marriage for Same-Sex Couples in European Countries" (2003–2004) 38 *New. Eng. L. Rev.* 569.
11 French Pacte Civil de Solidarité (Pact of Civil Solidarity).
12 Law Reform Commission, *Consultation Paper on the Rights & Duties of Cohabitees* (LRC CP 32-2004), p.4.
13 Civil Marriage Act 2005 (Ch.33).
14 *Fourie v Minister of Home Affairs* 2006 (3) B.C.L.R. 355 (CC).
15 *Goodridge v Department of Public Health* 440 Mass. 309; 798 N.E.2d 941; 2003 Mass. LEXIS 814.

tory legal manner one must analyse the moral arguments both for and against same-sex marriage, because implicit in this is the conflict between individual liberty and social conformity and paternalism. This conflict represents the kernel of the debate on whether to allow individuals to determine the form of marriage they wish to enter without the state pre-empting this decision for them. Notwithstanding this, it is pertinent to analyse the preliminary issue of the need to define marriage.

THE PROBLEM WITH DEFINING MARRIAGE

Debates concerning the status of marriage and other related matters typically open with the definition of marriage. From this basis authors then proceed with their arguments concerning separation, divorce, pre-nuptial agreements, etc. However, it is submitted that generally these arguments suffer from a fundamental weakness in that they fail to consider the issue of why marriage is defined, and possibly how it should be defined. Not only is the definition of marriage a matter that needs to be tackled, but so is state regulation of this definition. There are two inherent problems that need to be addressed before one considers how marriage ought to be recognised. These are:

1) Should marriage be defined?
2) The issue of a state definition of marriage.

Should marriage be defined?

The definitional argument has always found favour with those arguing for the retention of the traditional definition of marriage. Courts constantly refer to the original definition as enunciated in *Hyde v Hyde*,[16] or variations thereof, and apply it to the modern era, albeit with the modification effected by the divorce referendum.[17] Simply, the definitional argument consists of stating the definition of marriage, as understood by the courts, and determining whether the parties before it fit within that definition; if not, there can be no possibility of there being a marriage. Therefore, as marriage is traditionally construed as being between a man and a woman it cannot permit a same-sex couple to be married. As is evident, the root of the problem facing those who seek to expand the institution of marriage so as to include all who seek to benefit from its status, lies in the actual definition of marriage as it now stands.

---

[16]   *Hyde v Hyde and Woodmansee* [1861–1873] All E.R. Rep. 175.
[17]   See *Foy v An t-Ard Chlaraitheoir*, unreported, High Court, July 9, 2002 at 130; *Murray v Ireland* [1985] I.R. 532; *TF v Ireland* [1995] 1 I.R. 321.

As noted, the traditional definition of marriage was enunciated by Lord Penzance in the case of *Hyde v Hyde*[18] where he stated:

> "that marriage, as understood in Christendom, may for this purpose be defined as the voluntary union for life of one man and one woman, to the exclusion of all others."

This definition of marriage stood for almost 120 years in Ireland, until marriage was to undergo a seismic alteration. Following the referendum of 1995, divorce became legal in Ireland and as a result "the permanency aspect of marriage no longer applies".[19] As such, the definition of marriage underwent a metamorphosis unforeseeable 30 years ago, illustrating that marriage as an institution can be altered so as to reflect changing times. This demonstrates that the definitional argument is not as strong as it first seems because it is contingent on the current definition of marriage. As Murray J. (as he then was) pointed out in *DT v CT*, Art.41 of the Constitution must be interpreted in a contemporary manner[20]; yet, as illustrated in Chapter 1, there has been a palpable failure of the courts to do so.

A contemporary analysis of marriage provides one with a broader picture as to how marriage ought to be recognised beyond the stringent confines of an under-inclusive definition. Under the traditional definition of marriage, certain assumptions are made that do not necessarily correspond with social reality. It was traditionally assumed that a marriage between a man and a woman would result in the man being the sole breadwinner and the woman being a homemaker. Weitzman describes such assumptions as being "anachronistic and inappropriate"[21] as they do not accord with social reality. This is becoming evident in Ireland as more and more women join the workforce and contribute equally with their husband to the marriage.

Such assumptions inherent in the traditional definition of marriage create gender roles and deny individual autonomy. As noted above, the traditional definition of marriage in Ireland has reflected Roman Catholic teachings and has resulted in certain sections of society being restricted in the form of marriage they may enter. This has had the effect of failing to recognise and account for family diversity. In today's progressive society the needs of the individual are becoming more important, so as to preserve the cohesion that keeps society intact. The satisfaction

---

[18] *Hyde v Hyde and Woodmansee* [1861–1873] All E.R. Rep. 175.

[19] *Foy v An t-Ard Chlaraitheoir*, unreported, High Court, July 9, 2002 at 130.

[20] *DT v CT* [2003] 1 I.L.R.M. 321.

[21] Weitzman, *The Marriage Contract: Spouses, Lovers and the Law* (The Free Press, New York, 1981), p.135.

that one seeks from life will invariably differ from person to person and people are beginning to look beyond the traditional form of marriage to other relationship models to satisfy their needs and wants.

This trend is indicative of the need to modify the focus on the meaning of marriage from one of *form* to one of *function*. The current definition of marriage is under-inclusive in the sense that it focuses on the *form* marriage ought to take rather than its *function* intra the parties to it. Factors such as love, commitment, loyalty and trust ought to take the place of traditional formal requirements such as gender. The *form* approach is an anachronism in that it is based on the pretence that it can shape social norms.

Other jurisdictions have taken the approach of recognising that a marriage is not merely a unit but is in fact a partnership of two individuals; because of this it is becoming increasingly important for the law to appreciate the needs of these individuals. The US Supreme Court realised this in *Eisenstadt v Baird*[22] where the applicant sought to have the decision of *Griswold v Connecticut*[23] extended so as to permit non-marital couples to obtain contraceptives. In what has been criticised as a case of judicial activism,[24] the court did make the following pertinent comment:

> "It is true that in *Griswold* the right of marital privacy in question inhered in the marital relationship. Yet the married couple is not an independent entity with a mind and heart of its own, but an association of two individuals each with a separate intellectual and emotional makeup. If the right of privacy means anything, it is the right of the *individual*, married or single, to be free from unwarranted governmental intrusion into matters so fundamentally affecting a person as the decision whether to bear or beget a child."[25]

It is submitted that the Irish courts are becoming more aware of the fact that a marriage is not merely a unit in society but is in fact a partnership of two people.[26] Indeed, Murray J. (as he then was) defined marriage as "a

---

[22] 405 U.S. 438 (1972).
[23] 381 U.S. 479 (1965).
[24] See Wellington, "Common Law Rules and Constitutional Double Standards: Some Notes on Adjudication" (1973) 83 Yale L.J. 221, at 296–97.
[25] *Eisenstadt v Baird* 405 U.S. 438, 453 (1972) (emphasis in original).
[26] For further analysis see Chap.5 below.

solemn contract of partnership"[27] and it is clear from divorce case law that the courts are becoming more aware of the individual role that each spouse plays in the marriage. In determining the division of property and wealth in a divorce, the courts consider the parties as separate and autonomous individuals and consider the contributions that each made to the marriage. Therefore, if the law is prepared to recognise that marriage consists of two individuals in partnership at the termination of the marriage, why can it not do so at the formation of the marriage? It is submitted that this ought to be the case and, accordingly, the law would then be capable of recognising the ever-present diversity in Irish society and adapt to it so as not to discriminate.

Not only does the definitional argument not accord with the realities of society, but its application in the exclusion of same-sex couples from marriage is also fundamentally flawed. The US case of *Baker v Nelson*[28] is illustrative of this point. In that case the court refused to grant an order of mandamus compelling the county clerk to issue a marriage licence to a same-sex couple. The court took a traditional approach to interpreting the statute. Even though the statute did not expressly prohibit same-sex marriages, the court held that the language used in the statute, *e.g.* "husband and wife", implied that marriage was to be given its ordinary meaning deriving from the Book of Genesis.[29] Consequently, the court held that same-sex couples were excluded from entering marriage. Culhane criticises this approach, and the approach taken in general by courts when dealing with cases involving homosexuals.[30] He makes the point that, when courts analyse cases advocating same-sex marriage, they tend to concentrate on what same-sex partners do instead of what constitutes marriage. Preferably a court should desexualise such a case as there is no physical difference between parties seeking a same-sex or mixed-sex marriage.[31]

---

27   *DT v CT* [2003] 1 I.L.R.M. 321.

28   *Baker v Nelson* 191 N.W. 2d 185 (Minn. 1971); see also *Singer v Hara* 522 P.2d 1187 (Wash. Ct. App. 1974).

29   191 N.W. 2d 185, at 186.

30   Culhane, "Uprooting the Arguments Against Same-Sex Marriage" (1998–1999) 20 *Cardozo L. Rev.* 1119.

31   The need for this was recognised by Cameron JA in the South African Supreme Court of Appeal decision in *Fourie v Minister of Home Affairs* 2005 (3) B.C.L.R. 241 (SCA) stating, at para.19 of the judgment, that it is necessary to:
      "…look beyond the unavoidable specificities of our condition—such as race, gender and sexual orientation—and consider our intrinsic human capacities and what they render possible for all of us. In this case, the question is whether the capacity for commit-

Seeking to decide a case on the basis of the definition of marriage is a tautology as marriage has always been defined by those who have access to it. The circular nature of this argument can be established by dissecting its intrinsic logic. Generally such an argument, in the context of the same-sex marriage debate, is based on the following rationale:

- The state adopts a definition of marriage excluding same-sex couples because the traditional definition of marriage excludes same-sex couples.
- The traditional definition of marriage excludes same-sex couples because the majority of married couples within the state are mixed-sex couples.
- The majority of married couples within the state are mixed-sex because the traditional definition of marriage has always excluded same-sex couples.

The circularity of this argument has not only received academic support[32] but also judicial support. In holding that the refusal to grant a same-sex couple a civil marriage licence was a prima facie discrimination on the grounds of sexual orientation in violation of the state constitutional guarantee of equal protection, the Hawaiian Supreme Court noted the tautology that is the traditional definitional argument for excluding same-sex couples from marriage.[33]

This weakness in the definitional argument has already been exploited by the American courts in declaring unconstitutional the anti-miscegenation laws prohibiting mixed-race marriages. The US Supreme Court declared such laws unconstitutional in the triumphant case of *Loving v Virginia*.[34] Before this case, marriage in America, was defined as a "union of a man and a woman of the same race"; following this decision marriage was defined as a "union between a man and a woman". This illustrates the point that the definition of marriage is established by those who presently have access to it. Therefore, if same-sex couples were permitted to marry, the definition of marriage would no longer be a "union between a man and a woman", but instead might be a "union between two people".

---

ment, and the ability to love and nurture and honour and sustain, transcends the incidental fact of sexual orientation. The answer … is, 'Yes'."

[32] See Culhane, "Uprooting the Arguments Against Same-Sex Marriage" (1998–1999) 20 *Cardozo L. Rev.* 1119; Cruz, "Just Don't Call It Marriage: The First Amendment and Marriage as an Expressive Resource" (2000–2001) 74 *S. Cal. L. Rev.* 936.

[33] *Baehr v Lewin* 852 P.2d 44, at 63 (Haw. 1993).

[34] 388 U.S. 1 (1967).

The rigid and arbitrary nature of a definition is incompatible with an organic concept such as marriage. Emotions, feelings and other intangible concepts cause a marriage to be formed, not clear and concise criteria. By engaging in a definitional argument the courts fail to engage in the underlying substantive issues in these types of cases, such as the rights to equality, privacy, autonomy and dignity. Society should not seek to rely on a rigid definition of marriage; instead we should seek to illustrate the characteristics and elements of marriage so as to enable us to recognise it in its various possible forms. Instead of relying on a definition instructing us what to do in relation to marriage, we should adopt an approach illustrating what marriage is.[35] A definition should not be the basis of a decision as to whether two parties can enter into marriage; instead it should act as a conceptual framework setting out the factors that a court should be aware of in determining whether there is the possibility of a marriage in those circumstances. "[T]he decision whether and whom to marry is among life's momentous acts of self-definition"[36]; therefore, it should be defined by those who enter it and not by those who seek to regulate it.

The miscegenation analogy

In debates concerning the under-inclusiveness of the institution of marriage, comparisons are made to past discriminations concerning the availability of marriage, most notably the anti-miscegenation statutes of the United States of America. Prior to the emergence of the civil rights movement in America, racial discrimination was widespread even within the legal system. Many states had anti-miscegenation statutes that prohibited mixed-race marriages. The rationale behind this palpable discrimination was illustrated in the opinion of the trial judge in the case of *Loving v Virginia*,[37] who stated:

> "Almighty God created the races white, black, yellow, malay and red, and he placed them on separate continents. And but for the interference with his arrangement there would be no cause for such marriages. The fact that he separated the races shows that he did not intend for the races to mix."[38]

---

[35] Culhane, "Uprooting the Arguments Against Same-Sex Marriage" (1998–1999) 20 *Cardozo L. Rev.* 1119, at 1183–1184.

[36] *Goodridge v Department of Public Health* 440 Mass. 309; 798 N.E.2d 941 (2003) at 322 and 955, respectively.

[37] *Loving v Virginia* 388 U.S. 1 (1967).

[38] *ibid.* at 4.

The Supreme Court in *Loving* declared the Virginia anti-miscegenation statute to be a violation of the equal protection clause under the Fourteenth Amendment of the Constitution and thereby struck it down. These laws were deemed to promote white supremacy and it has been argued in academic circles that the laws prohibiting same-sex marriage are just as discriminatory, as they also impose a hierarchy within society on the basis of flawed assumptions concerning the nature of same-sex relationships.[39] Furthermore, these laws violate fundamental rights, such as equality, privacy, and autonomy; rights which were respected and celebrated in the abandonment of the anti-miscegenation statutes. The Supreme Court of Massachusetts recognised the parallels between these two arguments and declared that just as before "history must yield to a more fully developed understanding of the invidious quality of ... discrimination."[40]

Those in favour of the miscegenation analogy to same-sex marriage argue that not only are there obvious similarities in the discrimination suffered, but both also have a similar negative impact upon society. Appleton has argued that laws prohibiting same-sex marriage promote a gender hierarchy within which women are subordinate to men, just as anti-miscegenation laws promoted white supremacy before the *Loving* decision.[41] Her argument here is founded upon the traditional family model that promotes the husband as the superior figurehead of the family. It is submitted, however, that such an argument is not compelling as it is no longer cognitive of the realities of society. The male is no longer recognised as the sole figurehead of the family; both husband and wife contribute equally to the family in today's society, especially now that women play a more pivotal role in the workforce.

---

[39] See "Uprooting the Arguments Against Same-Sex Marriage" (1998–1999) 20 *Cardozo L. Rev.* 1119.

[40] *Goodridge v Department of Public Health* 440 Mass. 309; 798 N.E.2d 941 (2003) at 329 and 959 respectively.

[41] Appleton, "Missing in Action? Searching for Gender Talk in the Same-Sex Marriage Debate" (2005) *16 Stan. L. & Pol'y Rev*. 97, at 107. Merin adopts a similar stance: see Merin, *Equality for Same-Sex Couples: The Legal Recognition of Gay Partnerships in Europe and the United States* (University of Chicago Press, 2002), p.43; quoting from Graff, *What is Marriage For?* (1999) at 223, where he states:
  "Once the theory of white supremacy had been toppled, interracial marriage could no longer be barred. In just the same way, once the theory of male supremacy and female inferiority was dismantled—the theory that man must rule and women must serve—there is no longer any justification for barring marriage between two women and two men."

Nevertheless, a valid comparison can be drawn between the reasoning surrounding the introduction of anti-miscegenation statutes and the current majority opinion against same-sex marriage. Ross argues that the debate surrounding same-sex relationships is overly sexualised, as was the debate concerning interracial marriages prior to the introduction of anti-miscegenation statutes.[42] Focusing on the sexual aspect of such relationships can have negative social implications, as was apparent in relation to the segregation laws in America:

> "the obsession with sexuality played a key role in maintaining the racist power imbalance and the continued second-class treatment of certain relationships."[43]

It is argued that the debate concerning same-sex marriages needs to be desexualised in order for reason to prevail. There is no logic in concentrating on the physical relationship between those who choose to marry. Indeed, when a person marries someone of the opposite sex it attracts public recognition of their relationship but does not attract interest in their private sex lives. Therefore, why is it that when same-sex marriage is debated one of the common arguments against it is that it would be tantamount to public recognition of deviant sexual acts? It is no longer rational to conceive marriage as the legitimisation of engaging in sexual activity; instead it represents the symbolic act of expressing a lifelong commitment to a person one loves.

Whilst this analogy between the anti-miscegenation statutes and laws prohibiting same-sex marriage is useful, it is submitted that this is as far as it can go as there is a fundamental difference between inter-racial marriages and same-sex marriages. The common argument against the miscegenation analogy is that race is an immutable characteristic but sexual orientation is not. Bamforth has defined immutability in the context of sexual orientation as:

> "the idea that a person's sexual orientation is either biologically predetermined, or is at least fixed at such an early stage in life that they cannot be held morally responsible for it."[44]

---

[42] Ross, "The Sexualization of Difference: A Comparison of Mixed-Race and Same-Gender Marriage" (2002) 37 *Harv. C.R.-C.L.L. Rev.* 255.

[43] *ibid.* at 261.

[44] Bamforth, *Sexuality, Morals and Justice: A Theory of Lesbian and Gay Rights Law* (Cassell, 1997), p.203 (footnotes omitted).

The rationale behind the decision in *Loving* was that race is an immutable characteristic and any discrimination based solely on race would violate a person's dignity. Those who argue in favour of the miscegenation analogy in same-sex marriage discourse claim that sexual orientation is immutable and therefore any law seeking to limit or alter one's sexual orientation imposes an inhumane burden on that person and should be declared unconstitutional. The fundamental flaw in such an argument is that no study to date has found sexual orientation to be immutable. Instead, Byrne and Parsons concluded that the origins of homosexuality are to be found in a "complex mosaic of biologic, psychological and social/cultural factors".[45] Nevertheless, it is interesting to note the dicta of Henchy J. in *Norris v Attorney-General* where he seems to have declared sexual orientation as being a "quasi-immutable" characteristic:

> "What appears clear from the evidence is that his sexual condition was predestined from birth or from childhood rather than adopted by choice …"[46]

Moreover, Bamforth argues that such an argument is flawed because in everyday life distinctions are legitimately drawn between people on the basis of certain immutable characteristics. He gives the example of the legitimacy of refusing to allow a blind person to become a driving instructor, but if a law was made prohibiting all white people from becoming driving instructors then this would give rise to a legitimate claim of discrimination. Therefore, he is of the opinion that an argument based on principles of immutability may draw attention to the plight of gays and lesbians in their quest for equal treatment, but it is an insufficient basis upon which one can postulate a normative argument.[47]

Nevertheless, it has been argued that, although sexual orientation may not be an immutable characteristic, it can be categorised as one of life's "certain choices [that] are so important to self-definition that these too should be protected."[48] Therefore, as sexual orientation is a defining

---

[45] See submissions of "European Life Network" and "Focus on the Family Ireland" in All Party Oireachtas Committee, "10th Progress Report: The Family" (Government Publications, 2006) at A61 and A80 respectively. Quoting from William Byrne and Bruce Parsons, "Human Sexual Orientation: The Biologic Theories Reappraised" (1993) 50 *Archives of General Psychiatry* 228–239.

[46] *Norris v Attorney-General* [1984] I.R. 36 at 67.

[47] Bamforth, *Sexuality, Morals and Justice: A Theory of Lesbian and Gay Rights Law* (Cassell, 1997), p.204.

[48] Kentridge in Chaskalson, *Constitutional Law of South Africa*, (1998) Revision Service 2 at 14–26.

characteristic of one's life it ought to be treated in a similar manner to race and gender. Failure to do so would have negative implications for one's dignity and, as shall be seen below, this can form the framework for a substantial moral argument in favour of reformulating marriage.

As is clear, the miscegenation analogy may be useful so as to draw attention to the need to expand the availability of the institution of marriage, but on its own it would be insufficient to form any persuasive argument. An analysis of the underlying rights and principles is necessary in order to determine why marriage ought to be developed and in what manner. I shall endeavour to engage this issue below and attempt to postulate a logical argument supporting the need for marriage to meet the requirements of the individual. But, first, the State's role in the institution of marriage needs to be examined.

The State definition of marriage

Marriage is often regarded as public matter; it is the public recognition of a committed relationship between two parties. Yet this was not always the case. Indeed, it is generally thought that marriage originated in the form of a private arrangement. Under Roman law, a marriage was not a legal relationship but a social fact; therefore, it was generally not regulated by law. A marriage was created if the parties intended to treat their relationship as a marriage and there was no need for any legal recognition.[49] This remained the case until the influence of the Roman Catholic Church expanded and, with the establishment of the Ecclesiastical Courts in the 13th century, marriage became an institution regulated by the Church in accordance with its teachings, as enforced within its courts.[50] This caused marriage to be controlled in a manner that limited its availability to those deemed eligible under Church teachings. The commingling of Church and politics throughout the Middle Ages resulted in the institution of marriage being regulated by those who ruled the land. On this basis marriage gradually moved from being a private affair to a public institution.

Modern justifications for the state regulation of marriage are centred on the premise that marriage plays an important role in family life and promotes stability in society. Worthen sets out four categories of societal interests that support the privileged position of marriage and

---

[49] Dannenbring, *Roman Private Law* (2nd ed., Butterworths, 1968), in particular Pt V.

[50] Merin, *Equality for Same-Sex Couples: The Legal Recognition of Gay Partnerships in Europe and the United States* (University of Chicago Press, 2002), p.11.

thereby accords governments the right to define marriage as they deem fit:

1) Society's interest in promoting procreation and responsible child rearing.

2) Society's interest in fostering a particular moral atmosphere.

3) Society's interest in promoting the individual wellbeing of its members by facilitating the kind of intimate relationships that promote individual fulfilment.

4) Society's interest in the equitable distribution of economic and other tangible benefits.[51]

States have not only protected marriage as an institution but have also promoted it. This is apparent in Ireland by virtue of the constitutional recognition of the institution of marriage as the foundation upon which the family is built,[52] coupled with the approach that has been taken by the courts to date.[53] Nonetheless, this is not solely an Irish phenomenon; the definition of marriage has become a topical political subject in America in recent times.[54]

The inherent problem with the State definition of marriage is that it leads to discrimination. When we seek to define an object, not only are we describing what that object is but we are also describing what it is not.

---

[51] Worthen, "Who Decides and What Difference Does It Make?: Defining Marriage in 'Our Democratic, Federal Republic'" (2004) 8 *BYU J.Pub.L.* 273, at 275–276.

[52] Art.41.

[53] See *State (Nicolau) v An Bord Uchtála* [1966] I.R. 567; *Ennis v Butterly* [1996] 1 I.R. 426.

[54] Following the dramatic decision of the Hawaiian Supreme Court in *Baehr v Lewin* 852 P.2d 44 (1993), the US Government moved to quell the concerns of traditionalists throughout America. The Federal Government enacted the Defense of Marriage Act (DOMA), which defined marriage as the union of a man and a woman (See Pub. L No. 104-199, 110 Stat 2419 (1996) (codified as amended in 1 U.S.C. § 7; 28 U.S.C. § 1738C (2000)); see generally Duncan, "Doma and Marriage" (2004–2005) 17 *Regent U. L. Rev.* 203. This paved the way for individual states to enact their own DOMA legislation and pursuant to the "Full Faith & Credit Clause" within the United States Constitution such state laws would allow a DOMA state to refuse to recognise a same-sex marriage contracted in a non-DOMA state. Interestingly, 14 states enacted their own DOMA legislation within a year of the federal law. By the end of 2004 39 States had DOMA Acts; see www.lc.org/DOMAs.html. The issue of defining marriage is of particular interest in the United States of America, with President Bush lobbying for such a development. See in general "Bush renews gay marriage ban call", June 6, 2006, available at http://news.bbc.co.uk/2/hi/americas/5050550.stm; Border, "Bush supports campaign to ban gay marriages" *The Irish Times*, June 6, 2006.

This is particularly precarious when one seeks to define a social phenomenon such as marriage.

In Ireland there is a distinct controversy in relation to the State definition of marriage in that, to date, it has coincided with the Roman Catholic Church's definition of marriage. This apparent approval of Roman Catholic teachings has been at the expense of other faiths and beliefs. Indeed, it is arguable that such an entanglement between State approval and Roman Catholic Church teachings is in fact unconstitutional as it favours one belief to the detriment of others.[55]

The main problem with the State defining marriage in a manner akin to that of the Catholic Church is that the Church is entitled to promote its teachings in a constant manner irrespective of social developments, but the State cannot take such an approach. The State is required to acknowledge and indeed reflect developments and changes in society so as to adequately meet the needs of its citizens.[56] Up until approximately 20 years ago a definition of marriage based on Roman Catholic teachings was representative of the majority view in Irish society. Nevertheless, there have been dramatic changes in Ireland, as alluded to in Chapter 1, most notably the introduction of divorce, and therefore it is no longer accurate to define marriage in a manner akin to that of the Catholic Church. Irish society has developed from one of a prevailing communitarian ethos to one of pluralism. With an ever increasing multitude of cultures, faiths and beliefs, it is clear that Irish society is no longer a mirror image of Roman Catholic life and therefore should not be regulated as such. Rev Earl Storey, before the General Synod, alluded to this phenomenon, stating:

> "In terms of religion, [Ireland] will soon be unrecognisable. People are finding their places of community and spirituality in new places other than the church."[57]

As noted in Chapter 1, family diversity is an emerging phenomenon in Ireland and ought to be recognised and protected. The family based on marriage can no longer be the rationale behind maintaining the current definition of marriage; instead it should only be an ideal to be aspired to instead of a direct reflection of Irish society. In order to truly respect and

---

[55] Art.44.2.3°.

[56] See in general Cox, "A Question of Definition: Same-Sex Marriage and the Law" presented at Trinity College Dublin Conference, *Legal Recognition of Committed Relationships*, April 30, 2005.

[57] McGarry, "Republic in religious terms becoming 'unrecognisable'" *The Irish Times*, May 11, 2006.

protect the rights of the citizens of Ireland, concepts such as marital privacy and family autonomy need to be expanded to the extent that the courts and legislature adopt a "neutral" approach to family law rather than imposing a "one size fits all" ideology on all families. To adopt such a "neutral" approach the law must shy away from trying to regulate the "family" through the proxy of marriage.[58] Marriage is truly an institution built upon the ideals and desires of the parties entering it; it is not for the State to determine.

One of the main arguments in favour of the State definition of marriage is that marriage promotes procreation and child-rearing. This argument has proved particularly popular in the case against same-sex marriage, often in tandem with a natural-law-based argument. However, it can be dismissed on the basic ground that it no longer accords with social reality, and has not since the legalisation of contraceptives.[59] As a result of the use of contraceptives in marriage, procreation no longer represents a necessary incident of marriage. Instead, the parties to a marriage have a choice; they may choose to have children, or may limit the possibility of such an event by using contraceptives. As marriage no longer automatically represents a forum within which children can be reared, the procreation aspect should no longer be deemed a necessary factor in the State definition of marriage. According to the 2002 census, 24 per cent of children were born outside of marriage, thereby illustrating that marriage is no longer the sole realm for the rearing of children. Also, a fundamental flaw in this argument is its failure to contend with the possibility of an infertile married couple, or couples who marry after childbearing age, or couples who adopt, or couples who choose not to have children. Following the philosophy of the procreation argument, one is compelled to assume that such a married couple is inferior to other married couples who can have children, or perhaps is party to a sham marriage, thus demeaning their dignity.[60] It is clear that neither of these possibilities would enjoy any endorsement in today's society; as such it is submitted that this argument for State regulation of marriage cannot stand.

The representation of a married couple as being an indivisible unit forming the bedrock upon which society operates is no longer accurate.

---

[58] See Milot, "Restitching the American Marital Quilt: Untangling Marriage from the Nuclear Family" (2001) 87 *Va. L. Rev.* 701.

[59] *McGee v Attorney-General* [1974] I.R. 269.

[60] See the judgment of Sachs J. in *Fourie v Minister of Home Affairs* 2006 (3) B.C.L.R. 355 (CC).

Social order and contentment now seem to be generated by the ability of individuals to freely enter into relationships, whether they be business or personal. As such, there is an increasing recognition of the need for society as a whole to give way to the wishes and choices of the individual. As has been demonstrated, the tenets upon which the State traditionally justified its interference in marriage no longer stand up to scrutiny. Yet the language synonymous with the traditional definition of marriage still manifests itself in modern discourse. This represents the "shell" of an ancient culture and way of thinking that is no longer coherent with the modern day logic of the State's norms. As Pelikan so aptly stated:

> "[t]radition is the living faith of the dead; traditionalism is the dead faith of the living."[61]

Nevertheless, it has been argued that marriage is not a "civil contract" but instead is a "civil status" and therefore ought to be subject to State definition.[62] Support for this argument is based on the rationale that marriage concerns religion and society as a whole and therefore must conform with standards as set out by the State so as to retain its uniqueness and "status".[63]

It is proposed that such an approach is too regimental because the definition of status[64] lacks the capacity to distinguish the essential elements of a marriage. To adopt such an attitude would be to take marriage out of the hands of those individuals who are party to it and allow the State to control the nature of the marriage. Marriage, however, is an evolving entity subject to the emotions of the parties to it and therefore needs to be responsive to their needs and wants in order to survive. By removing it from the control of those who are party to the marriage, the law would be damaging the very institution it seeks to protect.

---

[61] Jaroslav Pelikan, *The Vindication of Tradition* (New Haven, Yale University Press, 1984), p.65.

[62] See generally Foster, "Marriage: A Basic Civil Right of Man" (1968–1969) 37 *Fordham L. Rev.* 51 at 52.

[63] See Rasmussen, "Interspousal Contracts: The Potential for Validation in Massachusetts" (1974–1975) 9 *Suffolk U. L. Rev.* 185, at 187:
"Traditional marriage is not a contractual relationship with negotiable terms but rather a status relationship, in that no private agreement can change any of the legal rights and obligations which adhere to an individual upon his or her undertaking of the position of a spouse."

[64] "A legal position imposed by law on the basis of public policy rather than a condition voluntarily assumed by the individual", referred to by Rasmussen, "Interspousal Contracts: The Potential for Validation in Massachusetts" (1974–1975) 9 *Suffolk U. L. Rev.* 185 at 187, n.10.

Not only does the current State definition of marriage not reflect the pluralist nature of our society, but one can argue that the time has come to eliminate the State's role in regulating the availability of marriage. To achieve equality and enhance dignity marriage should be available to all people irrespective of their tendencies. The State regulation of marriage represents an unjust encroachment into the privacy, autonomy and dignity of individuals. Marriage is one of the most important commitments that an individual will make in his/her lifetime and as such the meaning given to marriage ought to reflect what it means to that person and not a state-imposed meaning.

The grounds for declaring such State interference illegitimate can be set out under the headings of:

- equality;
- privacy;
- autonomy;
- dignity.

Each of these shall be analysed in due course.

3. The Legal Philosophy of Marriage

"Even if morality is not based on rights it may include rights in its foundations."[1]

While there is no right, *per se*, to choose the type of marriage one wishes to enter, it does concern a moral question which at present is centred on the conflict between individual autonomy and paternalism. The current position of marriage, as a public institution regulated by the State, is founded on the rationale that it is in the common good to formulate marriage as a unique and privileged entity so as to promote social stability. In order to overcome this justification it is necessary to present a satisfactory argument to rebut such a perception. It shall be argued that the current regulation of marriage is at the expense of individual rights, such as privacy and autonomy. Nevertheless, as it is now generally accepted that marriage is a publicly recognised institution, moral arguments for the validity of privately formulated marital relationships must be capable of achieving public approval also. Therefore, an argument based solely on the right to privacy or autonomy will not prevail unless it is incorporated with a publicly recognised moral basis—that being equality. As shall be seen, an argument based solely on equality will not prevail as it is intrinsically reliant on principles such as autonomy and privacy. So to provide a compelling argument it is necessary to analyse these various moral propositions.

EQUALITY

Proponents of the reform of the legal institution of marriage generally compose their arguments in egalitarian terms. They argue that the traditional model of marriage should be replaced by a more inclusive, egalitarian model.

Typically such arguments are asserted in the following manner:

- Marriage is an intangible good as it provides a person with a certain status in society.
- Denying the institution of marriage to a certain class of people, or formulating it in a manner such as to limit their options, is to deny them the status they seek in society.

---

[1] Raz, *The Morality of Freedom* (Clarendon Press, Oxford, 1986), p.217.

- This implies that such persons are inferior to those who can enter marriage and therefore results in discrimination.

As is clear, arguments couched in equality terms illustrate an injustice and are easily communicated to the masses and therefore tend to be popular. The current definition of marriage represents both a direct and indirect discrimination. A direct discrimination is one that is prima facie evident from the law in question. By defining marriage as between a man and a woman there is a direct discrimination against same-sex partners. An indirect discrimination is "the recognition that there may be measures which, although neutral on their face, effect classifications between individuals".[2] Simply defining marriage discriminates against those who wish to enter marriage on their own terms. By restricting a person's choice in matters, a law affects their human dignity, as a person should have the right to choose the manner in which to conduct their lifestyle. Herbert J.'s observations in *Redmond v Minister for the Environment*[3] are persuasive in this regard. The case concerned the requirement for candidates in certain elections to pay electoral deposit fees pursuant to s.47 of the Electoral Act 1992 and s.13 of the European Parliament Elections Act 1997. Herbert J. found the provisions to be unconstitutional with regard to Arts 16.1 and 40.1 of the Constitution. In relation to Art 40.1 he stated:

> "[A] law which has the effect, even if totally unintended, of discriminating between human persons on the basis of money is an attack upon the dignity of those persons as human beings who do not have money ... The history of poverty and social deprivation in Ireland ... demonstrates overwhelmingly the extent to which the essential dignity of persons as humans beings is involved."[4]

As shall be seen below, the dignity of those who are denied access to the institution of marriage in a manner that accommodates their lifestyle has become a central issue in various jurisdictions[5] in the debate surrounding

---

[2]   Doyle, *Constitutional Equality Law* (Round Hall, 2004), p.77.
[3]   *Redmond v Minister for the Environment* [2001] 4 I.R. 61.
[4]   *ibid.* at 80.
[5]   *Goodridge v Department of Public Health* 440 Mass. 309; 798 N.E.2d 941 (2003); *National Coalition for Gay and Lesbian Equality v Minister for Home Affairs* 2000 (2) SA 1; 2000 (1) B.C.L.R. 39 (CC); *National Coalition for Gay and Lesbian Equality v Minister for Justice ("The Sodomy Case")* 1999 (1) SA 6; 1998 (1) B.C.L.R. 1517 (CC).

marriage. The Supreme Court of Hawaii largely based its decision in the case of *Baehr v Lewin*[6] on equality grounds when it held that the refusal to grant a same-sex couple a civil marriage licence was prima facie discrimination on the grounds of sexual orientation. Also, the South African Constitutional Court relied heavily on egalitarian reasoning in determining that the traditional definition of marriage was a violation of its equality guarantee under the Constitution.[7] Herbert J.'s observations in *Redmond* represent a fresh approach to the equality guarantee under Art.40.1 of the Constitution and, it is submitted, ought to form a part of any moral argument presented to the courts examining the institution of marriage.

Despite the apparent attractiveness of the egalitarian argument in this context, there are two intrinsic problems that must be contended with:

1) The inherent weakness within any egalitarian argument due to its reliance on other principles and rights.
2) The weak interpretation by the Irish courts to date of Art.40.1 and in particular their use of the "due regard" clause.

1) Egalitarian arguments and the ability to determine equality from inequality

The equality guarantee under Art.40.1 imports an Aristotelian concept of equality, that is, that equals should be treated equally and unequals unequally.[8] Such a concept of equality has been criticised as lacking foundation. Westen queries how one can move from a fact that two people are alike, to a normative conclusion that they ought to be treated alike. Essentially he is asking the question of "how can one move from an 'is' to an 'ought'?".[9] He claims that equality is an entirely circular concept because:

> "[i]t tells us to treat like people alike; but when we ask who 'like people' are, we are told they are 'people who should be treated alike'. Equality is an empty vessel with no substantive moral content of its own. Without moral standards, equality remains meaningless, a formula that can have nothing to say about how we should act."[10]

---

6   *Baehr v Lewin* 852 P.2d 44 (1993).
7   *Fourie v Minister of Home Affairs* 2005 (3) B.C.L.R. 241 (SCA), affirmed in *Fourie v Minister of Home Affairs* 2006 (3) B.C.L.R. 355 (CC).
8   *De Burca v Attorney-General* [1976] I.R. 38 at 68.
9   Westen, "The Empty Ideal of Equality" (1982) 95 *Harvard Law Review* 537 at 543.
10   *ibid.* at 547.

Therefore, to formulate an argument entirely in egalitarian terms is a tautology as it presupposes the existence of certain rights from which the claim for equality derives. In cases involving a deprivation of a right, any argument based on equality is superfluous because a valid claim can be made solely by reference to the underlying right or principle of the case without any recourse to equality. On this basis he claims that "equality is an entirely formal concept: it is a 'form' for stating moral and legal propositions whose substance originates elsewhere, a 'form' of discourse with no substantive content of its own."[11] Therefore, equality is merely a label for arguments based on the underlying rights or principles concerning a case.

There is case law that would tend to support Westen's theory, most notably from South Africa. In dealing with claims of unfair discrimination, the South African courts have adopted a mode of analysis set out in terms of equality, but fundamentally based on dignity. The approach that has been followed thus far was set out in the case of *Harksen v Lane NO*[12] where, in seeking to determine if there was unfair discrimination, the court stated:

> "The prohibition of unfair discrimination in the Constitution provides a bulwark against invasions which impair human dignity or which affect people adversely in a comparably serious manner ... If it is on a specified ground, then discrimination will have been established. If it is not on a specified ground, then whether or not there is discrimination will depend upon whether, objectively, the ground is based on attributes and characteristics which have the potential to impair the fundamental human dignity of persons as human beings or to affect them adversely in a comparably serious manner."[13]

It is evident that such an equality analysis is essentially based on an examination of the underlying right to dignity, thereby illustrating the tautology expressed by Westen.

Such an interpretation of the equality guarantee under the South African Constitution[14] has caused some to state that s.9 of the Constitution no longer acts as the "guarantor of substantive equality [but as the] gate-

---

[11]   *ibid.* at 577–578 (footnotes omitted).
[12]   1997 (11) B.C.L.R. 1489; 1998 (1) SA 300 (CC).
[13]   *ibid.* at paras 50–53.
[14]   s.9.

keeper for claims of violation of dignity."[15] By virtue of such an approach taken by the South African courts it is clear that there is some weight to Westen's theory; however, it is submitted that, although compelling, Westen's arguments are slightly too radical and overbroad. Nonetheless, Westen's theory can be tempered when considered in tandem with that of Raz.[16]

Raz acknowledges the criticism that egalitarian arguments tend to lack normative force but he draws a distinction between "strictly" egalitarian arguments and "rhetorical egalitarianism"; the former being a substantive argument and the latter being merely a formal and empty concept, only fit for use in political slogans. He defines "rhetorical egalitarianism" as "arguments and claims invoking equality but not relying on strictly egalitarian principles".[17] Such arguments are those commonly termed in the language of equality but having nothing to do with egalitarian principles. These arguments are used to invoke the emotive appeal and benefit of the positive connotations that surround an argument couched in equality terms in today's liberal society, and therefore make the particular cause in question seem more attractive. But such arguments lack the competence to detect an inequality and to then explain it. In contrast, "strictly" egalitarian principles can be used to indicate when a wrong is present and also to explain why there is a wrong. It would appear that Westen's view of equality would be deemed "rhetorical egalitarianism" under Raz's theory.

In relation to "strict" egalitarianism Raz states:

> "Moral theories are strictly egalitarian if they are dominated by strictly egalitarian principles. A theory is dominated by a (group of) principle(s) if and only if the principles are never or rarely overridden by other considerations and, secondly, they apply to the main cases to which the theory applies".[18]

It is submitted that his theory of "strict egalitarianism" is not very convincing. Indeed, his explanation of "strict egalitarianism" is flagrantly circular. Therefore, Raz does not go far enough to totally discount Westen's

---

[15]   *National Coalition for Gay and Lesbian Equality v Minister for Justice ("The Sodomy Case")* 1999 (1) SA 6; 1998 (1) B.C.L.R. 1517 (CC), *per* Sachs J. at para.120 in relation to a claim made by the Centre for Applied Legal Studies in the case of *S v Mhlungu* 1995 (3) SA 867 (CC); 1995 (7) B.C.L.R. 793 (CC).

[16]   Raz, *The Morality of Freedom* (Clarendon Press, Oxford, 1986).

[17]   *ibid.* at 228.

[18]   *ibid.* at 227.

theory. In fact, a correlation can be drawn in how both Raz and Westen regard equality as being incapable of illustrating an injury or wrongdoing. Both remark that there is a difference between making a claim of wrongful treatment and making a claim of inequality. A claim for wrongful treatment can be made ad-lib, but a claim of inequality requires further evidence so as to identify the nature of the wrong committed. Indeed the wrong committed could be alien to the inequality itself, causing Raz to comment that in such circumstances equality "functions contextually rather than normatively".[19] Westen goes further and seeks to explain this void in egalitarian jurisprudence and concludes that analysis based solely on egalitarian principles cannot determine whether two people are "alike" or "unalike". Therefore, an analysis of the underlying right or principle in question will determine if a person has suffered an injury.

While egalitarian arguments are not the answer to one's quest to have the institution of marriage expanded so as to meet the needs of all individuals seeking to enter it, they do serve an important purpose. As noted, marriage is generally regarded as a public institution, therefore any argument for its reformulation must be expressed on the public stage. The strongest argument in favour of the preservation of marriage is that based on natural law principles. It is not sufficient to merely discount natural law principles if one seeks to reformulate marriage. Instead it is necessary to counter it with a strong moral argument. Despite its flaws, Westen acknowledges that egalitarian arguments "tend to carry greater moral and legal weight than they deserve on their merits". That is why arguments in the form of equality invariably place all opposing arguments on the defensive.[20]

Therefore, in constructing an argument for state interference in marriage to yield to the preferences of individuals, it ought to be expressed in terms of equality but supported by underlying rights and principles such as privacy, autonomy and dignity.

---

[19] *ibid.* at 229.

[20] Westen, "The Empty Ideal of Equality" (1982) 95 *Harvard Law Review* 537 at 593 (footnotes omitted). See Bamforth, "Same-Sex Partnerships and Arguments for Justice" in Wintenmute and Andenæs (eds), *Legal Recognition of Same-Sex Partnerships: A Study of National, European and International Law* (Hart Publishing, Oxford, 2001), pp.41–42, where Bamforth expresses similar sentiments, stating:

"This does not mean, however, that there is no role whatever for equality arguments. Given their popularity and clear, emotive appeal it may well be felt that it is useful to employ such arguments, so long as they are seen as a purely rhetorical flourish reinforcing a coherent, independent and deeper argument …"

2) Searching for equality in Ireland

The problem of egalitarian argument being an "empty vessel" is particularly acute in Ireland by virtue of the approach taken by the courts to date in relation to Art.40.1. Not only has an Aristotelian concept of equality been imported into Irish jurisprudence, but Art.40.1 also contains a "due regard" clause which states:

> "this shall not be held to mean that the State shall not in its enactments have due regard to differences of capacity, physical or moral, and of social function."

Therefore, there is no guarantee of absolute equality for all citizens in all circumstances. Distinctions can be permissibly drawn between different groups of people on the basis of differences between those groups. For example, due to religious reasons the opening hours of a kosher butcher's may differ from those of regular butchers.[21] It was argued in *State (Nicolau) v An Bord Uchtála*[22] that discrimination between natural fathers and other categories of persons identified in the Adoption Act 1952 was unconstitutional under Art.40.1. Yet, the court justified this discrimination by distinguishing between the role natural fathers tend to play and that of those enumerated under the Adoption Act; speaking for the court Walsh J. stated:

> "When it is considered that an illegitimate child may be begotten by an act of rape, callous seduction or by an act of casual commerce by a man with a woman, as well as by the association of a man with a woman in making a common home without marriage in circumstances approximating to those of married life, and that, except in the latter instance, it is rare for a natural father to take any interest in his offspring, it is not difficult to appreciate the difference in moral capacity and social function between the natural father and the several persons described in the sub-section in question."[23]

Such reasoning has been staunchly criticised as being the antithesis of equality jurisprudence. In his judgment in *WO'R v EH,* Barrington J. succinctly demonstrated the fundamental flaw in the reasoning of Walsh J. by virtue of the following syllogism:

---

[21] See *Quinn's Supermarket v Attorney-General* [1972] I.R. 1.
[22] *State Nicolau v An Bord Uchtála* [1966] I.R. 567.
[23] *ibid.* at 641.

1) Many natural fathers show no interest in their offspring and the State may properly exclude them from all say in their children's welfare.
2) The prosecutor is a natural father.
3) Therefore, the State may properly exclude him from all say in his child's welfare.[24]

Unfortunately, the failure of the courts to properly grasp the potential of Art.40.1 was not limited to the *Nicolau* decision. The equality guarantee has been consistently trumped by other constitutional rights. In *Murphy v Attorney-General*,[25] Kenny J. justified a discrimination against married couples in relation to unmarried couples in the area of tax on the basis of the special position of marriage under the Constitution.

O'B v S[26] probably represents the lowest point of Irish equality jurisprudence. This case concerned ss.67 and 69 of the Succession Act 1965, whereby illegitimate children were discriminated against by virtue of the intestacy rules. Walsh J., for the Supreme Court, held that:

> "legislation which differentiates citizens or which discriminates between them does not need to be justified under the proviso if justification for it can be found in other provisions of the Constitution."[27]

In this case the discrimination against illegitimate children was justified on the basis of the constitutional guarantee to protect the marital family.

Not only have the Irish courts been willing to find means of trumping the equality guarantee by means of existing rights, they have also had recourse to enunciate unenumerated rights so as not to base a decision on Art.40.1. Kenny J. was quite fond of this approach and has in doing so founded the enumerated rights of access to the courts[28] and the right to work.[29] Doyle refers to this approach as resulting in the "neutrality of the equality guarantee".[30]

This approach is the epitome of the "empty vessel" of equality which Westen was referring to. It is therefore apparent that any egalitarian-based argument to have marriage expanded so as to meet the needs of all citi-

---

24   *WO'R v EH* [1996] 2 I.R. 248 at 280.
25   *Murphy v Attorney-General* [1982] I.R. 241.
26   *O'B v S* [1984] I.R. 316; [1985] I.L.R.M. 86.
27   *ibid.* at 335 and 95 respectively.
28   *Macauley v Minister for Posts and Telegraphs* [1966] I.R. 345.
29   *Murtagh Properties v Cleary* [1972] I.R. 330.
30   Doyle, *Constitutional Equality Law* (Round Hall, 2004), p.76.

zens will have to be based on other underlying rights and principles if it is to find favour with the Irish courts.

The ability of equality arguments to reveal potential remedies

As noted above, moral argument couched in terms of "equality" is compelling, as it tends to necessitate opposing arguments to adopt a defensive stance. A further advantage of expressing an argument for the reformulation of marriage in terms of "equality" is that it forces one to consider potential remedies. The very fact that there is an alleged inequality causes those involved to contemplate means of eliminating the inequality. This gives rise to the debate as to whether to remedy an inequality by levelling up or down.

In the present context, by "levelling up" the State would be according all "committed" relationships the same rights and privileges currently available to marriage. Such a remedy found favour with the Constitutional Court of South Africa.[31] However, the practicality of such an approach is debatable. It would not be feasible to provide a state system of support to "committed" relationships as it would be impossible to determine the level of commitment required to be eligible. As such it is submitted that the state should not seek to support revocable relationships, as it would be impossible to monitor.

Following the Divorce Referendum, marriage can also be categorised as a revocable relationship. Therefore, it is proposed that the most suitable remedy to the current inequality is to "level down". This embraces the point of view postulated above concerning the withdrawal of State regulation of the institution of marriage.[32] For marriage to represent a universal acknowledgment of a "committed" relationship, the State ought not be a party to it because, as is evident, its current role leads to discrimination.

Equality arguments therefore represent a publicly sustainable moral argument, although inherently reliant on other principles. More importantly, such argument enlightens us as to potential remedies, and it is clear that the only feasible remedy to the current State-imposed discrimination as to the availability of marriage is for the State to be removed from the equation. Although the remedy is readily apparent, it is still necessary to analyse the underlying principles that provide the substance needed to present an argument formed in terms of equality.

---

[31]   *Fourie v Minister of Home Affairs* 2006 (3) B.C.L.R. 355 (CC).
[32]   See above, pp.27–32.

PRIVACY

The right to privacy is not a specified right under the Irish Constitution; rather it is one of the unenumerated rights flowing from the "Christian and democratic nature of the State".[33] The judicial recognition of this right has resulted in it being divided into two categories. The Supreme Court in *McGee*[34] held that legislation prohibiting the sale and use of contraceptives in Ireland was unconstitutional as a violation of the right to marital privacy. But it was not until the case of *Kennedy v Ireland*[35] that the right to individual privacy was recognised. In this case the applicants successfully argued that their right to privacy had been breached due to phone-tapping by the State. Hamilton P. stated:

"Though not specifically guaranteed by the Constitution, the right to privacy is one of the fundamental personal rights of the citizen which flow from the Christian and democratic nature of the State. It is not an unqualified right. Its exercise may be restricted by the constitutional rights of others, or by the requirements of the common good, and it is subject to the requirements of public order and morality ... The nature of the right to privacy must be such as to ensure the dignity and freedom of an individual in the type of society envisaged by the Constitution, namely, a sovereign, independent and democratic society."[36]

The "common good" limitation on the exercise of personal rights was first alluded to by Kenny J. in his judgment setting out the foundations for the doctrine of unenumerated rights when he stated:

"None of the personal rights of the citizen are unlimited: their exercise may be regulated by the Oireachtas when the common good requires this."[37]

This adoption of the "common good" limitation is a clear reference to the natural law background running throughout the Irish Constitution and in particular Arts 40–44 concerning personal rights. Walsh J. acknowledged this in *McGee* stating:

---

[33] *Ryan v Attorney-General* [1962] I.R. 294 at 312.
[34] *McGee v Attorney-General* [1974] I.R. 269.
[35] *Kennedy v Ireland* [1987] I.R. 587, [1988] I.L.R.M. 472. It is noted that this right was previously, unsuccessfully, asserted in *Norris v Attorney-General* [1984] I.R. 36; [1985] I.L.R.M. 266.
[36] *ibid.* at 592; 476. Subsequently approved by the Supreme Court in *Haughey v Moriarty* [1999] 3 I.R. 1.
[37] *Ryan v Attorney-General* [1962] I.R. 294 at 312.

"Articles 41, 42 and 43 emphatically reject the theory that there are no rights without laws, no rights contrary to the law and no rights anterior to the law. They indicate that justice is placed above the law and acknowledge that natural rights, or human rights, are not created by law but that the Constitution confirms their existence and gives them protection. The individual has natural and human rights over which the State has no authority".[38]

There are numerous versions of natural law theory, but it is generally accepted that the Thomistic model was the basis upon which the 1937 Constitution was drafted.[39] The fundamental concept within the Thomistic model is that "the individual is a part of the entire community just as one portion is part of an entire living organism, and as such, the needs of the whole are superior to the needs of the part."[40] Therefore, such a philosophy is conducive to a paternal role being played by the State in society whereby in seeking to achieve the "common good" the State is justified in putting the interests of the majority ahead of those of the individual. Walsh J., writing extra-judicially, recognised and approved this approach, asserting that:

"In ... the Constitution where the common good is referred to it is clear that the Constitution, while acknowledging the higher status of individual values, does not preclude the application of the guiding principle that gives priority to the common good over the individual interest and recognises that private interest must surrender to the common good in particular fields."[41]

However, one must not be mistaken in believing that this is merely an academic point; on the contrary, there has also been judicial recognition of the Thomistic model within Irish jurisprudence. In *McGee,* Walsh J. directly referred to this by stating:

"the individual, as a member of society and the family, as a unit of society, have duties and obligations to consider and respect the good of that society."[42]

---

[38]   *McGee v Attorney-General* [1974] I.R. 269 at 310.

[39]   See in general Millen, *The Right to Privacy in the United States and Ireland* (Blackhall Publishing, 1999), in particular Chap.6.

[40]   *ibid.* at 138.

[41]   Walsh, "Existence and Meaning of Fundamental Rights in the Field of Education in Ireland" (1981) 2 *Hum. Rts. L. J.* 319 at 327.

[42]   *McGee v Attorney-General* [1979] I.R. 285 at 310. Also, in *Norris v Attorney-General* [1984] I.R. 36 at 60, O'Higgins C.J. implicitly acknowledged such an approach in rejecting

Before entering a discussion on the principles underlying what constitutes the "common good", it is salutary to draw a distinction between the approaches taken by the US and Irish courts. It is thought necessary to do so, as those who argue in favour of the expansion of the definition of marriage on the basis of the right to privacy, often refer to American case law where the right has received significantly more judicial protection than its Irish counterpart.

McCarthy J., in his dissenting judgment in *Norris*, referred with approval to the definition of privacy as enunciated by Brandeis J. who proclaimed it to be "the right to be left alone".[43] As commendable as this definition is for its succinctness, it is nonetheless submitted that it is unhelpful in terms of Irish jurisprudence for two reasons:

1) Its construction is based on an altogether different philosophy than that followed in Irish law.
2) It does not refer to the scope of the right or why the right ought to be protected.

1) Privacy for the American *individual* and privacy for Irish *society*

There is a fundamental divergence between the right to privacy as interpreted in US and Irish law, based on the differing philosophies underpinning both Constitutions. The secular natural law theory, as illustrated by John Locke, provides the reasoning behind the fundamental rights as developed in US constitutional law.[44] This philosophy has developed the protection of the life, liberty and property of the individual in America. Under such an approach it is thought that the best means of achieving the common good is through providing each person with "his due". Therefore, the rights of the individual take precedence in US constitutional law and are not so readily restricted by the wishes of the majority. As a result, the procedure for determining rights under the secular natural law is to take the interests of the individual first and then those of the majority last; evidently it is the opposite to the Thomistic approach. The only le-

---

the plaintiff's claim that the criminalisation of homosexual acts had negative effects on his mental health and as such violated his right to bodily integrity. It was held that, once legislation was validly enacted, the mere difficulty which compliance causes the applicant does not render it unconstitutional. In such circumstances "the exigencies of the common good must prevail".

[43] *Norris v Attorney-General* [1984] I.R. 36 at 101.

[44] See in general Millen, *The Right to Privacy in the United States and Ireland* (Blackhall Publishing, 1999), in particular Chap.7.

gitimate curtailment on the rights of an individual is the need to protect the rights of another individual, *i.e.* I cannot exercise my rights in a manner that would encroach upon the rights of another individual. In contrast, the Irish Constitution is centred on the Thomistic philosophy. Such an interpretation of the right to privacy is narrower than that in the US because the primary purpose in determining rights is to enhance the common good. As such there is an element of conformity with the majority in determining rights in Irish law. As Millen notes, under the Thomistic model, *"the first and most important consideration in any adjudication concerning fundamental rights ought to be the common good."*[45]

From this philosophy it becomes clear why natural law arguments have found favour with those who wish for the current definition of marriage to be preserved. They argue that the traditional definition of marriage ought to be retained as it is in the interests of the "common good" to do so, and it is not an unjust infringement on the privacy of those who may wish to enter a different form of marriage. As is evident, the linchpin of this argument is the interpretation of what the "common good" is. Traditional arguments based on the common good tend to reconcile it with the teachings of the Catholic Church, but is this a true indicator of the "common good"? Also, would the expansion of the definition of marriage, to meet the needs of those currently not accommodated for, be detrimental to the common good? These are questions that need to be analysed in order to determine the true meaning of the "common good", which in turn will reveal whether traditional Thomistic theory arguments form persuasive grounds for the retention/expansion of the current definition of marriage.

2) The right to privacy and the "common good"

The balance between the right of individuals to conduct their private life in any manner they choose and the right of society to regulate the private lives of its citizens, has always been a contentious one. The justification for state intervention has traditionally been heralded under the banner of the "common good". Aquinas was one of the first to attempt to grapple with this ambiguous concept.[46] He acknowledged that the "common good" is achieved by a collective effort, as not all humans are impervious to suggestion and iniquity.[47]

---

[45]   *ibid.* at 86 (emphasis in original).
[46]   Aquinas, *Treatise on Law* (Hackett Publishing, 2000).
[47]   Millen, *The Right to Privacy in the United States and Ireland* (Blackhall Publishing, 1999), p.128; quoting Aquinas, *Treatise on Law*, 96, 2:

Hence, the ultimate objective of preserving the "common good" is to enhance human society; as such it must be asked whether in seeking to achieve this there is a need to regulate the private lives of individuals. Mill contended that the law could only regulate one's conduct if it had the potential to cause harm to another, but one's own mental, physical and moral protection was not a matter in which the law could regulate.[48] Therefore, the law could enforce morality. Such a theory was accepted by the Wolfenden Committee Report in 1957, titled *The Report of the Committee on Homosexual Offences and Prostitution*, which recommended that the criminal law should not interfere in the private lives of people unless necessary. In its seminal paragraph the Committee stated:

> "[u]nless a deliberate attempt is made by society, acting through the agency of the law, to equate the sphere of crime with that of sin, there must remain a realm of private morality and immorality which is, in brief and crude terms, not the law's business".[49]

This approach interprets the "common good" as only justifying state regulation of behaviour if such behaviour was to inflict injury on another and not simply because such behaviour might be deemed immoral. However, an opposing interpretation has been adopted by the Irish courts which justifies state regulation into private acts on grounds including immorality. This interpretation is based on the reasoning that there are a certain number of morals of general consensus within society and that these provide stability and order to society and as such ought to be upheld.[50] The case of *Norris v Attorney-General*[51] is demonstrative of this. The applicant claimed that ss.61 and 62 of the Offences Against the Person Act 1861, criminalising sodomy, and s.11 of the Criminal Law Amendment Act 1885, prohibiting acts of gross indecency between males, were unconstitutional on grounds of equality, bodily integrity and freedom of

---

> "And therefore human law does not prohibit all vices from which the virtuous abstain but only the more serious ones from which it is possible for the majority to abstain and especially those which are harmful to others and which, if not prohibited, would make preservation of human society impossible: Thus human law prohibits murders, thefts and the like."

[48] Mill, *On Liberty,* in Lerner (ed.), *The Essential Works of John Stuart Mill* (Bantam Books, 1965).

[49] Wolfenden Committee, *Report of the Committee on Homosexual Offences and Prostitution* (1957), at para.61.

[50] Devlin, *Morals and the Criminal Law*, reprinted in Devlin, *The Enforcement of Morals* (1965).

[51] *Norris v Attorney-General* [1984] I.R. 36.

expression. However, the kernel of the applicant's case was that the State had no business in the field of private morality and consequently had no right to legislate in relation to the private sexual conduct of consenting adults.

O'Higgins C.J., for the majority, dismissed the applicant's claims on all grounds; of pertinent interest, however, is his dicta in relation to the right to privacy. Not only did he conclude that the State has the right to regulate the private actions of individuals that may cause harm to another, but also he:

> "regard[ed] the State as having an interest in the general moral well-being of the community and as being entitled, where it is practicable to do so, to discourage conduct which is morally wrong and harmful to a way of life and to values which the State wishes to protect."[52]

It is submitted that such an interpretation of the Thomistic model of natural law within the Constitution is incorrect for two reasons:

1) A true interpretation of the "common good" justification under the Thomistic model limits it to regulating acts that may cause harm to another and not merely on the grounds that they are immoral.

Henchy J. in his dissent recognised this fundamental difference stating that the acts in question in this case:

> "would all appear to fall within a secluded area of activity or non-activity which may be claimed as necessary for the expression of an individual personality, for purposes not always necessarily moral or commendable, but meriting recognition in circumstances which do not engender considerations such as State security, public order or morality, or other essential components of the common good."[53]

In seeking to include morality in the equation for determining the "common good", O'Higgins C.J. ventured into the muddy waters of attempting to gauge public consensus. This is a flawed analysis, however, as majority consensus does not always equate with the "common good". The Supreme Court recognised this point in *McGee* where it held that the private mor-

---

[52] *ibid.* at 64.
[53] *ibid.* at 72.

als of a husband and wife, which may lead them to use contraceptives, does not justify intervention by the State merely because it offends the morals of the majority of citizens. For the State to intervene it must be in the interests of the common good. Not only was the basis of the analysis of the "common good" by O'Higgins C.J. flawed but he further compounded his error by determining that Christian teachings were an accurate guidepost from which one can gauge public opinion as to what constitutes a moral or immoral act. This approach filters into the next objection to the majority's determination of the "common good".

> 2) The judgment of O'Higgins C.J. was heavily influenced by Catholic teachings and it is felt that his determination of the "common good" was based on this.

Under a true Thomistic approach to determining the "common good" it is not permissible to equate the "common good" with the teachings of the Roman Catholic Church. Church and State ought to be treated as two separate and distinct entities. Again, Henchy J. in his compelling dissent recognised the need for this distinction, arguing that the preservation of a pluralist society required such a division.[54]

Furthermore, just because the vast majority of the population profess to be practising Catholics does not necessarily correlate with the fact that the vast majority of society follows the teachings of the Church. This fact is illustrated when one analyses the result of the 1995 Divorce referendum. Divorce is contrary to Catholic teachings and, at the time of the 1995 referendum, approximately 90 per cent of the population were Catholics,[55] yet over 50 per cent voted to allow divorce, thus demonstrating a direct divergence between those who profess to be Catholics and those who actually follow such teachings.[56]

---

[54]　*ibid.* at 78. Similar judicial support can be seen for this approach in the dicta of Denham J. in *Re a Ward of Court (withholding of medical treatment) (No.2)* [1996] 2 I.R. 79; [1995] 2 I.L.R.M. 401 where she stated that the Supreme Court is a "court of law, and the Constitution and law are applied; not moral law."

[55]　Census 2002, available at www.cso.ie.

[56]　One may argue that this example does not gauge public consensus at the time of the *Norris* case. This criticism is accepted; the purpose of the example is merely illustrative of a greater point, that being that those who claim to be Catholic do not always follow such teachings. Also, it is submitted that the results of the Divorce Referendum of 1986 (two years after *Norris*) substantiates this point as 36.5 per cent voted for divorce, again representing a significant divergence from the number who then claimed to be Catholics (approximately 93 per cent of the population).

Also, the limiting of the right to privacy in this case on the partial basis that it would be contrary to Catholic teachings reveals an intrinsic contradiction within the reasoning of the Supreme Court in this case and that of *McGee*. In *McGee* the court allowed married couples to use contraceptives despite it being virulently against Catholic teachings, yet in *Norris* the court submitted to the teachings of the Catholic Church in upholding the criminalisation of male homosexual sex.

Therefore, it is submitted, that if one seeks to invoke an argument based on the "common good", the correct interpretation to be given is that it permits the limitation of acts if they are potentially harmful to others and not solely based on the ground that they may be deemed immoral by some. Based on this interpretation it is now necessary to define or seek to set out the factors of the "common good".

Walsh defines the "common good" as:

"the satisfaction (in so far as possible) of the greatest proportion of interests of all persons with the least sacrifice, the least friction, and the least waste…"[57]

Costello defines it as:

"the whole ensemble of conditions which collaboration in a political community brings about for the benefit of every member of it."[58]

Thus, as is evident, the concept of the "common good" is an organic one, dependent upon the interests of society at any particular moment in time. However, the fundamental tenets underlying it can be traced back to the works of Aquinas, summarised by Millen as incorporating the principles of:

- preserving the life and health of humans;
- not discriminating against certain sections of society;
- prohibiting certain acts that society deems contrary to the preservation of the life and health of humans, *e.g.* murder;
- to maintain peace and justice.[59]

---

[57] Walsh, "Existence and Meaning of Fundamental Rights in the Field of Education in Ireland" (1981) 2 *Hum. Rts. L. J.* 319 at 327.

[58] Costello, "Limiting Rights Constitutionally" in O'Reilly (ed.), *Human Rights and Constitutional Law: Essays in Honour of Brian Walsh* (Round Hall Press, 1992), p.178.

[59] Millen, *The Right to Privacy in the United States and Ireland* (Blackhall Publishing, 1999), p.129.

In order to promote these ideals it is necessary to interpret the "common good" in a contemporary manner. It has been accepted by the courts that no interpretation of the Constitution is intended to be final for all time,[60] therefore a natural law argument based on the "common good" cannot be used as an impediment to constitutional change if the "common good", as presented, does not accord with a contemporary reflection of the needs of society. The judgment of O'Higgins C.J. in *Norris* again provides an illustrative example of a failure to recognise this. Part of his reasoning in determining male homosexual acts to be immoral, was based on the fact that for over two thousand years Christian teachings had declared them to be so.[61] Reference to the teachings of the Christian Church for the past two thousand years is the antithesis to a contemporary interpretation. McCarthy J., in his dissent, directly opposed this aspect of the majority judgment declaring:

> "I cannot accept the approach based upon applying the test of the then contemporary mores to the issue of constitutionality. It must be the mores contemporaneous with the raising of the issue itself."[62]

Therefore, if one adopts a contemporaneous analysis of the "common good" in today's society, can it be legitimately argued that by expanding the definition of marriage it would be detrimental to the "common good"? It is submitted that it would not. As was argued in Chapter 1, the current definition of marriage excludes many de facto families from obtaining the constitutional protection as currently enjoyed by the marital family. This is out of sync with social reality as there is a substantial number of non-marital families within Irish society today. Also, by defining marriage in the current sense, it is restricting certain sections of society from expressing their wish to enter marriage, most notably same-sex couples. There is a current need within society for the definition of marriage to be expanded and as such the "common good" should recognise this. Walsh J., writing extra-judicially, acknowledged this, stating:

---

[60]   *McGee v Attorney-General* [1974] I.R. 269, at 319. This approach to constitutional interpretation was again endorsed by the Supreme Court in *State (Healy) v Donoghue* [1976] I.R. 325 where at 347 O'Higgins C.J. stated: "the Constitution did not seek to impose for all time the ideas prevalent or accepted with regard to these virtues at the time of its enactment. Walsh J. expressed this view very clearly in *McGee v Attorney General*."

[61]   *Norris v Attorney-General* [1984] I.R. 36 at 64.

[62]   *ibid.* at 99.

"It would appear to follow that, as the quality of life improves and the requirements necessary to maintain the quality of life need to be defended, the courts will in the natural order of things declare such matters to be protected rights and, therefore, will give constitutional protection to those who seek to invoke these rights."[63]

It is submitted that by permitting couples to determine the form of marriage they wish to enter, rather than imposing a rigid state definition, the dignity and personality of individuals would be enhanced,[64] thereby benefiting the "common good". Although the "common good" is often discussed in terms of being superior to the interests of the individual, it must be acknowledged that the individual contributes to promoting and enhancing the "common good":

"only when individual rights are protected is the common good promoted and only by promoting the common good can the rights of all be fairly protected."[65]

The Thomistic model of the "common good" ought not to be confused with a Utilitarian model. This point was emphasised by Costello J., writing extra-judicially, stating that:

"… the common good is not the good of the political community as such (which is a concept inherent in the totalitarian State and inimical to the protection of human rights) but is an end to be promoted for specific purposes, which include the furtherance of the dignity and freedom of every individual in society."[66]

Therefore, the promotion of human dignity and individual autonomy enhance the "common good". However, in order for dignity and autonomy to flourish there is a need for a realm of privacy; as such, it is submitted

---

[63] Walsh, "Existence and Meaning of Fundamental Rights in Ireland" (1980) 1 *Hum. Rts. L. J.* 171 at 177.

[64] In relation to this point the dicta of the South African Courts is particularly interesting, most notably in the cases of *National Coalition for Gay and Lesbian Equality v Minister for Home Affairs* 2000 (2) SA 1; 2000 (1) B.C.L.R. 39 (CC); *National Coalition for Gay and Lesbian Equality v Minister for Justice ("The Sodomy Case")* 1999 (1) SA 6; 1998 (1) B.C.L.R. 1517 (CC); *Fourie v Minister of Home Affairs* 2005 (3) B.C.L.R. 241 (SCA), affirmed in *Fourie v Minister of Home Affairs* 2006 (3) B.C.L.R. 355 (CC).

[65] Millen, *The Right to Privacy in the United States and Ireland* (Blackhall Publishing, 1999), p.143 (emphasis in original).

[66] Costello, "Limiting Rights Constitutionally" in O'Reilly (ed.), *Human Rights and Constitutional Law: Essays in Honour of Brian Walsh* (Round Hall Press, 1992), p.178.

that by according individuals the privacy necessary to enter the form of marriage they wish, it will enhance dignity and autonomy, thereby promoting the "common good" and as such the "common good" should not be used to regulate the privacy of those wishing to enter marriage.

AUTONOMY

Individualism v paternalism

At the core of the argument concerning the availability of marriage is the conflict between the State's role in seeking to regulate marriage and the ability of the individual to choose the form of marriage he/she wishes to enter. In philosophical terms this is a conflict between the concepts of paternalism (the State's role) and autonomy (individual choice). The State's traditional justification in regulating the availability of marriage was based on a number of factors already alluded to.[67] Briefly, these factors include:

1. Protection of children;
2. Control on sexuality;
3. The assumption of sex and procreation being connected.[68]

As time has passed, however, these justifications have diminished in stature as society has developed.[69] We have moved from a State based on communitarian ideals to one now beginning to focus on the needs and wants of the individual. Autonomy, and not paternalism, is becoming the new idiom of social debate. The traditional paternalistic approach to marriage promoted gender roles, exclusivity and permanence. The introduction of divorce into Irish law has extinguished the irrevocable nature of marriage, and social and economic developments have caused gender equality to become the norm. As is apparent, the traditional justifications for regulating marriage have been on the decrease; nevertheless, the concept of paternalism is still the guiding force behind the regulation of marriage. It is submitted that there is a need to eradicate this in favour of an autonomy-based model.

The right to marry has been described as "one of the vital personal rights essential to the orderly pursuit of happiness by free men", thereby representing a "basic civil right of man" and that such freedom is "funda-

---

[67]   See p.31 above.
[68]   As prior to the judgment of *McGee v Attorney-General* contraceptives were not legally available in Ireland.
[69]   See Chap.1.

mental to our very existence and survival".[70] Furthermore, it has been said that "[t]he right to marry is the *right of individuals…*".[71] From this the popularity of autonomy-based arguments amongst those seeking to eliminate the state regulation of marriage becomes evident. As a starting-point, however, one needs to examine why and how state interference in the institution of marriage is a violation of individual autonomy. Two rationales present themselves.

First, state interference in the institution of marriage violates the autonomy of those currently excluded from marriage by virtue of its definition. This is because, with marriage, certain rights and privileges are attached which those who do not fit within the state definition of marriage are being deprived of. This violates the autonomy of such individuals as it is not presenting them with the opportunity to choose whether to enter marriage or not.[72] Not only does this stigmatise those excluded from marriage, but it also dehumanises them by depriving them of some of the basic rights of man such as autonomy, liberty, dignity and equality.[73]

Secondly, by imposing a form of marriage, the State is violating the autonomy of each and every person in society. The rationale for this argument is based on the view that marriage is one of life's most defining moments and therefore should be entered into on the basis of the choice and free will of the parties to it. This found favour with the South African Supreme Court of Appeal in the case of *Fourie v Minister of Home Affairs*[74] where Cameron JA stated:

> "… marriage and the capacity to get married remain central to our self-definition as humans … The capacity to choose to get married enhances the liberty, the autonomy and the dignity of a couple committed for life to each other."[75]

On the other hand, those in favour of a paternalistic approach argue that the introduction of autonomy and notions of individualism into family law and family structure would lead to the destruction of the communal

---

[70] *Loving v Virginia* 388 U.S. 1 (1967) at 12.

[71] *Perez v Lippold* 198 P.2d 17 at 20 (Cal. 1948) (emphasis added).

[72] For judicial support of this argument see the judgment of Marshall C.J. in *Goodridge v Department of Public Health* 440 Mass. 309; 798 N.E.2d 941 (2003).

[73] See in general Bamforth, "Same-Sex Partnerships and Arguments for Justice" in Wintenmute & Andenæs (eds), *Legal Recognition of Same-Sex Partnerships: A Study of National, European and International Law* (Hart Publishing, 2001).

[74] *Fourie v Minister of Home Affairs* 2005 (3) B.C.L.R. 241 (SCA).

[75] *ibid.* at para.14.

backbone of the family and allow "loose" connections to constitute a marriage/family. Traditionalist concerns are centred on the fear that an autonomy-based model of marriage will change the institution of marriage from the once interdependent union promoting state goals to an institution of self-gratification, whereby the interests of those associated with a marriage, *e.g.* children, would be dispensed with. On the contrary, however, it has been argued that an autonomy-based model of marriage would not alter the status and respect enjoyed by the institution of marriage. Instead, it would ensure that those entering marriage would do so as equals and that the mutuality needed in a relationship would be ensured. By dispensing with the traditional model of marriage and its imposing gender roles, etc., autonomy would, through the element of choice, give couples the opportunity to carve out their own roles in a marriage in a manner that they deem necessary for it to be a success.[76]

It is not argued that there should be total freedom in relation to entering into marriage. It is acknowledged that marriage as an institution is a very special and unique entity; nevertheless, it should not be available to some and not others. Notwithstanding this, a certain degree of state involvement would be permissible in relation to one's respect and commitment toward the institution of marriage. This was acknowledged by Traynor J. in *Perez v Sharp*,[77] one of the first miscegenation cases ultimately leading to the seminal case of *Loving v Virginia*,[78] where he said:

> "There can be no prohibition of marriage except for an important social objective and by reasonable means."[79]

Importantly, Traynor J. qualified this statement by stating that the test for such legislation must always be based on the individual rather than arbitrary societal concerns. As such, state involvement would be impermissible if it were to discriminate against a certain element of society, but if it were merely to act in a manner so as to ensure that marriage as an institution was respected, then this would be permissible. An example of such an approach is the three-month notification period required before one can enter into a marriage in Ireland.[80] This is viewed as a means of preventing a "Las Vegas style" wedding where a couple may hastily marry

---

[76] See in general Wriggins, "Marriage Law and Family Law: Autonomy, Interdependence, and Couples of the Same Gender" (1999–2000) 41 *B. C. L. Rev.* 265.

[77] 32 Cal. 2d 711, 198 P.2d 17 (1948).

[78] 388 U.S. 1 (1967).

[79] 198 P.2d 17, at 19 (1948).

[80] Civil Registration Ireland Act 2004, s.46.

without giving marriage the thought and respect that it deserves, and subsequently seek to terminate the marriage. This formality is for the common good and ultimately for the benefit of the individuals that choose to get married and constitutes a permissible state action in this area as it is not prima facie discriminatory.[81] Another example of permissible state involvement in marriage is the age limits imposed on those seeking to marry.[82] In particular this protects young girls from being taken advantage of by paedophiles.

Autonomy in Irish law

The right to autonomy is recognised in Ireland as an unenumerated right and came to prominence in the case of *Re Ward of Court (withholding medical treatment) (No.2)*.[83] This case concerned a woman who, following complications from an operation, was in a near-vegetative state for over 20 years. Her family sought an order for all artificial feeding to cease. Lynch J. in the High Court granted the order, but this was appealed to the Supreme Court where the original High Court order was upheld by a 4:1 majority. While the Supreme Court majority recognised the right to autonomy, it did not deal with the meaning of autonomy in a satisfactory manner. In circumstances such as those in the *Ward* case it becomes apparent that there are two potential meanings to autonomy:

> "[If it means] an expression of the desirability of people being free from interference by others, even a patient who is entirely incompetent can be said to have an interest in autonomy. On the other hand, if autonomy involves a capacity for the exercise of choice and judgement, a mentally ill patient may (depending on the nature of the illness) suffer from a lack or impairment of autonomy."[84]

Unfortunately the majority of the Supreme Court adopted the former meaning on the basis that, by virtue of the equality guarantee in Art.40.1, each and every citizen is entitled to exercise their rights. Such reasoning has been criticised as failing to appreciate the "due regard" clause of

---

[81] An argument could be made that it prevents a terminally ill person from marrying a loved one expediently if necessary and therefore discriminates. However, s.47 of the 2004 Act provides a means of exemption from the three-month notice requirement and therefore alleviates any potential discriminatory impact.

[82] Family Law Act 1995, s.32 declares that one may not marry until the age of 18.

[83] [1996] 2 I.R. 79; [1995] 2 I.L.R.M. 401, hereinafter referred to as the *Ward* case.

[84] Feldman, "Human Dignity as a Legal Value: Part 2" [2000] *P.L.* 61 at 69.

Art.40.1 of the Constitution which justifies differential treatment between people by virtue of their physical and moral capacity and social function, causing Byrne and Binchy to comment:

> "A non-autonomous person, by definition, cannot exercise the right to autonomy even if the law … were to ascribe such a right to that person."[85]

The majority failed to determine the scope and origins of this right, arguably being more concerned with *achieving* the "right" decision than the *means* of getting there.[86] Instead the court seemed content in paraphrasing English case law, supplementing it with "incantations of 'privacy', 'dignity', 'bodily integrity' and 'autonomy'. A rigorous analysis [of which] is notable by its absence."[87]

Nevertheless, the Irish Supreme Court is not alone in adopting such an interpretation to autonomy. The German Constitutional Court, although dealing with the origins of autonomy, reached the same conclusion.[88] American courts have adopted a more individualistic interpretation of autonomy[89]; this is not surprising, however, having regard to the secular natural law basis upon which its Constitution has been developed, and therefore ought not to be given undue weight in relation to Irish jurisprudence.[90]

One thing that is apparent from the *Ward* case is that the right to autonomy does exist in Irish law. That said, it is now pertinent to examine the origin and scope of this right. In *Groundwork of the Metaphysic of Morals* (1785) Kant embarked on a thorough study of autonomy and its effects. It was Kant's belief that, because humans were rational and autonomous beings, they possessed a unique value or attribute and therefore should be treated in a manner reflective of this. One of the essential elements of Kant's theory was that the moral law requires individuals to act in a manner so as to treat others as "ends" and never as only "means". To treat someone as an end is to view them as an objective or good to be achieved. Autonomy, however, by its nature, causes people to act in their

---

[85] Byrne and Binchy, *The Annual Review of Irish Law 1995* (Round Hall Sweet & Maxwell, 1997) at 159.

[86] See in general O'Carroll, "The Right to Die: A Critique of the Supreme Court Judgment in 'The Ward' Case" (1995) 84 *Studies* 375.

[87] Keown, "Life and Death in Dublin" [1996] 55 C. L. J. 6 at 7.

[88] BverfGE 87, 209, 228 (1992).

[89] See in particular *Schloendorff v Society of N.Y. Hospital* 211 N.Y. 125; 105 N.E. 92 (1914) and *Olmstead v United States* 277 U.S. 438 (1928).

[90] See pp.48–49 above.

own self-interest, consequently increasing the risk of using others as a "means". To resolve this conflict it is necessary to obtain another person's consent/permission before one can embark on a course of conduct benefiting their own self-interest, which in turn may cause them to treat others as a "means" to their own cause. Because of this Kant accentuates the need to respect the autonomy of others. To do this it is necessary to appreciate their dignity, so they are not merely used as a "means" throughout life. Therefore, it is necessary to give others the opportunity to agree to helping a person pursue his own self-interest, thus avoiding the immorality of people being merely used as a "means" without their permission or even knowledge. As such, the right to autonomy derives from this concept of dignity, which in turn imposes limitations on the right to autonomy:

> "In a broad and general sense, respect for dignity implies respect for the autonomy of each person, and the right of everyone not to be devalued as a human being or treated in a degrading or humiliating manner."[91]

The concept of dignity is essentially the driving force behind any claim for autonomy, because, combined, they create a compelling argument, bringing notions such as free choice and the "good life" to the forefront of any discussion. In the debate concerning the expansion of the institution of marriage, free choice and the "good life" represent the shift from traditional communitarian views of marriage to those associated with a pluralist society. Both are interconnected in the sense that by promoting individual autonomy it is thought that the individual will flourish as a person, thereby enhancing his/her dignity.

Dignity

Dignity, as a legal concept, came to prominence in the aftermath of World War II. Following the outcry of the holocaust, nations gathered in an attempt to prevent such an atrocity recurring, resulting in the United Nations Declaration of Human Rights (1948). Since then the concept of "dignity" has occupied an aspirational role in the preamble to many inter-

---

[91]   Chaskalson, "Human Dignity as a Constitutional Value" in Kretzmer & Klein (eds), *The Concept of Human Dignity in Human Rights Discourse* (Kluwer Law International, 2002), p.134.

national charters[92] and constitutions.[93] However, a study of this notion of "dignity" reveals a complex and in some places contradictory meaning, thereby leading to assorted conceptions as to its nature.[94] Furthermore, "dignity" can operate on a number of different levels:

(i)   The dignity attaching to the whole human species.
(ii) The dignity of groups within the human species.
(iii) The dignity of human individuals.[95]

Consequently, there is no clear and concise meaning or interpretation that can be given to the concept of dignity. On the contrary "[i]t is a notion which is culturally dependent and eminently malleable."[96] Despite this myriad of possibilities, one can glean two forms of argument based on the concept of dignity, both of which have found support.

The first form of argument is a subjective one, whereby "dignity" is portrayed in a manner so as to protect each individual's moral self-worth.

---

[92] Charter of the United Nations (1945); UN Universal Declaration on Human Rights (1948); International Covenant on Economic, Social and Cultural Rights; International Covenant on Civil and Political Rights (1966); and European Convention of Human Rights.

[93] Dignity is a fundamental right in the German Grundgesetz, set out in Art.1, and also in the South African Constitution, set out in Art.10.

[94] Meyer articulates four categories of "dignity" which are capable of attaching to human beings:

1. Social Dignity—This is simply the endowment of dignity by virtue of one's position in a social hierarchy. This conception originates from Edmund Burke set out in *Reflections on the Revolution in France 1790* (Anchor, New York, 1973).

2. Egalitarian account of Human Dignity—This is the counter argument to social dignity and is evident in the works of Kant. Under such a philosophy dignity is seen as being of special moral value, and status attaches to all humans irrespective of social standing, race, gender and other social markers. This is quite an expansive account of dignity.

3. Sense of Dignity—If a person has a sense of his own dignity then he will be more likely to assert it and resist the humiliation and inhumane treatment which others may seek to impose on him. However, even if a person does not appreciate his own sense of dignity it does not debar him from dignity altogether. Instead he still has the benefit of the status of having human dignity which in itself demands the respect and protection of others.

4. Virtue of Dignity—This notion of dignity derives from the second account of dignity, that being Human Dignity. By acting as a virtue it attends to the moral and ethical framework of the concept of dignity so as to illustrate its virtuous character amongst mankind. This conception originates from the work of Thomas Paine in *The Rights of Man (1791–1792)* (Anchor, New York).

See Meyer, "Dignity as a (Modern) Virtue" in Kretzmer & Klein (eds), *The Concept of Human Dignity in Human Rights Discourse* (Kluwer Law International, 2002), p.195.

[95] Feldman, "Human Dignity as a Legal Value: Part 1" [1999] P.L. 682 at 684.

[96] *ibid.* at 698.

Under this interpretation, "dignity" commands respect for the autonomy of the individual, thereby prohibiting state action that might exclude the individual from a course of conduct he/she wishes to pursue. Such an argument tends to draw support from those in favour of expanding the availability of marriage. The second form of argument is an objective one, which tends to approach the concept of dignity from the perspective of society as a whole. "Dignity" is seen as a virtue that attaches to society or mankind as a whole and not merely to the individual. Under this approach it is the collective nature of mankind that gives dignity and autonomy their vitality, leading some to declare such an interpretation as a "euphemism, or even a deception".[97]

Although "dignity" is the source from which autonomy germinated, it can also provide the means by which autonomy is restricted, if not defeated. The objective intimation of "dignity", set out above, can be used to form an argument supporting paternalism, the antithesis of autonomy, thereby justifying state interference in marriage. If the state is of the opinion that the dignity of the people as a whole would be protected by introducing certain regulations that may restrict/interfere with the dignity of an individual, then this may be permissible. Therefore, this argument, expressed in terms of "dignity", actually supports a paternalistic course of action.

The basis for such an argument is found in natural law theory, in particular that of John Finnis.[98] Finnis claimed that the law is derived from a pre-ordained set of basic goods.[99] Throughout life each person will seek to achieve and promote these basic goods. Finnis later added marriage as a basic good, committed to the ultimate objective of rearing children. Therefore, any sexual acts beyond marital vaginal intercourse are seen to be immoral. As such, the law can enter the realm of privacy to ensure that other sexual acts are not taking place. For natural law theorists bodily integrity/dignity can only be preserved by using one's body in the manner in which God envisaged. Therefore, sexual acts are permissible only if procreation is the ultimate objective. As such, masturbation, oral and anal

---

[97] Wood, "Autonomy as the Ground of Morality" O'Neill Memorial Lectures, University of New Mexico, March 1999, available at http://www.stanford.edu/~allenw/papers/Autonomy.doc.

[98] See Finnis, *Natural Law and Natural Rights* (Clarendon Press, 1980) and Finnis, "Law, Morality, and 'Sexual Orientation'" (1993–1994) 69 *Notre Dame Law Review* 1049.

[99] According to Finnis these are life, knowledge, play, aesthetic experience, friendship, practical reasonableness and religion; Finnis, *Natural Law and Natural Rights* (Clarendon Press, 1980).

sex, even with a spouse, is a violation of that person's bodily integrity as their partner is merely using their body as a means to an end, that being pleasure. Consequently, natural law theorists would be against an autonomy-based model of marriage as it would use marriage, a basic good, to promote self-interest. Instead, the "dignity" of mankind would be better protected by prohibiting the expansion of marriage to a level where the parties to the marriage are free to determine its course and form.

Bamforth attempts to rebut this argument by honing in on the theological basis to Finnis's theory, claiming it to be either centred on Roman Catholic teachings or, otherwise, self-referential.[100] Despite the persuasive argument postulated by Bamforth in relation to Finnis's theory, it does not refute the argument that "dignity" can indeed support a theory of paternalism. "Dignity" as a concept does not rely on a Roman Catholic basis; on the contrary, it can claim origins from a number of sources including religious, philosophical, secular and moral.[101]

As such, "dignity" as a concept is a double-edged sword, thus raising the question of whether it should be treated as a right or not.

A right to dignity?

Due to the ambiguous nature of "dignity" it ought not be declared a justiciable right. Different interpretations of "dignity" have the potential to reach results which are polar opposites of each other, thereby providing too great a scope for judicial activism. The principle underpinning dignity, that being the protection of the lifestyle of a person, can be undermined by the very concept itself becoming a "screen behind which paternalism or moralism are elevated above freedom in legal decision-making."[102]

Admittedly there are jurisdictions where dignity has been declared a right; however, such countries are those seeking to transcend past indiscretions whereby sections of their society were treated in an inhumane manner. Article 1 of the German Grundgesetz[103] and Art.10 of the South

---

[100] Bamforth, "Same-Sex Partnerships and Arguments for Justice" in Wintenmute & Andenæs (eds), *Legal Recognition of Same-Sex Partnerships: A Study of National, European and International Law* (Hart Publishing, 2001), p.50.

[101] See in general Kretzmer & Klein (eds), *The Concept of Human Dignity in Human Rights Discourse* (Kluwer Law International, 2002).

[102] Feldman, "Human Dignity as a Legal Value: Part 1" [1999] P.L. 682 at 697.

[103] "The dignity of man shall be inviolable. To respect and protect it shall be the duty of all state authority".

African Constitution[104] are illustrative examples of this, as both countries seek to eradicate their respective past atrocities, the holocaust and apartheid. It is submitted, however, that it is not worthwhile to talk of an actual right to dignity in a legal sense as it can lead to conflicting interpretations depending on whether one adopts a subjective or objective approach. Instead, it would be prudent to regard "dignity" as a descriptive concept instead of a normative one. Statman defines a descriptive concept as one that refers "to some given feature that all humans possess and by virtue of which they enjoy privileged status in the world."[105] Therefore, the law ought to have regard for the notion of "dignity", in the sense that it seeks to preserve it in everyday life by protecting and promoting fundamental human rights. Feldman articulates this approach stating:

> "Dignity is thus not an end in itself, or even a means to an end. It is rather an expression of an attitude to life which we as humans should value when we see it in others as an expression of something which gives particular point and poignancy to the human condition. By its nature, dignity can be neither pursued nor used, but only lived, fostered, enhanced and admired. It follows that it can generally make little or no sense to talk of a right to dignity. The law can at best provide a circumscribing circle of rights which, in some of their effects, help to preserve the field for a dignified life."[106]

Although Denham J. declared "dignity" to be one of the unenumerated rights under the Constitution,[107] it has remained a relatively untapped concept in Irish law. As stated above, it is not prudent to refer to a "right to dignity"; instead "dignity" should be used as a framework within which more specific claims can be made and, despite the dicta of Denham J. in the *Ward* case, this has been the approach of the Irish courts to date. "Dignity" ought to be interpreted as a value to be pursued[108] through the implementation of other rights. Walsh J. acknowledged such an approach in

---

[104]   "Everyone has inherent dignity and the right to have their dignity respected and protected."
[105]   Statman, "Humiliation, Dignity and Self-Respect" in Kretzmer & Klein (eds), *The Concept of Human Dignity in Human Rights Discourse* (Kluwer Law International, 2002), p.211.
[106]   Feldman, "Human Dignity as a Legal Value: Part 1" [1999] P.L. 682 at 687.
[107]   *Re Ward of Court (withholding medical treatment) (No.2)* [1996] 2 I.R. 79 at 163.
[108]   *Foy v An t-Ard Chlaraitheior*, unreported, High Court, McKechnie J., July 9, 2002. Relying on *Re Article 26 Offences Against the State (Amendment) Bill* [1940] I.R. 470 and *Re Philip Clarke* [1950] I.R. 235.

Quinn's Supermarket v Attorney-General where, in relation to Art.40.1, he commented that it:

> "…is not a guarantee of absolute equality for all citizens in all circumstances but is a guarantee of equality as human persons and is a guarantee related to their dignity as human beings and a guarantee against any inequalities grounded upon an assumption, or indeed a belief, that some individuals or classes of individuals, by reason of their human attributes or their ethnic or racial, social or religious background are to be treated as the inferior or superior of other individuals in the community."[109]

In a similar vein, but in the context of achieving justice before the courts and in particular the entitlement to legal aid, O'Higgins C.J. stated:

> "…the concept of justice, which is specifically referred to in the Preamble in relation to freedom and dignity of the individual appears again in the provisions of Article 34 which deal with the Courts. It is justice which is to be administered in Courts and this concept of justice must import not only fairness, and fair procedures, but also with regard to the dignity of the individual. No court under the Constitution has jurisdiction to act contrary to justice."[110]

Furthermore, in *G v An Bord Uchtála*,[111] O'Higgins C.J. stated that the natural rights that attach to a child are those necessary so as to provide the child with the opportunity of "realising his or her full personality and dignity as a human being."[112]

Therefore, "dignity" ought not to be used as a means of resolving rights issues; instead it should be used as a means of expressing such problems. "Dignity" as a concept carries with it a sense of universality; it can be the binding force of any claim for a breach of rights. It should therefore function as an umbrella concept expressing the need for action, but within which fundamental rights provide the substantive content of the claim. Despite enumerating "dignity" as a fundamental right, the South African courts have implicitly adopted this approach, whereby in

---

[109]   [1972] I.R. 1 at 13.
[110]   *State (Healy) v Donoghue* [1976] I.R. 325 at 348.
[111]   [1980] I.R. 32.
[112]   *ibid.* at 55.

dealing with the "right to dignity" the court invariably associates it with the rights to equality,[113] privacy,[114] or autonomy.[115]

In conclusion, the "dignity" of individuals is being infringed by the State's interference in the institution of marriage. Such interference is preventing individuals from asserting the form of marriage they wish to enter and defining the lifestyle they seek to pursue. However, in the quest to eliminate paternalism from the private lives of individuals, "dignity" should only be used for its emotive and broadcasting merits and not as a substantive right in itself. It can be used to draw attention to the gradual decline of state justifications for the role of paternalism in marriage and to illustrate the shift in attitudes from viewing marriage as an institution to a mutual caring and compassionate relationship between two individuals. It is time to abandon the "shell" of marriage which, at the behest of the State, has dominated Irish society in modern times. As Barlow and James note:

> "...the reality of the situation remains that marriage has simply lost its power to hold people together and to entice them into lifelong partnerships in the first place. The social structures which gave it this power have been greatly weakened by lack of religion, women's financial independence, state support for lone parents, separation of sex from marriage and of childbearing from marriage, ease of divorce, ease of cohabitation. Hence, we are currently in a state of transition where individuals are viewing marriage less as an institution and more as a companionate relationship."[116]

Whilst an argument couched in terms of "dignity" draws attention to this, it is the rights of equality, privacy and autonomy that ought to provide the substantive content for the argument that marriage ought to be left to the free will of those who seek to enter it. Marriage 20 years ago meant something altogether different from what it does today. In the past marriage was seen as a safe haven, an institution of security where both hus-

---

[113] *National Coalition for Gay and Lesbian Equality v Minister for Home Affairs* 2000 (2) SA 1; 2000 (1) B.C.L.R. 39 (CC).

[114] *National Coalition for Gay and Lesbian Equality v Minister for Justice ("The Sodomy Case")* 1999 (1) SA 6; 1998 (1) B.C.L.R. 1517 (CC).

[115] *Fourie v Minister of Home Affairs* 2005 (3) B.C.L.R. 241 (SCA), affirmed in *Fourie v Minister of Home Affairs* 2006 (3) B.C.L.R. 355 (CC).

[116] Barlow and James, "Regulating Marriage and Cohabitation in 21st Century Britain" (2004) 67 M.L.R. 143 at 176.

band and wife had predetermined gender roles in which it was their objective to contribute to the development of society by procreating children. Today, however, marriage is viewed more in terms of how it affects people's emotions. It is a junction on life's path whereby people stop and seek to achieve emotional fulfilment with the one they love. There are no predetermined roles and the only constant between all marriages is the element of love. This needs to be promoted and protected instead of being arbitrarily regulated. It is submitted that the way to do so is to allow each and every individual, party to a couple, to determine the manner and course their marriage ought to take. It is submitted that a contractual model of marriage would be conducive to such an approach.

THE CONTRACTUAL MODEL OF MARRIAGE

As discussed above, marriage ought to be based on a model easily accessible to all who wish to enter it. The connotations surrounding the institution of marriage are socially defining and therefore cannot be offered to some to the exclusion of others. Egalitarian arguments, supported by principles of privacy and autonomy, have demonstrated the need for a fresh approach, one that enhances the choice of the person seeking to enter marriage. For a person to have the ability to choose the form of marriage he/she wishes to enter, there must be a range of options from which he/she can determine what best suits his/her needs. Such a private ordering of one's relationship promotes equality of choice amongst all citizens, as well as individual autonomy and privacy. As such the "veil of ignorance shrouding marriage" should be lifted so as to make way for a contemporary interpretation of the true meaning of marriage.[117] Inherent in this is the need to dispense with the traditional mindsets and language that typically surround debates on marriage.

As noted previously, strands of individualism are gradually entering the marriage domain and it is no longer accurately described simply as a "unit"; instead it is more representative of a partnership between two individuals. These individuals have their own needs and expectations which they seek to be satisfied within the marital relationship. More and more, marriage is becoming a bargaining forum, whereby the parties to it set out the manner in which they envisage the relationship progressing, and seek the benefit of the services that the other party can provide them. Therefore, references to the contractual model of marriage are under-

---

[117]   See in general Rasmussen and Stake, "Lifting the Veil of Ignorance: Personalizing the Marriage Contract" (1997–1998) 73 Ind. L. J. 453.

standable. Although marriage was traditionally viewed as a social status, people's interpretation of marriage has developed in modern times, reflecting social changes, and providing support for a contractual model of marriage.

The introduction of divorce into Ireland is illustrative of these changes. Marriage is no longer a perpetual commitment; instead there is now scope for an element of negotiation within the marriage. With the availability of divorce, spouses can become concerned with the possibility of their partner terminating the marriage, thereby giving rise to the possibility of the need to consider this before entering marriage. Such an element of negotiation prior to a marriage has contractual connotations to it and is representative of the shift in thinking.[118] Furthermore, Ireland's adoption of a "no-fault" divorce regime provides added support for this point. This is because a no-fault termination of marriage renders the termination amoral, *i.e.* there is no moral judgment *per se* cast against either of the parties to the marriage. A party could terminate the marriage simply because he/she is tired of it. Thus, a morally neutral approach has been injected into our interpretation of marriage, similar to what one would expect from a contract.

Subsequently, it is apparent that the private ordering of family life is becoming a realisation. The State has already acceded to a certain level of private ordering of family life, including the education of the children of the family,[119] the form of primary school education children in a marital family undertake,[120] as well as their religious upbringing,[121] the care of children in a family,[122] the regulation of family size[123] and the division of family property.[124] It is submitted that the acceptance of the private ordering of the marital relationship is the natural fruition of the approach taken to date.

Although still a minority thesis, the courts have acknowledged the individualistic model of marriage. In *DPP v JT*[125] the Court of Criminal Appeal upheld a decision in which the wife of the appellant, who was

---

[118] See in general Barlow and James, "Regulating Marriage & Cohabitation in 21st Century Britain" (2004) 67 M.L.R. 143.

[119] Art.42.1 of Bunreacht na hÉireann.

[120] *Re Art 26 and the School Attendance Bill 1942* [1943] I.R. 334.

[121] *Tilson v Attorney-General* [1951] I.R. 1.

[122] *North Western Health Board v HW* [2001] 3 I.R. 622.

[123] *McGee v Attorney-General* [1974] I.R. 269.

[124] *Re Art 26 and the Matrimonial Home Bill 1993* [1994] I.L.R.M. 241.

[125] 3 Frewen 141 (1988).

convicted of sexually assaulting their mentally disabled daughter, gave evidence against him at trial. The appellant argued that this violated the autonomy of the family unit. In rejecting this argument the court held that the offences in question were in themselves a violation of the autonomy of the family unit and therefore ought to be punished, thereby legitimising the need for the wife to testify against the husband. This judgment implicitly realises the fact that a marriage is indeed made up of two individuals and that it is not an impervious unit.

The recent statutory incentive for married couples to engage in a mediation process[126] as an alternative to going through the courts to determine whether a marriage has broken down, provides further evidence of the increasing acceptance of the private ordering of marital affairs.

A contractual model of marriage represents a natural progression in this field as it facilitates the private ordering of relationships without state interference in the substance of the relationship. The only role the State plays under such a model is in the court enforcement of contractual formalities, which is acceptable, as under contract principles the State would not be at liberty to impose its own morality upon the status of the relationship. Contract's popularity derives from the fact that it facilitates a malleable resource, whereby parties to a relationship can enter into the form of marriage they seek to enjoy. Inherent in this is the protection of equality, privacy, autonomy and dignity.[127]Traditional boundaries and impediments are dispensed with in favour of individual choice.

Advantages of the contract model of marriage

The direct advantages of a contractual model of marriage can be summarised as follows[128]:

> 1) The accommodation of diversity that reflects contemporary social reality.

---

[126] Judicial Separation and Family Law Reform Act 1989, ss.5–7; Family Law (Divorce) Act 1996, ss.6–8.

[127] See Pateman, *The Sexual Contract* (Polity Press, 1988), p.166–167, where she states:
"Contract appears as the solution to the problem of patriarchal right (status) … Contract in the public world is an exchange between equals (between individuals) so it appears that, if contract is extended into the private sphere, inequalities of status between men and women in marriage must disappear."

[128] See Weitzman, *The Marriage Contract: Spouses, Lovers and the Law* (The Free Press, 1981), pp.227–228; and McLellan, "Contract Marriage—The Way Forward or Dead End?" (1996) 23 *Journal of Law & Society* 234.

2) Abandonment of traditional stereotypes for the adoption of an egalitarian framework for all relationships.
3) Promotion of autonomy and privacy by allowing couples to order their personal relationships in any manner they choose.
4) Inclusion of those who have been traditionally barred from marriage, *e.g.* same-sex couples.
5) Creation of a framework for the resolution of marital disputes.

The contract model of marriage is directly responsive to the needs of the parties to a marriage, in that it can accommodate their vision of the marriage they wish to enter. Whereas the traditional form of marriage, which adopts the "one size fits all" mentality, inevitably falls short of the precise needs of all couples.

As noted previously, the "common good", as a social concept, is enhanced by the happiness and well-being of each and every individual; as is human dignity, if one adopts an objective interpretation. The contract model of marriage facilitates and indeed engenders these interests by virtue of the fact that by allowing people to construct their own relationships it will provide them with a sense of happiness and fulfilment incapable of being attained under the rigid traditional model. Also, it creates the further benefit of providing parties to a marriage with an incentive to make the marriage work, because within the human psyche there is an inherent will to succeed at tasks that we set ourselves. Therefore, by virtue of the parties to a marriage formulating their personal "ideal" marriage, they will not wish to fail in achieving this.

A contractual model of marriage would eliminate the "shell" of the traditional form of marriage representing patriarchal notions of the wife being the property of her husband.[129] Although not all marriages today represent the traditional patriarchal approach taken to marriage, the possibility is still present. Therefore, a distinction needs to be drawn between individual marriages and the institution of marriage itself. An individual marriage may be based on equality, etc., thereby the husband does

---

[129] See Pateman, *The Sexual Contract* (Polity Press, 1988), p.167, where she states:

"There can be no predetermined limits on contract, so none can be imposed by specifying the sex of the parties. In contract, the fact of being a man or a woman is irrelevant. In a proper marriage contract two 'individuals' would agree on whatever terms were advantageous to them both. The parties to such a contract would not be a 'man' and a 'woman' but two owners of property in their persons who have come to an agreement about their property to their mutual advantage."

not exert what has traditionally been his dominant role over his wife. Nonetheless, such an example cannot be used to argue that this ought to be the case in general for the institution of marriage, as traditionally interpreted. Instead, when a man marries a woman and becomes a "husband" this automatically entails patriarchal connotations.[130] Within the traditional institution of marriage there is a gender distinction embedded, which no longer accords with modern philosophies. As already argued, the gender distinction inherent in traditional marriage ought to be removed so as to accommodate a more expansive institution. References to "husband" and "wife" are no longer beneficial because they bring with them the baggage of the past whereby the husband effectively owned his wife. Instead, marriage ought to be viewed as a partnership, within which the parties may choose to refer to themselves as "husband" and "wife", or simply as partners. The "husband" and "wife" dichotomy is beginning to prove troublesome for the courts as the quest for same-sex relationship recognition begins to gain momentum. Courts have resigned themselves to interpreting "husband" and "wife" in a substantive, functional context, rather than literally.[131] However, it is submitted that such an approach is not sustainable. For the sake of clarity and equality, the "husband" and "wife" discourse ought to be removed from marriage so as to finally eliminate gender roles, and instead it should be left to the preferences of the couple to decide how they wish to be referred to. The contractual model provides a forum for such a development. Even if the parties to a marriage wish to enter a traditional form of marriage entailing patriarchal connotations, then they may do so, as the contractual model would facilitate such a relationship. Equality, privacy, autonomy and dignity are not only foundations for the expansion of the institution of marriage, but also for the retention of the traditional model of marriage for those who wish to choose to enter it.

Disadvantages of the contractual model of marriage

The move towards a contractual model of marriage is generally seen as a shift in the interpretation of marriage from status to contract. However, there are still trenchant supporters of the traditional "status" interpretation of marriage. Arguments against the contractual model of marriage

---

[130]   See in general Pateman, *The Sexual Contract* (Polity Press, 1988).
[131]   See *Fitzpatrick v Sterling Housing Association Ltd* [1999] 4 All E.R. 705; [1999] 3 W.L.R. 1113; [2000] 1 F.C.R. 21; [2000] Fam. Law 14.

are typically formulated on grounds of instability, the promotion of self-interest at the expense of social cohesion and ambiguity.[132]

It is generally argued that the perceived lack of commitment of the contractual model of marriage is to the detriment of the weaker spouse, typically the female. This has been the mantra of feminist objection to the adoption of a contractual model of marriage. It is thought that such an approach fails to emphasise the need for duties and obligations within marriage and as such does not appreciate the interdependence that has traditionally been found in marriage. It is generally assumed that the wife fares the worst in the break-up of a marriage, and due to the perceived weaker bargaining position of women, it is claimed that the introduction of a contractual model of marriage would exacerbate the "feminisation of poverty".[133]

Pateman is a supporter of the above argument and indeed adopts a hard-line approach. She argues that under a contractual model, marriage is essentially an unwritten contract that promotes a patriarchal social order, thereby facilitating the male in exerting his greater bargaining power over the female and as such entitling him to the physical pleasures of his wife. Pateman essentially argues that under the traditional contract theory of marriage a woman is being exchanged as a piece of property.[134]

Similarly, Naffine argues that the law fails in its function to allow a marriage contract to be drawn up in a manner whereby both parties have the right to choose the terms of the contract from which they both stand to benefit, as the law does for all other contracts. Instead, the law allows a husband to benefit from his entitlement to the unpaid services of his wife.[135]

Olsen argues that by importing the contract theory into the sphere of the family it crystallises the weaker spouse's position as it imports her

---

[132] See Scott and Scott, "Marriage as a Relational Contract" (1998) 84 Va. L. Rev. 1225 at 1245 (footnotes omitted):

"Communitarian critics associate contract with limited, narrowly self-interested arrangements in which each party negotiates for a short-term commitment that best serves his or her personal ends, one that can be readily set aside if breach is efficient."

[133] The genesis of this phrase comes from the work of Lenore Weitzman in *The Divorce Revolution: The Unexpected Consequences for Women and Children in America* (Free Press/MacMillan, 1985). However, it must be noted that Weitzman is in favour of a contractual model of marriage; see in general Weitzman, *The Marriage Contract: Spouses, Lovers and the Law* (The Free Press, 1981).

[134] Pateman, *The Sexual Contract* (Polity Press, 1988).

[135] Naffine, *Law and the Sexes: Explorations in Feminist Jurisprudence* (Allen and Unwin, 1990).

marketplace inequality into the family, *e.g.* her unequal earning capacity. Therefore, by adopting such an approach it will not lead to the expression of the will of the parties but instead will lead to the greater power governing the relationship, *i.e.* the man.[136]

Whilst these feminist arguments may prove persuasive under the traditional contract model of marriage, it is submitted that they fail to discredit a relational contractual model of marriage, as shall be demonstrated below.

The argument has also been made that, even though it is plausible to speak in terms of men and women choosing whether or not to contract to marry, that is where the contract analogy with marriage must end "because the terms and conditions of the relationship are dictated by the state", thereby depriving the parties of the freedom which contract entails.[137] However, such an argument can be refuted on the grounds that, as already argued, the State has no legitimate role in the regulation of marriage on the basis of the rights of equality, privacy and autonomy. Therefore, the terms and conditions within the marriage contract are in fact at the discretion of the parties to it.

Arguments have also been postulated against the contractual model of marriage on the grounds that such a contract would be unenforceable due to its inherent uncertainty. Such arguments claim that it is impossible for a couple entering into marriage to foresee all future contingencies, thereby rendering it impossible to set out a clear, concise and enforceable contract. However, as shall be exemplified below, the potential ambiguity of a contractual model of marriage can be neutralised by adopting the relational contractual model of marriage.

The contractual model—a new wave of thinking

Under the traditional contract theory, the duties and obligations of spouses are generally portrayed as being commercial in nature. Traditional feminists opposed contract theory on this basis as it was felt that the incorporation of the morals of the marketplace into the marital relationship would

---

[136]　Olsen, "The Family and the Market: A Study of Ideology and Legal Reform" (1983) 96 Harv. L. Rev. 1497.

[137]　Weitzman, *The Marriage Contract: Spouses, Lovers and the Law* (The Free Press, 1981), p.xix. See also Cohen, "Marriage: The Long-Term Contract" in Dnes and Rowthorn (eds), *The Law and Economics of Marriage & Divorce* (Cambridge University Press, 2002), pp.10–35; Brinig and Crafton, "Marriage and Opportunism" (1994) 23 *Journal of Legal Studies* 869.

result in the wife's economically inferior position being exacerbated. However, contract theory has been evolving as of late and has moved from principles based on *caveat emptor* and *laissez-faire* philosophies to an era of judicial activism. The terms of a contract and the form of consent given are becoming less decisive, as concepts such as fairness and conscionability begin to establish a prominent role in contract law. This shift in contract theory has led to more of an emphasis on the relationship of the contracting parties than on the commercial aspect of the arrangement. Kingdom therefore argues that this transposition is illustrative of a sociological shift from the norms of self-interest and competitiveness toward the norms of altruism and cooperation.[138]

Traditionally, feminists have argued that a contractual model of marriage would cement the inferior economic status of women. However, it is submitted that not only does the new wave in thinking surrounding the contractual model of marriage alleviate these fears, but also such an argument is inherently contradictory. Such an argument is the catalyst whereby the economic bargaining position of women would be even further weakened because its natural fruition is to undermine the ability of women to enter any form of contract, thereby further deteriorating their already, allegedly, inferior bargaining position.

As noted, the traditional model of contractual marriage is evolving from one associated with commerce to one now concerned with the nature of the relationship. In relation to this form of argument the work of Wightman is relevant.[139] Wightman draws a distinction between two types of agreement, agreements for exchange and agreements for use. Agreements for exchange are typical commercial contracts whereas agreements for use are personal contracts.[140] He argues that agreements for use are more concerned with the ideals of altruism and cooperation, whereas agreements for exchange are fundamentally motivated by the ideals of individualism and selfishness. Such an analysis leads to one adopting the view that personal contracts should reflect the mutual interest of the parties concerned; therefore, for such a contract to be enforceable it should refer to the interests of the marital/family unit, thereby causing the individuals entering the contract to agree on complementary duties and responsibilities within their relationship. This analysis finds favour with

---

[138] Kingdom, "Cohabitation Contracts and the Democratization of Personal Relations" (2000) 8 *Feminist Legal Studies* 5 at 11.
[139] Wightman, *Contract: A Critical Commentary* (Pluto Press, 1996).
[140] *ibid.* at 96 and see Chap.8.

hostile feminists because, as stated, the interests of the family should be expressed in the contract and not solely those of the individuals. Therefore, it could be formulated that the husband's career does not automatically take precedence over the wife's even if the wife could potentially earn more than the husband. Such a contract is concerned with the best interests of the marital/family unit and this would be achieved by the wife pursuing her career and the husband making whatever sacrifices would be necessary to accommodate this.

MacNeil also draws a distinction between two types of contract:

1) The Discrete Transaction: whereby the agreement is of a specific nature and all duties and obligations terminate upon completion of the activity. He gives the example of buying petrol with cash; in such a situation no obligations exist between the parties before or after the transaction.

2) The Relational Contract: the parties to such a contract are in a relationship that develops over time and allows for a flexible approach to the manner in which the obligations are carried out.[141]

Similar to Wightman, MacNeil relates the "discrete transaction" model of contract law to the concepts of individualism and self-interest. The "relational contract" model is in turn based on the concepts of trust and cooperation. MacNeil argues that although the traditional contract law preferred to view contracts under the "discrete transaction" model, this is no longer viable as it is becoming all too apparent that the interests and rights and duties of the parties to a contract are becoming more evident and as a result in need of more protection. Such protection can be found under the "relational contract" model in its promotion of trust and cooperation.[142]

Therefore, contrary to popular feminist argument, the introduction of individualism into marriage negotiations will not result in marriage being altered from an interdependent union to an institution of self-fulfilment. Instead, it promotes equality and seeks to provide an incentive for the parties to the marriage to make it work as it demands that the concept of mutuality form a significant factor in such a relationship. It is important to note that under a contractual model of marriage the con-

---

[141] MacNeil, *The New Social Contract* (Yale University Press, 1980), at 10–13 and 20–35 respectively.

[142] *ibid.* at 85–102.

cepts of autonomy and obligation are not at war.[143] Rather, they complement each other under the relational contract model.

The relational contract model of marriage

Relational contracts are used where the parties are unable to accurately foresee all future possibilities. Such relationships tend to be dynamic in nature, spanning a long period of time, resulting in the predictability of future occurrences becoming complex and uncertain:

> "A contract is relational to the extent that the parties are incapable of reducing important terms of the agreement to well-defined obligations. Such definitive obligations may be impractical because of inability to identify uncertain future conditions or because of inability to characterise complex adaptations adequately even when the contingencies themselves can be identified in advance."[144]

Although long-term contracts tend to fall under the scope of relational contracts, time is not a determining factor. Nevertheless, the agreement to marry epitomises the essence of the relational contract. When entering marriage the parties rarely, if indeed ever, are capable of reducing all future contingencies to paper. Marriage, by its nature, requires a "take it as it comes" mentality which can be facilitated under the relational contract model. Traditional arguments based on ambiguity can be discarded as the relational contract model accommodates unpredictable future scenarios, whilst at the same time providing certainty and clarity to the relationship. This is achieved by virtue of the framework it constructs, within which the parties to the contract are furnished with a method and reason for addressing unforeseen issues.

A further benefit of the relational contract model of marriage is that it provides a composition supportive of augmenting the mutuality necessary for a marriage to function successfully. Under such a model the relationship is a reciprocal one, in that a loss suffered by one party is shared by the other, as is a gain. This approach is cognitive of the necessity for the duties and obligations of a marriage to be apportioned equally upon the parties, thereby engendering equality and respect within the relationship.

---

[143]   Scott and Scott, "Marriage as a Relational Contract" (1998) 84 Va. L. Rev. 1225.
[144]   Goetz and Scott, "Principles of Relational Contracts" (1981) 67 Va. L. Rev. 1089.

Not only does the relational contract model promote mutuality within the marriage, it also induces both parties to develop the relationship in a positive manner by virtue of the performance standard implicit in such a contract. The performance standard in a contract is the means by which the behaviour of both parties is evaluated; failure to abide by this can give cause for one party to seek a remedy for a breach of contract. The standard of performance under relational contracts tends to be that of "best efforts" as it is thought it would be wrong to impose a set of stringent standards when the foreseeability of future contingencies is unclear. The "best efforts" standard has been defined as "the duty of each party to invest sufficiently to produce the maximum joint value from the relationship."[145] Such a standard thereby induces the parties to the relationship to strive to make it work as they both stand to benefit under the mutuality inherent in a relational contract. A further advantage of such a standard is that it is capable of regulating all forms of behaviour whether it is economic, emotional, intellectual or ameliorative.

CONCLUSION

A contractual model of marriage is favourable because it facilitates individual commitment in today's diverse society. As such the contractarian model of marriage promotes the concepts of privacy and autonomy, which can be generalised as individual dignity. By virtue of its accommodation of diverse relationships, the contractual model of marriage has the advantage of not being under-inclusive contrary to the traditional model; as a consequence it does not suffer from claims of discrimination and inequality.

Furthermore, marriage as a relational contract does not neglect the traditional objectives of commitment and structure; on the contrary, it accentuates the mutuality necessary for any relationship to prosper. Under the relational contract ethos, parties are encouraged to cooperate and contribute as equals as both stand to benefit from any investment put into the relationship.

By virtue of this new wave in contractual thinking, the contractual model of marriage can no longer be interpreted simply as a contract in isolation. Instead, under the relational contract model one is required to have regard to the social relevance of the contract, thereby necessitating

---

[145]   Scott and Scott, "Marriage as a Relational Contract" (1998) 84 Va. L. Rev. 1225 at 1266.

the need to adopt an altruistic viewpoint so as not to permit the contract model to develop marriage into an institution of self-fulfilment. Such an approach inevitably leads to the law incorporating egalitarian and democratic ideals into contracts on personal relationships rather than imposing its own traditional form of regulation on such contracts. It is submitted that the relational contractual model of marriage ought to replace the traditional model of marriage so as to protect the commitment necessary for a successful marriage, but on the basis of egalitarian norms promoting privacy and autonomy, thereby enhancing the common good and human dignity. On this basis it becomes plausible for one to discuss prenuptial agreements and their enforceability as a direct consequence of the adoption of a contractual model of marriage.

4. International Approach to Pre-Nuptial Agreements

Having concluded in preceding chapters that marriage ought to be considered as a contract, it now becomes necessary to examine the manner in which parties to a marriage can introduce this contractarian philosophy into their individual marriages.

The pertinent time period for such consideration is the pre-marital stage. By engaging in such deliberation, a couple can set out their individual needs and expectations, which they associate with marriage. The resultant agreements are conventionally termed "pre-nuptial agreements".[1] A pre-nuptial agreement typically means an agreement entered into, in the contemplation of marriage, relating to the conduct of the marriage and, if necessary, the distribution of assets upon its termination. Marriage can be terminated in two ways, by the death of one of the parties, or divorce, and it will be necessary for a pre-nuptial agreement to consider both eventualities for it to be enforceable.

Despite popular opinion, pre-nuptial agreements are not a modern phenomenon born out of the hills of Hollywood. On the contrary, pre-nuptial agreements were in existence in Aramaic society,[2] and even more so in Britain during the Middle Ages.[3] In that era, marriage signified an exchange of property and wealth, and the alliance of two families. Often an agreement was required so as to stipulate the exact terms of possession, as one family did not wish to lose its fortune to another by virtue of a marriage. Also, as a woman had no real individual identity following marriage, a pre-nuptial agreement was used to retain specified rights in relation to her husband.

In the modern era marriage still involves a substantial investment. Not only are there significant financial investments, but also one party may sacrifice his/her career so as to care for children of the marriage. Evidently, marriage involves a degree of risk-analysis and a pre-nuptial agreement provides an appropriate forum to engage in this.

Traditionalists find pre-nuptial agreements to represent the antithesis of love and romance associated with marriage. Nevertheless, each

---

[1] Literature in this area also adopts the phrases "premarital" or "antenuptial" agreements. These phrases, along with "pre-nuptial" agreements are interchangeable; it is therefore irrelevant which phrase is adopted as they all relate to the same concept.

[2] See Barton, "Pre-Marital Contracts and Equal Share on Divorce" (1998) 28 Fam. L. J. 423.

[3] See Younger, "Perspectives on Antenuptial Agreements" (1988) 40 Rutgers L. Rev. 1059.

and every "traditional" marriage entered into implicitly incorporates a pre-nuptial agreement; that being the "unwritten contract that is imposed by law."[4] By marrying, a couple is agreeing in advance to have the assets of their marriage distributed upon its termination, in accordance with the laws of the State. Following divorce, the assets of a marriage are distributed by the court in accordance with the Family Law (Divorce) Act 1996. Alternatively, upon death, a party's assets are distributed in accordance with the succession laws of the State. Such an agreement, before marriage, to abide by the laws of the State in the event of the termination of the marriage constitutes all the elements that typically represent a pre-nuptial agreement. Rather than submitting to the state regulation of marriage, it is asserted, on the basis of the moral argument postulated in Chapter 3, that each and every party to a marriage ought to be permitted to formulate their own pre-nuptial agreement.

With the transposition of marriage from status to contract, the acceptance of pre-nuptial agreements has become more evident. As noted, entering marriage involves an element of risk-analysis. By rendering marriage a revocable contract, divorce has increased the need for such risk-analysis. Weitzman states:

> "Ends may influence beginnings ... a radical change in the rules for ending marriage inevitably affects the rules for marriage itself and the intentions and expectations of those who enter it."[5]

The legislature's modification to the termination of marriage also requires a modification to the formation of marriage; otherwise the balance within the family configuration is unequal. As already postulated, there is a need to reassess marriage and its availability. The law needs to appreciate the individual nature of each and every marriage so as to truly protect and promote this institution, which so many seek to enjoy.

The reason behind adopting a pre-nuptial agreement is personal to each and every couple about to enter marriage. Typically, however, it is thought that by entering a pre-nuptial agreement a couple is seeking to obviate the State laws concerning dissolution of marriage and the distribution of assets. Bix sets out four purposes behind adopting a pre-nuptial agreement:

---

4 Weitzman, *The Marriage Contract: Spouses, Lovers and the Law* (The Free Press, 1981), p.xv.
5 Weitzman, *The Divorce Revolution: The Unexpected Social and Economic Consequences for Women and Children in America* (Free Press/MacMillan, 1985).

1. Safeguarding specific family assets in the event of a divorce;
2. Ensuring that children from a previous marriage retain a portion of the family wealth for inheritance purposes, thereby avoiding state succession laws and elective share statutes;
3. Attempting to ease the potential conflict of a divorce;
4. Protecting the economically weaker spouse in the event of a divorce. [6]

These purposes are representative of the different categories of pre-nuptial agreements, summarised by Cohen as traditional, remarriage, counterculture and feminist.[7] A traditional pre-nuptial agreement is one where a spouse wishes to protect the assets that he/she accumulated prior to the marriage from any potential divorce litigation arising from the imminent marriage. The remarriage model arises where the parties to the new marriage have children with other people and wish to ensure that their inheritance will be protected. Such a pre-nuptial contract would deal with the division of the property of the spouses upon death or divorce, bearing in mind the needs of their children. The counterculture pre-nuptial contract is one designed to avoid the traditional form of marriage. It sets out various rights, duties and obligations to be adhered to by the spouses. The feminist model is designed to protect the interests of the wife upon divorce, *i.e.* designed to prevent the "feminisation of poverty".[8]

As is evident, pre-nuptial agreements are not an alien concept and therefore should not be treated with scepticism. In fact, as shall be seen, pre-nuptial contracts and their formulation offer many positive attributes to marriage in modern society. First, it is necessary to trace the judicial response to such contracts throughout history so as to better understand the context in which pre-nuptial agreements are understood today. Also, appreciation of the factors giving rise to the popularity of pre-nuptial agreements provides further understanding of the scope they ought to benefit from. Upon this basis it will then be possible to analyse the extent to which a pre-nuptial agreement can regulate the course and conduct of

---

[6]   Bix, "Bargaining in the Shadow of Love: The Enforcement of Premarital Agreements and How We Think About Marriage" (1999) 40 Wm. & Mary L. Rev. 145 at 150.

[7]   Cohen, "Marriage the Long-Term Contract" in Dnes & Rowthorn (eds), *The Law & Economics of Marriage & Divorce* (Cambridge University Press, 2002), p.29.

[8]   See in general Weitzman, *The Divorce Revolution: The Unexpected Consequences for Women and Children in America* (Free Press/MacMillan, 1985).

a marriage and, if necessary, its dissolution. Intertwined with the study of this is the need to adequately regulate pre-nuptial contracts. This has proven to be a contentious point to date, with no uniformity apparent from other jurisdictions. One must adopt an element of caution at this juncture, as it would be foolhardy to proceed on the assumption that pre-nuptial agreements are flawless. On the contrary, emerging litigation and academic arguments show that pre-nuptial agreements need to be handled with care, so as to avoid the scenario in which they cause the very headaches they were designed to ease. An analysis of this shall be undertaken later in this chapter. Finally, an examination of the recent developments in English law concerning this area shall be embarked upon. Due to the striking similarities between the English law regulating ancillary relief,[9] and the corresponding Irish legislation,[10] it is hoped that such an examination will shed light on potential modifications to the Irish approach.

CASTING ASIDE THE TRADITIONAL APPROACH TO PRE-NUPTIAL AGREEMENTS

Traditionally courts have refused to enforce pre-nuptial agreements on the basis that they are contrary to public policy. There were two main reasons supporting such an approach:

1. Such agreements were made in the contemplation of divorce, thereby facilitating the breakdown of marriage.
2. Such agreements sought to oust the jurisdiction of the courts by modifying the incidentals to marriage, *e.g.* spousal support.

The House of Lords, in *Hyman v Hyman*,[11] expressed such an opinion in holding an agreement precluding a wife from spousal support in the future to be void on the grounds of public policy. Lord Hailsham stated:

> "The power of the court to make provision for a wife on the dissolution of her marriage is a necessary incident of the power to decree such a dissolution, conferred not merely in the interests of the wife, but also of the public in that the wife cannot by her own covenant preclude herself from invoking the jurisdiction of the court or preclude the court from the exercise of that jurisdiction."[12]

---

9   Matrimonial Causes Act 1973.
10 Family Law (Divorce) Act 1996.
11 [1929] All E.R. 245.
12 *ibid.* at 251.

The rationale for this decision was to avoid the wife becoming a charge on the public purse. Instead, the court was of the opinion that the husband's common law duty to support his wife could not be contracted away from.

Furthermore, in *Fender v St John Mildmay*[13] pre-nuptial agreements in anticipation of future separation were deemed void as against public policy on the basis that they encouraged marital instability. Lord Wright, in the House of Lords, stated:

> "What was not enforced was a contract before marriage or before the spouses actually separated or agreed to separate. It was held that an agreement for future separation was against the policy of the law. The distinction between that and the cases of actual separation is obvious. If a separation has actually occurred or becomes inevitable, the law allows the matter to be dealt with according to realities and not according to fiction. But the law will not permit an agreement which contemplates the future possibility of so undesirable a state of affairs."[14]

Similar dicta can also be found in Irish case law. In *Wilson v Carnley,*[15] Kennedy L.J. stated:

> "no court has ever yet held that a deed providing *in futuro* for the contingency of separation between husband and wife is in accordance with public policy."[16]

Irish academic opinion seems to follow along a similar line of thinking. Duncan has stated, in relation to Irish law, that:

> "a contract made in contemplation of a separation which may occur at some future date, and which is not inevitable, probably remains unenforceable. The assumption is that such a contract might tend to encourage or too readily facilitate the breaking of the marriage vows. It seems, therefore, that it is void for reasons of public policy."[17]

---

[13]   [1938] A.C. 1.

[14]   *ibid.* at 44.

[15]   [1908] 1 K.B. 729. Later relied on in *Brodie v Brodie* [1916–1917] All E.R. Rep. 237; (1917) 33 T.L.R. 525

[16]   *ibid.* at 743.

[17]   Duncan and Scully, *Marriage Breakdown in Ireland: Law and Practice* (Butterworths, 1990), p.416 (footnotes omitted). Shatter would seem to concur with this opinion: see Shatter, *Family Law* (4th ed., Butterworths, 1997), p.329.

In support of this opinion Duncan relies on the judgment in *Fender v St John Milmay*, in particular the dictum as noted above. However, Conneely argues that the dictum in *Fender* cannot form an authoritative basis for such an opinion. She argues that the dictum in relation to pre-nuptial agreements was merely *obiter*, as the case concerned an action taken by a third party against a spouse for a breach of promise made after a decree *nisi* for the dissolution of marriage had been proclaimed.[18] In spite of this, there has been no great movement in the Irish courts in recent times dealing with this matter. As such, case law still maintains that pre-nuptial agreements, in contemplation of divorce, are unenforceable in Ireland as they are contrary to public policy. Nevertheless, the same cannot be said for other jurisdictions.

Courts in the United States of America, following English case law, also adopted the public policy rationale for rendering pre-nuptial agreements void.[19] Divorce-orientated pre-nuptial agreements were deemed contrary to public policy in that they "invite[d] dispute, encourage[d] separation and incite[d] divorce".[20] Nonetheless, in 1970 the Florida Supreme Court cast aside the traditional rationales rendering pre-nuptial agreements void *ab initio*, and instead held that such contracts may be deemed valid subject to judicial review.[21] In light of this, courts began to adopt the rationale that pre-nuptial agreements promoted and enhanced marital stability rather than reduced it[22]:

> "It may be equally cogently argued that a contract which defines the expectations and responsibilities of the parties promotes rather than reduces marital stability."[23]

The traditional approach of the American courts was steeped in paternalism, but following the decision in *Posner* this shroud of paternalism dissipated, as the courts began to embrace fresh moral arguments centred on autonomy, privacy and equality:

---

[18]   Conneely, "Pre-Nuptial Agreements: Back to the Future" (1999) 17 I.L.T. 9 at 9.

[19]   See *Graham v Graham* 33 F. Supp. 936 (Mich. 1940) (pre-nuptial agreement void as against public policy because it sought to alter the state imposed terms of marriage.); *Norris v Norris* 174 N.W.2d 368 (Iowa 1970) (pre-nuptial agreement void because it encouraged divorce).

[20]   *Fricke v Fricke* 42 N.W.2d 500, 502 (Wis. 1950).

[21]   *Posner v Posner* 233 So. 2d 381 (Fla. 1970).

[22]   See in general *Volid v Volid* 6 Ill. App. 3d 836;286 N.E.2d 42 (1972); *Tomlinson v Tomlinson* 352 N.E.2d 785 (Ind. Ct. App. 1976); *Scherer v Scherer* 292 S.E.2d 662 (Ga. 1982).

[23]   *Volid v Volid,* 6 Ill. App. 3d 836; 286 N.E. 2d 46 (1972).

"No longer will the courts in viewing antenuptial contracts invariably begin with the realisation that between persons in prematrimonial state there is a mystical, confidential relationship which anaesthetises the senses of the female partner."[24]

America proved to be the first jurisdiction of note to recast the "public policy" argument in a manner that reflected social reality, thereby recognising the enforceability of pre-nuptial agreements. As shall be seen, with the growing popularity of pre-nuptial agreements amongst society, "public policy" in various other jurisdictions has developed (or is developing) in such a manner so as to render pre-nuptial agreements valid.

THE GROWTH IN POPULARITY OF PRE-NUPTIAL AGREEMENTS

In popular discourse pre-nuptial agreements are associated with the lives of the rich and famous and have even been immortalised by contemporary music.[25] Whilst pre-nuptial agreements are commonplace amongst the rich and famous, they have also proven useful for the not so rich and famous. People entering marriage, in particular those entering a second marriage, sought to formulate their own marriages. The courts acknowledged this and, as illustrated above, began to recognise pre-nuptial agreements as enforceable. Following this lead, legislatures in many jurisdictions set out guidelines governing the formation and enforcement of pre-nuptial agreements so as to provide clarity and certainty to the law. The following is a brief overview of those developments.

As noted above, the Florida Supreme Court was the first court in the United States of America to recognise the modern-day pre-nuptial agreement designed to regulate the dissolution of a marriage upon divorce.[26] Various jurisdictions followed suit until the National Conference of Commissioners on Uniform State Law decided to produce a piece of uniform legislation to govern this area. The result was the Uniform Premarital Agreement Act[27] (UPAA) promulgated in 1983. This Act sought to govern the formalities for entering a pre-nuptial agreement,[28] the contents[29]

---

24   *Potter v Collin*, 321 So. 2d 128, 132 (Fla. Dist. Ct. App. 1975) quoting Gamble, "The Antenuptial Contract" (1972) 26 *U. Miami L. Rev.* 692, at 719.

25   See Kanye West, "Gold Digger", taken from the album *Late Registration* (Roc-A-Fella Records, 2005).

26   *Posner v Posner* 233 So. 2d 381 (Fla. 1970).

27   9B U.L.A. 376 (1987).

28   *ibid.* § 2.

29   *ibid.* § 3.

and the regulation and setting aside of such agreements.[30] To date there are 24 contracting states to the UPAA.[31] Pre-nuptial agreements are becoming increasingly popular in America with approximately 5 per cent of all marriages based on a pre-nuptial contract, with 20 per cent of remarriages similarly formulated.[32] One must not be mistaken in believing that this is strictly an American phenomenon; on the contrary it is very much an international one. Approximately 25 per cent of all marriages in the Netherlands contain a pre-nuptial contract.[33]

In 2000 Australia amended its Family Law Act 1975 so as to recognise pre-nuptial contracts.[34] This was against a backdrop of strong lobbying and previous failed attempts. The Australian Law Reform Commission in 1987,[35] and the Joint Select Committee in 1992,[36] both concluded in their respective reports that pre-nuptial agreements ought to be enforceable under Australian law. The Joint Select Committee's recommendations were translated into a Bill,[37] but did not progress any further due to a change of government that year following a general election.[38] Nevertheless, following the 2000 amendment, Pt VIII of the Family Law Act 1975 was inserted, resulting in pre-nuptial agreements becoming enforceable under the rubric of "financial agreements".[39] Similar to the UPAA, the Australian provisions deal with the content,[40] regulation[41] and termination[42] of these agreements.

---

[30] *ibid.* § 6.

[31] Arizona, Arkansas, California, Connecticut, Hawaii, Idaho, Illinois, Iowa, Indiana, Kansas, Maine, Montana, Nebraska, Nevada, New Jersey, New Mexico, North Carolina, North Dakota, Oregon, Rhode Island, South Dakota, Texas, Utah and Virginia.

[32] Marston, "Planning for Love: The Politics of Prenuptial Agreements" (1997) 499 Stan. L. Rev. 887 at 891.

[33] Smith, "The Law and Economics of Marriage Contracts" (2003) 17 *Journal of Economic Surveys* 201.

[34] Family Law (Amendment) Act 2000.

[35] Australian Law Reform Commission, *Matrimonial Property* (Report No. 37, AGPS, Canberra, 1987).

[36] Joint Select Committee, *Report of the Joint Select Committee on Certain Aspects of the Operation and Interpretation of the Family Law Act* (AGPS, Canberra, 1992).

[37] Family Law Reform Bill (No.2) 1995 (Cth).

[38] See in general Nygh, "Asset Distribution on the Breakdown of Marriage in Australia" in Bailey-Harris ed., *Dividing Assets on Family Breakdown* (Jordan Publishing, 1998), p.11.

[39] Family Law Act 1975, s.90B (as amended). "Financial agreements" are defined in s.4(1) of the Family Law Act 1975, as amended. For the sake of ease, the term "pre-nuptial agreements" shall be ascribed to these "financial agreements".

[40] *ibid.* ss.90B, 90E and 90F.

[41] *ibid.* s.90G.

[42] *ibid.* ss.90J and 90K.

Unlike America and Australia, Canada has yet to adopt uniform legislation governing pre-nuptial agreements. At present only a number of provinces in Canada have governing provisions concerning pre-nuptial agreements.[43] Several European countries have also adopted similar legislation; some as parties to the Hague Convention on the Law Applicable to Matrimonial Property Regimes,[44] others with their own legislation.[45] Also, in both Brazil[46] and China[47] pre-nuptial contracts are binding.

It is thus pertinent to analyse the factors behind this growth in the recognition of pre-nuptial agreements internationally,[48] so as to examine the lack of such recognition in Ireland. The developments in divorce law around the world have caused many jurisdictions to restore balance to marriage by amending the law concerning the formation of marriage. It is submitted that it is these developments in the area of divorce and ancillary relief that justify the enforcement of pre-nuptial contracts.

The introduction of "no-fault" divorce and the "clean break" phenomenon

The argument has been made that the introduction of no-fault divorce has rendered the marriage contract illusory. Brinig and Crafton make the comment that as there are "no significant activities that trigger breach ... there can be no breach and no remedies, and the contract has become illusory."[49] By virtue of this, the risk factor in getting married greatly increases as a party to a marriage who has sacrificed his/her career to take care of the children could be left by their partner without having committed any acts of fault. The party generally left to suffer is the woman,[50] who by virtue of having no career and the "burden" of a child has little "value" when it

---

[43] See Family Relations Act, R.S.B.C. 1996, C-128 s.62; Family Law Act, R.S.N. 1990, C.F-2 s.62; Family Law Act, R.S.O. 1990, C.F-3 s.52.

[44] Austria, France (France also has domestic legislation in this area; see Art.1387 of the Civil Code.), Luxembourg and Portugal.

[45] Belgium, Denmark, Germany, Greece, The Netherlands, Norway, Spain, Sweden and Switzerland. See Shannon, "Pre-Nuptial Agreements in Ireland" (2003) I.J.F.L. 132.

[46] Civil Code, Art.256, II.

[47] Marriage Law 2001, Art.19.

[48] The absence of England is notable. For present purposes it can be taken that pre-nuptial agreements are quasi-enforceable in England. This shall be examined in greater detail below.

[49] Brinig and Crafton, "Marriage and Opportunism" (1994) 23 *Journal of Legal Studies* 869 at 882.

[50] See in general Weitzman, *The Divorce Revolution: The Unexpected Social and Economic Consequences for Women and Children in America* (Free Press/MacMillan, 1985).

comes to re-entering the "marketplace" looking for a new partner. Essentially the presence of a no-fault regime has a negative impact on the desire of women to commit to marriage.

This negativity is further exacerbated by the possibility of there being a "clean break" upon divorce. It is generally thought that the ancillary relief granted upon divorce to the claiming party is received on a continuous basis in the form of periodic payments, so as to satisfy the common law rule of spousal support. That said, in "ample resource" cases, a trend has emerged whereby the claimant receives one substantial lump sum and no periodic payments so as to achieve a "clean break" in the marriage. Although these lump sums are of such a magnitude that the claiming party generally can live comfortably thereafter, the mere possibility of a "clean break" injects a further sense of fear in the economically weaker party entering marriage. It is irrelevant that a couple, by virtue of their wealth and income, might never come under the scope of a potential "clean break". The knowledge of it as being a possible eventuality justifies the need to quell any fears.

These negative possibilities need to be counteracted so as to promote marriage as a viable option for women to enter into, without the fear of being left "high and dry" by a husband who has simply lost interest in a few years time. A means of achieving this is to formulate a pre-nuptial agreement whereby the marital promises are reinforced and justify a remedy in the event of a breach. A pre-nuptial agreement can act as a disincentive seeking to prevent husbands leaving wives simply because they have lost interest, and attaining a divorce as an economically viable escape, leaving him to pursue more "attractive interests".[51] By imposing significant financial penalties on a party who unilaterally terminates a marriage, the marriage as a union becomes more secure, thereby relieving any fear of investing one's time, effort and emotions into the relationship.

Ireland has embraced the no-fault divorce regime whereby the parties need only live apart for four of the five years prior to the divorce

---

[51] Dnes refers to this as the "greener grass effect"; whereby, in particular, wealthy people see divorce as a "cheap" escape from a marriage so as to pursue new interests in their life. See Dnes, "An Economic Analysis of a Proposal to Reform the Discretionary Approach to the Division of Marital Assets in England and Wales" (Lord Chancellor's Department, Research Series, No.6/98, September 1998), p.7. For a more in depth analysis of this concept see Dnes, "The Division of Marital Assets Following Divorce With Particular Reference to Pensions" (Lord Chancellor's Department, Research Series No. 7/97, 1997).

proceedings.[52] Furthermore, it is not necessary that the parties "live apart" in separate buildings.[53] Consequently, there is a significant element of risk in investing heavily in a marriage under Irish law. It is accepted that there is a constitutional imperative to ensure "proper provision"[54] to both spouses and any children upon divorce. Nevertheless, this might not be known to the majority of those entering into marriage, as the intricacies of divorce law ought to be far from their mind at that stage. In addition to this, the possibility of a "clean break" in Irish law[55] has increased the level of risk amongst parties entering marriage. There is a need to counteract this fear and it is submitted that the best means of achieving this is the recognition of pre-nuptial agreements as being binding in Irish law.

Judicial discretion in the granting of ancillary relief

Judicial discretion in the granting of ancillary relief in divorce cases has led to a heightened degree of uncertainty in recent times. Irish family law grants judges an unparalleled level of discretion in such cases and "[i]t is likely that the unfettered discretion afforded to the courts, in light of constitutional and statutory obligations, will continue to remain an integral part of Irish family law".[56] As a result of this there is an evident lack of certainty in the advice that lawyers can communicate to their clients in such cases. The difficulty in curbing this level of discretion, and at the same time seeking to achieve justice in individual cases, has been noted by the 17 judges of the High Court Family Division in England, stating:

> "In the law of ancillary relief the optimum tension between the predictability which flows from firm rules and the flexibility to secure justice in the individual case is notoriously difficult to achieve."[57]

As such, judicial discretion in the area of ancillary relief must be accepted as a given. Therefore it is necessary to regulate the discretion exercisable to each individual case. Following from the moral arguments

---

[52] Art.41.3.2°(i); as set out in the Family Law (Divorce) Act 1996, s.5.

[53] *MMcA v XMcA* [2000] 2 I.L.R.M. 48. For a critical commentary on this see Binchy, "Family Law—Divorce—Living Apart" (2000) 22 D.U.L.J. 216.

[54] Art.41.3.2°(iii).

[55] For an analysis of this see p.141 below.

[56] Shannon, "Pre-Nuptial Agreements in Ireland" (2003) I.J.F.L. 132 at 132. For an analysis of judicial discretion in Irish law see p.129 below.

[57] Wilson, "Ancillary Relief Reform—Response of the Judges of the Family Division to Government Proposals" (1999) 29 Fam. L. J. 159.

in the previous section, it is evident that the parties to a marriage and indeed a divorce ought to be allowed to determine the manner of the distribution of the marital assets. The optimum means of achieving this would be by means of a pre-nuptial agreement. Such an agreement would not only reflect the wishes of the parties, but also provide a level of certainty and clarity in the granting of any ancillary relief, that is at present notably absent.

Dnes expands upon this point and argues that a mathematical presumption, for example a 50/50 split, should act as the norm, so as to improve certainty in such cases, with a pre-nuptial contract acting as a rebuttal to this presumption.[58] He argues that the current level of judicial discretion in determining ancillary relief has led to a devaluing of the marital promises. Instead, a contractual model, incorporating expectation damages, would better compensate one for a breach of the marital promises. The expectations of the parties entering into a marriage need to be protected and enforced. Dnes suggests that this could be achieved if the following model was to be adopted:

> "It is possible that the setting of a statutory norm (equal shares) together with an opportunity for the couple to indicate their expectation over assets if it differs from the norm (using a prenuptial agreement) may overcome the problem of identifying marital expectations."[59]

Under such a methodology, the formulaic and possible presence of a pre-nuptial agreement would form the starting-point for a judicial decision rather than the automatic recourse to discretion that has been adopted to date. Judicial discretion would still be a possibility if the circumstances justified deviance from the mathematical formula or pre-nuptial agreement. Importantly, however, judicial discretion would only be present as an alternative and not as a rule.

The simplicity of such an approach is attractive; nevertheless, it is not without its critics. Wilson, on behalf of the judges of the High Court Family Division, argues that a mathematical formula methodology has been experimented with before and rejected on the grounds that it is too

---

[58] Dnes, "An Economic Analysis of a Proposal to Reform the Discretionary Approach to the Division of Marital Assets in England and Wales" (Lord Chancellor's Department, Research Series, No.6/98, September 1998).

[59] *ibid.* at 8.

arbitrary.[60] Nonetheless, following the House of Lords decision in *White v White*[61] the equal division argument was revived, leading to the next factor explaining the increase in popularity of pre-nuptial agreements.

50/50 division of assets emerging?

The case of *White* concerned a couple married for 36 years with two children. They were also business partners in agriculture, with a combined wealth of £4.6 million at the time of the divorce proceedings. The House of Lords judgment emphasised that the overriding goal in any ancillary relief proceedings was to achieve fairness. In formulating what is "fair", the court reverted back to traditional conceptions and concluded that the starting-point ought to be one of equality. It is on the basis of this dicta that proponents of pre-nuptial contracts have argued that a consequence of the decision in *White* is that upon divorce assets will be divided equally.[62]

On the contrary, this was not the *ratio* of the decision in *White*, as expressed by Thorpe L.J. in *Cowan v Cowan*, stating, "the decision in *White* does not introduce a rule of equality"[63] in the context of ancillary relief.[64] This is evident from a close examination of the judgment in *White*, and it becomes clear that equality was only intended to be a "yardstick"[65] against which a judge may measure the needs of the parties against the facts of the case.[66]

Although it is clear that there is not a rule of equal division of assets upon divorce, an emerging line of cases shows the genesis of a new point of contention surrounding the determination of ancillary relief. Following the Court of Appeal decision in the joined cases of *Parlour v Parlour* and *McFarlane v McFarlane*,[67] debate grew as to whether the eco-

---

[60] Wilson, "Ancillary Relief Reform—Response of the Judges of the Family Division to Government Proposals" (1999) 29 Fam. L. J. 159. Reference is made to the cases of *Calderbank v Calderbank* [1976] Fam. L.J. 93; *P v P* [1978] 1 W.L.R. 483; *Page v Page* (1981) 2 F.L.R. 198.

[61] [2000] 2 F.L.R. 981.

[62] Francis and Philips, "New Light on Prenuptial Agreements" (2003) 33 Fam. L. J. 164, referring to Bruce, "Premarital Agreements Following *White v White*" [2001] Fam. Law 304.

[63] [2001] 3 W.L.R. 684; [2001] 2 F.L.R. 192; [2001] Fam. Law 498; at para.53.

[64] See *Miller v Miller; McFarlane v McFarlane* [2006] 3 All E.R. 1, at para.4. See also, Barton and Hibbs, "Ancillary Relief and Fat Cat(tle) Divorce" (2002) 65 M.L.R. 79.

[65] *White v White* [2000] 2 F.L.R. 981 at 989.

[66] See in general Diduck, "Fairness and Justice For All? The House of Lords in *White v White* [2000] 2 F.L.R. 981" (2001) 9 *Feminist Legal Studies* 173.

[67] *McFarlane v McFarlane; Parlour v Parlour* [2005] Fam. 171, [2004] 2 All E.R. 921; [2004] 2 F.L.R. 893; [2004] 3 W.L.R. 1481.

nomically weaker party, the wife in both cases, ought to receive enough money to provide for her "reasonable needs", or whether she was entitled, by virtue of her sacrifices throughout the marriage, to receive an amount so as to sustain the lifestyle she had grown accustomed to. Traditionally, the economic value of the non-monetary contributions that a wife makes to a marriage have rarely, if ever, been taken into account when calculating ancillary relief. Generally, once a wife was given enough to provide for her "reasonable needs", any surplus was deemed the husband's. Both these cases share a common thread, namely, insufficient capital to effect a clean break, but there was a substantial earning capacity on the part of the husband. In the *Parlour* case the husband was a Premiership footballer, whose substantial income was expected to decrease dramatically within four to five years of the case, upon his retirement. In *McFarlane* the husband was a successful tax advisor with a potential net income of £750,000. It was held in the Court of Appeal that a clean break should be achieved over a period of time. Bearing this in mind the court made an order for periodic payments to the wives in both cases that would terminate after five years. It was thought that this would encourage financial independence amongst the parties, and thereby facilitate the possibility of a clean break in five years' time. Both these cases saw the wives receive periodic payments well in excess of their "reasonable needs", thus striking fear amongst potential divorcing husbands.[68] Nonetheless, with the finite duration of these payments it is clear that it was the courts' intention to have the wives invest this excess, so as to achieve financial independence in the long run.

The *McFarlane* case was appealed to the House of Lords[69] where, in a clear and concise judgment, it was expressed that in granting a wife ancillary relief it was no longer to merely cater for her "reasonable needs" with the excess income benefiting the husband. The "reasonable needs" of a spouse is only one of three factors to be taken into account, the other two being compensation and contribution to the marriage.[70] As marriage is to be perceived as a partnership of equals,[71] and if both spouses could live above their "reasonable needs", then the appropriate order should be made. The court granted the wife periodic payments of £250,000 each

---

[68]   See Towler, "Pre-nuptials for High Earners After Footballer Pays Penalty" *The Solicitors Journal*, July 16, 2004.

[69]   *Miller v Miller; McFarlane v McFarlane* [2006] 3 All E.R. 1.

[70]   *ibid.* at paras 137–143.

[71]   *ibid.* at paras 16–19 and para.141. Relying on the authority of *R v R* [1992] 1 A.C. 599 at 617, [1991] 4 All E.R. 481, [1991] 3 W.L.R. 767.

year for as long as she may need it, thereby extinguishing the five-year limitation.

The cost of divorce

The cost of divorce litigation is becoming a disincentive for those seeking to formally terminate their marriages.[72] For the majority of cases, in which the marital assets are far from exorbitant, the level of costs is generally disproportionate to any relief achieved, thereby rendering it negligible. With the illustration of an economic "game" model, Dnes argues that there is a mindset whereby both parties in divorce proceedings feel the need to employ several lawyers so as not to be taken advantage of by the other party. The circular effect of such tactics is a significant reduction in the marital assets available for division.[73] Dnes feels that it is necessary to encourage parties to enter into a cooperative mode of resolution and to avoid unnecessary conflict, as ultimately this will cause both parties to lose out financially by virtue of the costs such an approach would entail. To help combat the waste of marital assets due to conflict litigation, Dnes proposes "a firm presumptive rule for property division [which] could, by reducing uncertainty, attenuate the incentive for wasteful legal representation."[74] As an alternative to such a presumptive rule the parties could have entered into a pre-nuptial agreement, whereby on the basis of their own cooperation and early resolution, future conflicts would be significantly reduced thereby limiting the need for further wasteful legal representation.

This has been a significant factor in the promotion and subsequent popularity of pre-nuptial agreements. Nonetheless, there is evidence to suggest that the ingenuity of certain lawyers has dissipated the cost-effectiveness of a pre-nuptial agreement, thus diminishing the future capacity of "cost" as being a factor promoting pre-nuptial agreements. This issue shall be addressed below.

As pre-nuptial contracts are now a familiar concept in contemporary society, it is necessary to understand the content and construction of

---

[72] This aspect of Irish Family Law was recently criticised by Hardiman J. in the case of *BD v JD*, unreported, Supreme Court, December 8, 2004; [2005] Fam L.J. Autumn 11. See Coulter, "Hidden World of Family Costs" *The Irish Times*, March 24, 2006.

[73] Dnes, "An Economic Analysis of a Proposal to Reform the Discretionary Approach to the Division of Marital Assets in England and Wales" (Lord Chancellor's Department, Research Series, No.6/98, September 1998), pp.9–11.

[74] *ibid.* at 11.

such contracts. On foot of this, one can then determine the means of regulating their use and enforcement.

THE CONSTRUCTION AND CONTENT OF PRE-NUPTIAL AGREEMENTS

A pre-nuptial agreement is a contract; therefore, it is subject to standard contract formalities. It must be in writing, be signed by the parties and be exchanged for consideration, although in some jurisdictions consideration is not required,[75] while in others the marriage itself is sufficient consideration. These contract formalities rarely present any significant problems on litigation. Instead, it is the substantive content of the clauses in a pre-nuptial contract that is of interest.

Standard clauses

A pre-nuptial contract is a long-term contract that is designed to regulate the course of a marriage, and if necessary, its dissolution. As already discussed, the appropriate model under which to treat such a contract is that of the "relational contract".[76] By virtue of its intended longevity, a pre-nuptial contract needs to be flexible in interpretation so as to remain applicable in light of changing circumstances. As such, a characteristic of pre-nuptial contracts is the broad and numerous clauses seeking to regulate each and every aspect of a marriage. The following is a brief overview of the type of clauses one would expect to find in a pre-nuptial contract:

- Aims and expectations of the parties;
- Duration of the contract;
- Division of property and income;
- Regulation of work and career, and household tasks;
- Domicile and living arrangements;
- Treatment of debt;
- Sexual relations and birth control;
- Decision to have children, and how such children would be reared;
- Religion;
- Health and medical matters;
- Wills and inheritance;
- Dispute resolution;

---

[75] UPAA § 2, 9B U.L.A. 371 (1987).
[76] See Chap.3 above.

- · Amending and renewing the agreement;
- · Provisions for the possibility of divorce.[77]

This is merely an overview of what types of clauses may be contained in a pre-nuptial contract. As marriage is a personal relationship, a pre-nuptial agreement reflects the personal needs of the parties to it. Therefore, the possibilities of the range of clauses in a pre-nuptial contract are limitless. This is accommodated, as best as possible, by legislation. Section 3(8) of the UPAA permits a pre-nuptial contract to contain clauses concerning "any other matter, including personal rights and obligations, not in violation of public policy, or a statute imposing a criminal penalty". Similarly, Australian legislation permits any "matters ancillary or incidental"[78] to marriage and its dissolution. Although not defined, "matters ancillary or incidental" are thought to include all incidentals of married life.[79]

Despite the possibility of infinitely different pre-nuptial agreements, there are a number of clauses and issues that it is thought prudent to include in such a contract; or that have proved to be contentious in the past. In light of this, it is deemed worthwhile to examine such matters.

The need for independent legal advice

A nuptial agreement, whether made before, during or after a marriage, is conceived in a time of "extreme emotional susceptibility".[80] The ability to think rationally is clouded by the emotional ties between the parties. In order to ensure some form of rational discussion and agreement, it is thought best that both parties receive separate independent legal advice before signing such an agreement.

In Australia, the need to receive independent legal advice is a prerequisite to the enforceability of a pre-nuptial agreement. Proof of this is satisfied by the attachment of a certificate to such effect by the parties' solicitors to the agreement.[81] In America it has been held that independ-

---

[77]   Taken from Weitzman, *The Marriage Contract: Spouses, Lovers and the Law* (The Free Press, 1981), Chap.11; and Marston, "Planning for Love: The Politics of Prenuptial Agreements" (1997) 499 Stan. L. Rev. 887, incorporating the research of Warner and Ihara, *California Marriage and Divorce Law* (7th ed., 1985), at 36–39.

[78]   Family Law Act 1975, s.90A(3).

[79]   Fehlberg and Smyth, "Binding Prenuptial Agreements in Australia: The First Year" (2002) 16 I.J.L.P.F. 127.

[80]   Wilson, "Ancillary Relief Reform—Response of the Judges of the Family Division to Government Proposals" (1999) 29 Fam. L. J. 159.

[81]   Family Law Act 1975, s.90G(1)(b).

ent legal advice is not in itself a prerequisite to the enforceability of a pre-nuptial agreement. Rather, the *opportunity* to attain independent legal advice is the prerequisite.[82] It is submitted that such an approach is incorrect and fails to fully appreciate the need for separate independent legal advice in such situations. The *opportunity* to consult counsel is always available to someone presented with a pre-nuptial agreement. The problem arises when someone is presented with a pre-nuptial agreement a few days before the wedding, told to sign or the wedding will be cancelled. Of course that person has the *opportunity* to consult counsel; but in such a situation that is an unlikely eventuality, as the party may sign due to the pressure. It is arguable that such a pre-nuptial contract would be set aside on grounds of duress if it was sought to be enforced. Nevertheless, this would only remedy the situation at the point of performance, whereas requiring independent legal advice as a prerequisite would eliminate any wrongdoing, thus saving unnecessary litigation upon performance.

At present, concerns surround the current requirements in Australia in relation to the possibility of professional negligence claims being asserted against solicitors who provide certificates of independent legal advice.[83] Nonetheless, it is submitted that the concept is favourable and ought to be a mandatory requirement in any legislation concerning pre-nuptial agreements.

Full disclosure of assets

In addition to independent legal advice acting as a means of injecting a sense of rationality into emotionally-fuelled negotiations, a clause requiring full disclosure of assets is regarded as having a similar effect.[84] Antagonists to pre-nuptial agreements tend to be sceptical about the ability of the parties to foresee all possible eventualities to their impending marriage.

Bix comments that "society should be sceptical about the ability of the earlier self to judge the interests and preferences of the later self".[85]

---

[82]   *Gant v Gant* 329 S.E.2d 106, at 108 (W.Va. 1985).

[83]   Furthermore, there is a concern that professional indemnity insurance will not cover such agreements, as they constitute *financial* advice as opposed to *legal* advice. See in general Fehlberg and Smyth, "Binding Prenuptial Agreements in Australia: The First Year" (2002) 16 I.J.L.P.F. 127.

[84]   Wilson, "Ancillary Relief Reform—Response of the Judges of the Family Division to Government Proposals" (1999) 29 Fam. L. J. 159.

[85]   Bix, "Bargaining in the Shadow of Love: The Enforcement of Premarital Agreements and How We Think About Marriage" (1999) 40 Wm. & Mary L. Rev. 145, at 197.

He presents a compelling and persuasive argument by drawing an analogy between a pre-nuptial agreement and a surrogacy agreement.[86] He argues that a not-yet-pregnant woman signing a surrogacy agreement does so blindly as to the potential changes that might occur during the nine months of pregnancy. It is quite plausible that, having carried the baby for nine months, the woman would view matters in an altogether different light and decide to renege on her contractual commitment.[87]

---

[86] *ibid.* at 196.

[87] See in general Gittleman, *"In the Matter of Baby M:* A Setback for Surrogacy Contracts" (1987–1988) 40 *Rutgers L. Rev.* 1313; Allen, "Privacy, Surrogacy, and the *Baby M* case" (1987–1988) 76 Geo. L. J. 1759; Kort, "Casenote—*Johnson v Calvert*: California Supreme Court Enforces Surrogacy Contract" (1994) 26 Ariz. St. L. J. 243; Abell, "Gestational Surrogacy: Intent-Based Parenthood in *Johnson v Calvert*" (1993–1994) 45 Mercer L. Rev. 1429; Gostin, "A Civil Liberties Analysis of Surrogacy Agreements" (2000-2001) 17 J. Contemp. Health L. & Policy 432.

There are opposing views concerning this point in the context of surrogacy agreements. Essentially, proponents of surrogacy agreements argue that, the right to privacy of a surrogate mother permits her to carry a foetus to term so as to provide another couple with a child to be reared as their own, without state interference. On the other hand, those against such agreements claim that a surrogate mother is not in a position to provide informed consent to such an agreement as she is incapable of realising the potential bond that may grow between her and the child.

Both sides of the argument have been posited in American case law. In *In the Matter of Baby M* 109 N.J. 396, 537 A.2d 1227 (1988), the New Jersey Supreme Court deemed surrogacy agreements illegal and unenforceable on the basis that such agreements forced the surrogate to irrevocably surrender her parental rights over the child before realising the nature of the bond between her and the child, resulting in the inability of the surrogate to reach an informed decision/consent.

Several years later the Californian Supreme Court favoured the other side of the argument, holding surrogacy agreements to be enforceable. In *Johnson v Calvert* 851 P.2d 776 (Cal. 1993), the court held that the law ought to foster the ideals of autonomy, privacy and equality and therefore, should permit women to decide on matters concerning their own bodies, without paternalistic interference. Commenting on this Gostin states:

"The gestational mother has a particularly strong right of privacy and autonomy, founded upon several factors: her experience of artificial insemination, the changes in her body, her emotional commitment, her nurturing of the fetus for nine months, and the labour and pain of giving birth. The fact that she did not originally intend to keep the child does not dispose of this complex constitutional and social issue. Her bonding and identification with a baby born of her own body is an understandable and real human experience."

See Gostin, "A Civil Liberties Analysis of Surrogacy Agreements" (2000–2001) 17 J. Contemp. Health L. & Policy 432 at 435.

For the sake of completeness, it is noted that the cases of *Baby M* and *Johnson v Calvert* can be distinguished on the facts. The *Baby M* case concerned the artificial insemination of the sperm into the surrogate woman, which then fertilised with the surrogate's own egg to create a foetus and ultimately a child. Whereas, *Johnson v Calvert* concerned a gestational surrogacy which involves the surrogate woman becoming im-

Similarly, the parties to a pre-nuptial agreement rarely act within the optimal sense of their rationality by virtue of the surrounding circumstances. Despite signing a pre-nuptial agreement designed to regulate the dissolution of marriage upon divorce, they hold the aspirational intent of never having to rely on it. This is conducted in an era of rising divorce rates and uncertainty surrounding ancillary relief. Yet, oblivious to these facts, some parties enter into pre-nuptial agreements without seriously contemplating future possibilities. The result of this can be an incomplete agreement leading to future conflict upon termination.

This is indeed a concern surrounding pre-nuptial agreements. That said, by causing the parties to sit down and discuss figures it does inject a business sense into the transaction, thereby encouraging rational behaviour. Not only does full disclosure of assets achieve this, but also it levels the playing-field so to speak. It eliminates the potential for one party to take advantage of the other.[88] This reasoning provides the rationale behind s.6(2)(i) of the UPAA, which permits a court to set a pre-nuptial agreement aside as being unconscionable on the basis of failure to fully disclose one party's assets to the other.

Property and maintenance clauses

Traditionally, pre-nuptial contracts concerning property distribution upon divorce were treated differently than those concerning maintenance payments. The ability of parties to contract as to property distribution did not prove too troubling for courts to accept. Property distribution is generally easy to achieve as assets are simply split in accordance with the intentions of the parties, and it has no real implications on the institution of marriage. On the other hand, pre-nuptial clauses seeking to regulate maintenance payments did not initially receive judicial recognition. Courts exercised their paternalistic ideals to restrict the enforceability of such agreements as they were believed to be contrary to one of the fundamental tenets of marriage, that being spousal support, thereby violating public policy.

Such reasoning derives from the old common law rule of providing for one's spouse, which upon marriage became a life-long obligation.

---

pregnated with an embryo formed from another woman's fertilised egg. Thus, there is said to be no genetic connection between the surrogate woman and the child in such a case.

Notwithstanding this basis for distinction, both sides of the argument still provide for dynamic debate, and the ability of a surrogate woman to give informed consent before pregnancy remains questionable.

88   *Norris v Norris* 419 A.2d 982, 985 (D.C. 1980).

Nevertheless, as time progressed there was a divestment in the paternalistic role played by the courts. This new approach was cemented in American law under s.3 of the UPAA, and parties to a pre-nuptial agreement can now contract as to maintenance issues in the event of divorce, provided it is not unconscionable.[89] Spouses are now permitted to not only modify maintenance payments, but eliminate them altogether. A safeguard to this is apparent under s.6(b) of the UPAA, whereby such a clause may be deemed unenforceable if it would result in the other spouse requiring public assistance in order to meet his/her needs.

Despite this safeguard, a recent South Carolina Supreme Court decision demonstrates the scope of judicial deference to the freedom to contract, at the expense of public policy. In *Hardee v Hardee*[90] a pre-nuptial agreement waived all rights to spousal maintenance for a wife who was severely ill. The wife was disabled and unable to work and would become a public charge; yet the court held that the agreement was not unconscionable as the wife's ill-health was apparent at the time of signing the agreement, which she did contrary to her counsel's advice. Such a decision comes from the recent shift in judicial opinion as to the status of the spousal support obligation. Initially it was held to be an essential incident of marriage; now it represents an ancillary financial issue, thereby coming under the scope of pre-nuptial agreements and the broad and loose doctrine of "unconscionability" in America.

The decision in *Hardee* represents an unfettered deference to the autonomy and privacy of couples in the determination of matrimonial matters. Following the introduction of divorce, traditional restrictions on marriage and its consequential affairs cease to possess the same influence as before. Autonomy is beginning to reign supreme within the marital context, with no room for paternalistic attitudes. As parties can now freely leave marriage, one must question the validity of imposing spousal support obligations upon its termination. It is submitted that divorce and the subsequent automatic imposition of lifelong spousal support are incompatible.

Traditionally, it was assumed that a maintenance obligation was indicative of marriage. Yet, in a society of increasing diversity in the context of the "family", such a view is no longer tenable as it discriminates against other forms of committed relationships.[91] Rather than mutual sup-

---

[89] UPAA § 6.
[90] 355 S.C. 382; 585 S.E.2d 501; 2003 S.C. LEXIS 185.
[91] See *Satchwell v President of South Africa* 2002 (9) B.C.L.R. 986 (CC).

port obligations being a resultant consequence of marriage, an agreement to commit to reciprocal support obligations ought to give rise to a "marriage-like" relationship, worthy of legal recognition and support.[92] Such relationships are typically referred to as "committed relationships". From such a standpoint, it is plausible to argue that support obligations are no longer necessary incidents of marriage. Instead they are indicative of there being a committed relationship. As such, spouses ought to be permitted to contract away from such obligations before, during or after marriage.

Monetary and non-monetary contribution clauses

Traditionally, there has been a distinction drawn between monetary and non-monetary contributions to a marriage in the calculating of ancillary relief. That being said, monetary contributions are included in the determination of ancillary relief and non-monetary contributions are not.[93] This

---

[92]   Support for such a proposition is evident in the dictum of Madala J. of the South African Constitutional Court, where in *Satchwell v President of South Africa* 2002 (9) B.C.L.R. 986 (CC), at para.25, he stated:

"The law attaches a duty of support to various family relationships, for example, husband and wife, and parent and child. In a society where the range of family formations has widened, such a duty of support may be inferred as a matter of fact in certain cases of persons involved in permanent, same-sex life partnerships. Whether such a duty of support exists or not will depend on the circumstances of each case."

[93]   Interestingly, the reluctance of the courts to engage in this issue in actions directly concerning the marital context, does not reflect the approach adopted in other scenarios, notably actions taken for damages by dependants of parties fatally injured by another person's wrongful act. Section 48(1) of the Civil Liability Act 1961, as amended by the Civil Liability (Amendment) Act 1996, provides the dependants of a deceased with a right to take an action against a party whose wrongful conduct caused the fatality, for damages compensating them for the expectant benefits associated with their relationship to the deceased.

A cause of action in the context of a dependant claiming for damages due to the death of their spouse raises alluring observations for present purposes. A number of factors, surrounding the role of the deceased spouse, can be taken into account in such cases. Barron J. alluded to the possibility of this in the case of *Fitzsimons v Bord Telecom and ESB* [1991] I.L.R.M. 276 at 292, where he stated:

"The basis of the assessment of damages for fatal injuries is the balancing of losses and benefits. Like any other balance sheet, it seems appropriate to determine first what items can appear on the balance sheet and then secondly the amount of such items."

In *Cooper v Egan*, unreported, High Court, December 20, 1990, Barr J. was faced with an action brought by a widower for damages due to the wrongful death of his wife. The wife cared for their four-month-old baby, and also performed the role of homemaker. In awarding damages to the widower, Barr J. calculated the monetary value of the "services" that the wife provided for the husband in the marriage, and his resultant future loss of such benefit. He concluded that the plaintiff be awarded damages of £90,000 for the loss of the wife's contributions to the family, and £1,000 for occasional babysitting on weekends for the following eight years.

approach has been reciprocated in the formation stage of marriage in the sense that clauses concerning non-monetary contributions to an impending marriage have been held as being unenforceable clauses in a pre-nuptial agreement. Such clauses include those concerning "provision" of sex, the value of housework, childrearing and other "services".

Courts have adopted two grounds on which to justify such an approach:

1. It would be contrary to public policy to permit parties to a marriage to alter the essential incidents of marriage.
2. Such non-monetary clauses are unenforceable as they lack consideration.

The rationale behind this argument is that these "services" are incidents of the marital relationship, therefore under the pre-existing duty rule they cannot form sufficient consideration.[94]

This distinction seems prima facie arbitrary, in that there appears to be no legitimate justification in failing to recognise the economic value of these necessary "services". The family economy is comprised of both monetary and non-monetary factors, with no intrinsic hierarchy. Silbaugh defines the family economy as:

Furthermore, the courts have also placed a monetary value on the care given by a loved one to a plaintiff in an action for damages; see *Doherty v Bowaters Irish Wallboard Mills Ltd* [1968] I.R. 277. Although there is an issue as to the form such damages awards ought to take (See in general McMahon and Binchy, *Law of Torts* (3rd ed., Butterworths, 2000), paras [44.107]–[44.111]), the imposition of a monetary value on "carer" services provided by a loved one signifies the ability of the court to calculate the provision of non-monetary contributions to a family scenario.

These two points are of comparative interest for present purposes as they illustrate the ability of the courts to determine a monetary value for "services" provided within the home of a married couple. It displays a willingness to determine such factors outside the context of a matrimonial dispute; one must therefore question the apparent inability, or perhaps more pertinently the lack of enthusiasm, to engage in such matters within the context of matrimonial disputes.

[94]   The case of *Borelli v Brusseau* 16 Cal. Rptr. 2d 16 (Ct. Appeals 1993) adopted this mode of reasoning, where it was stated at 19–20:

"[C]ontracts whereby the wife is to receive compensation for providing [nursing-type] services are void as against public policy and there is no consideration for the husband's promise."

Similarly, the provision of marital "services" in a pre-nuptial agreement was held unenforceable in the case of *Kuder v Schroeder* 430 S.E.2d 271 (N.C. Ct. App. 1993) where the court held, at 273:

"So long as the coverture endures, this duty of [services] may not be abrogated or modified by the agreement of the parties to a marriage."

"[T]he daily informal exchange of money and nonmonetary components of marriage for the betterment of individuals within the family and the family as a whole."[95]

She argues that there is no justification in the current bias afforded by the law to monetary clauses in pre-nuptial agreements, at the expense of non-monetary clauses. She asserts that the current system fails to appreciate the "social meaning issue" in that:

"the quality of the things people bring to marriage differ; some things are easy to count, some are not; some are fungible, some are not; some are susceptible to traditional ideas about property rights, and some are not. But all are the product of spousal efforts, and all are valuable to both spouses and to some extent *to the culture*. A legal conception of marriage ought to support central positive social understandings of marriage, including an understanding that declines to prioritise the value of these disparate contributions."[96]

Courts are beginning to appreciate the need to reform this area, so as to ensure justice for women who contribute greatly to a marriage in a non-monetary sense. In determining equality as being the "yardstick" for the calculation of ancillary relief, the House of Lords in *White v White*[97] seemed to suggest a need to end such discrimination stating:

"In seeking to achieve a fair outcome, there is no place for discrimination between husband and wife and their respective roles … whatever the division of labour chosen by the husband and wife, or forced upon them by circumstances, fairness requires that this should not prejudice or advantage either party when considering [s.25(2)(f) of the Matrimonial Causes Act 1973] relating to parties' contributions…If, in their different spheres, each contributed equally to the family, then in principle it matters not which of them earned the money and built up the assets. There should be no bias in favour of the money-earner and against the homemaker and the child-carer."[98]

---

[95] Silbaugh, "Marriage Contracts and The Family Economy" (1993) 93 N.W.U.L. Rev. 65 at 100.

[96] *ibid.* at 108 (emphasis in original).

[97] [2000] 2 F.L.R. 981.

[98] *ibid.* at 989. This dictum was reiterated by the House of Lords in *Miller v Miller; McFarlane v McFarlane* [2006] 3 All E.R. 1 at para.1.

Courts should not use this dictum as a licence to examine and calculate the value of the contributions made by each party to the marriage; to do so would be to open a "forensic Pandora's box".[99] The futility of such an approach was elaborated on by Coleridge J., in the case of *G v G (Financial Provisions: Equal Division)*, stating:

> "[W]hat is 'contribution' but a species of conduct? ... Both concepts are compendious descriptions of the way in which one party conducted him/herself towards the other and/or the family during the marriage. And both carry with them precisely the same undesirable consequences. First, they call for a detailed retrospective at the end of a broken marriage just at a time when parties should be looking forward, not back ... But then, the facts having been established, they each call for a value judgment of the worth of each side's behaviour and translation of that worth into actual money. But by what measure and using what criteria? ... Is there such a concept as an exceptional/special domestic contribution or can only the wealth creator earn the bonus? ... It is much the same as comparing apples with pears and the debate is about as sterile or useful."[100]

It would appear that the law in England on this point makes no distinction between monetary and non-monetary contributions to a marriage. Simply, both are relevant factors in determining ancillary relief and ought to be treated equally:

> "Section 25(2)(f) of the 1973 Act does not refer to the contributions which each has made to the parties' accumulated wealth, but to the contributions they have made (and will continue to make) to the welfare of the family. Each should be seen as doing their best in their own sphere."[101]

It is submitted that the incorporation of non-monetary contributions to a marital relationship in the calculation of ancillary relief removes any justification for the current distinction at the formation stage. Silbaugh's conclusion is an altogether different one. Rather than "levelling-up", she is in favour of "levelling-down", thereby restricting the ability of parties to a marriage to contract as to monetary and non-monetary contributions.[102]

---

[99]   *G v G (Financial Provision: Equal Division)* [2002] 2 F.L.R. 1143 at 1154.
[100] *ibid.* at 1155.
[101] *Miller v Miller; McFarlane v McFarlane* [2006] 3 All E.R. 1 at para.146.
[102] Silbaugh, "Marriage Contracts and The Family Economy" (1993) 93 N.W.U.L. Rev. 65, at 137–138.

It is asserted that such an approach would not be favourable as it fails to appreciate the scope of relational contracts in improving this area of law. Also, it deprives individuals of the ability to formulate their own marriage as it reverts back to the state-imposed rules concerning marriage. This is deemed untenable for the reasons set out above.[103] Furthermore, recent developments in England adopt an alternative remedy, as shall be discussed below.

The position and effect of children to a pre-nuptial agreement

As already noted, one of the reasons for entering into a pre-nuptial agreement is to protect the inheritance of children from a former marriage. It is clear that the existence of children at the time of executing the pre-nuptial agreement should not present any problems in terms of the enforceability of the contract, provided proper provision has been made for them.[104] It is the birth of children subsequent to the execution of an agreement that appears to be problematic. Shannon, adopting a somewhat cautious tone, predicts this to be a potential constitutional stumbling-block for pre-nuptial agreements in Ireland.[105] He feels that the constitutional requirement to make "proper provision"[106] for children upon divorce would render any pre-nuptial agreement failing to contemplate potential children as being unenforceable. In considering the possibility of reforming the law in this area, the British Government reached a similar conclusion.[107]

There have been arguments against rendering pre-nuptial agreements void upon the birth of a child. It has been claimed that such a rule could act as a deterrent to having children, or alternatively, encourage abortion so as to save the pre-nuptial contract.[108]

---

[103] See Chaps 2 and 3.
[104] See *K v K (Ancillary Relief: Prenuptial Agreement)* [2003] 1 F.L.R. 120 where a pre-nuptial contract was entered into in the knowledge of the wife-to-be being pregnant. Although not binding in England, this pre-nuptial contract was heavily relied on by the court in reaching its decision irrespective of the knowledge of the impending child.
[105] Shannon, "Pre-Nuptial Agreements in Ireland" (2003) I.J.F.L. 132.
[106] Art.41.3.1°(iii).
[107] The Home Office, "Green Paper: *Supporting Families: A Consultation Document*" (TSO, 1998). A similar concern was expressed by the judges of the Family Division of the High Court in Wilson, "Ancillary Relief Reform—Response of the Judges of the Family Division to Government Proposals" (1999) 29 Fam. L. J. 159.
[108] See Hooker, "Prenuptial Contracts and Safeguards" [2001] Fam. Law 56. For criticism of this argument see Leadercramer, "Prenuptial Contracts—New Safeguards, New Problems?" (2001) 31 Fam. L. J. 295.

Nevertheless, there is an alternative. Conway postulates that in such circumstances the courts ought to be able to alter such an agreement so as to meet the justices of the case without arbitrarily declaring it void.[109]

Such an approach would be capable of accommodating the constitutional concerns posited by Shannon above. If the justice of the case required greater provision to be made for a child than originally provided for in the pre-nuptial contract, then so be it. As such, the agreement would still stand, thereby fulfilling the intentions of the parties to the greatest extent possible, having regard to any subsequent children.

Notwithstanding the prudent nature of such an approach, one must question whether maintenance obligations to a child can be contracted away from. If two autonomous individuals to a broken-down marriage can agree to terminate spousal support, then why not expand such reasoning to the support obligations of a child? Circumstances may lend themselves to an absolute clean break between the parties. If a wife and mother agrees to no financial support from the husband and father, then such a decision ought to be respected. Furthermore, if a frozen embryo is inseminated and brought to term, without the sperm donor's consent, ought he be obliged to provide support for the child?[110] One might foresee an estoppel-type argument being posited in such circumstances.[111] Moreover, if courts reduce child support obligations in light of subsequent changes to the financial circumstances of the father, then why not permit the father and mother to contract away from such obligations in the first place?

---

[109] Conway, "Prenuptial Contracts" (1995) 145 New L.J. 1290.

[110] For an overview of the recent debate concerning the "Embryo" case before the High Court at present, see "Husband's case on embryos upheld" *The Irish Times,* July 19, 2006; Coulter, "Ownership of Embryos case will raise very difficult questions" *The Irish Times,* July 3, 2006; Binchy, "Unborn share a common dignity with all other living human beings" *The Irish Times,* March 15, 2006.

Although the Irish courts are only now being faced with the status of an embryo for the first time, there is a wealth of academic opinion in this field. Furthermore, courts in the United States of America have contended with this issue. Of note, for present purposes, it is worth referring to the decision of the Tennessee Supreme Court in *Davis v Davis* 842 S.W.2d 588 (Tenn. 1992). In this case it was held that, in the context of a dispute surrounding the custody of a frozen embryo following the termination of a marriage, the husband had a constitutional right to evade unwanted parenthood, thus avoiding consequential obligations such as providing maintenance.

Furthermore, it was held in *JB v BZ* 421 Mass. 150; 725 N.E.2d 1051 (2000) that a contract concerning the disposition of frozen embryos was unenforceable as it violated the husband's right to refuse to procreate.

See in general Jost, "Rights of Embryo and Foetus in Private Law" (2002) 50 Am. J. Comp. L. 633.

[111] It is noted that estoppel-type arguments have not always found favour in the family

Dealing with changing circumstances—the need for periodic review

Although a pre-nuptial agreement may be fair at the time of execution, unforeseen circumstances at the time of performance may render it unfair. In Australia, if circumstances render the agreement "impracticable"[112] or effect a "material change"[113] causing a party to suffer hardship if the agreement was to be enforced, then the court can set it aside. In New Zealand, if the court concludes that to enforce a pre-nuptial contract would cause "serious injustice"[114] then it may be set aside. Similarly, the British Government, in contemplating the enforceability of pre-nuptial agreements, considered that such agreements ought to be set aside if enforcement would cause "significant injustice".[115]

The New Jersey Supreme Court reckoned with this issue in the case of *Lepis v Lepis*.[116] It was held that family maintenance provisions, whether imposed by a court or by the parties themselves, could be altered if there has been a significant change in the circumstances. Such a change would have to be substantial, unforeseeable at the time of determining the agreement and be of a permanent nature. To avoid having a pre-nuptial agreement set aside for failure to reflect the current realities of a marriage, it is submitted that a periodic review clause be inserted into all pre-nuptial agreements. Shannon recommends a three- to five-year period of review; or after the occurrence of a significant event, *e.g.* the birth of a child, or a change in career.[117] As is evident, this would have the added benefit of reformulating a pre-nuptial agreement (technically creating a nuptial

---

context, as within this domain the status of the parties is of particular importance *i.e.* a man is the husband/father, and the woman the wife/mother. With these statuses, certain legal rights and obligations are attached, thereby giving rise to consequent issues also. In cases concerning marriages based on invalid divorces, estoppel arguments have been posited so as to avoid ancillary relief obligations to the second spouse on the basis of the marriage being a nullity. See *Gaffney v Gaffney* [1975] I.R. 133 and *CK v JK*, unreported, Supreme Court, March 31, 2004. Both cases held that the concept of estoppel can play no role within the marital context. Summarising the principle enunciated by Walsh J. in *Gaffney*, Keane C.J. in *RB v AS* [2002] 2 I.R. 428 at 456 stated:

> "the doctrine of estoppel cannot operate so as to change a person's status where that status, as a matter of law, has not been changed."

[112] Family Law Act 1975, s.90K(c).
[113] Family Law Act 1975, s.90K(d).
[114] Property (Relationships) Act 1976, s.21J.
[115] The Home Office, "Green Paper: *Supporting Families: A Consultation Document*" (TSO, 1998).
[116] 83 N.J. 139; 416 A.2d 45; 1980 N.J. LEXIS 1357.
[117] Shannon, "Pre-Nuptial Agreements in Ireland" (2003) I.J.F.L. 132.

agreement) so as to make provision for a child, thereby reducing the risk of having the agreement deemed invalid as illustrated above.

Dispute resolution clauses

In recent times the role of the State in the regulation of marriage has been gradually diminishing. Increasingly, family law seeks to delegate the power to control and regulate the family, and marriage, to the interested parties. An example of this is the growth in popularity of mediation services.[118] The law now encourages the parties to a dispute to attempt to resolve any difficulties without recourse to litigation. Irish family law is no different. Sections 5 and 6 of the Judicial Separation and Family Law Reform Act 1989, and ss.6 and 7 of the Family Law (Divorce) Act 1996 require solicitors to recommend mediation talks between parties prior to embarking on legal separation proceedings. The objectives inherent in this policy are to increase communication amongst parties so as to avoid hostile conflict.[119] A pre-nuptial agreement would be a further means of promoting this philosophy.

---

[118] See in general Conneely, *Family Mediation in Ireland* (Ashgate, 2002).

[119] Feminists tend to argue against this point on the basis that the private ordering of family law disputes merely reaffirms the weaker position of a woman in a relationship by virtue of her perceived economic, social and emotional vulnerabilities. Conneely contends with this issue of gender discrimination in the context of the mediation process. She notes that feminist arguments in opposition to the mediation process tend to be based upon theoretical propositions, whereas proponents of mediation support their arguments with reference to empirical data.

It would seem that the empirical data used by those in favour of mediation has trumped opposition feminist arguments. There would appear to be several reasons for this, including the following:

First, the feminist school of thought is split within itself. One side claims the mediation process to be less favourable to women, due to the fact that women have less access to wealth, power and resources than men. The alternative argument claims that the interaction and cooperation necessitated in the mediation process tends to favour women.

Secondly, the traditional argument of mediation, and the private ordering of family law in general, solidifying the weaker position of women is more myth than reality. Studies depict power and bargaining position to be relative concepts. Power does not necessarily equate with wealth. Instead it has been argued that power is a fluid concept. As such, the close relationship between a mother and child may prove a more powerful bargaining device than any amount of money in custody disputes.

Although Conneely concludes that the empirical data employed by those in favour of mediation in family law is persuasive, she notes that it is difficult to uncover any substantive form of consensus due to the vast variety of cases arising from matters typically concerned with mediation.

See in general Conneely, *Family Mediation in Ireland* (Ashgate, 2002), pp.139–47.

A pre-nuptial agreement, by its nature, acts as a mediation device. It causes a couple to sit down and actively discuss their expectations and concerns of marriage. Possible points of conflict can be addressed before they become matters of serious concern. Furthermore, so as to maintain this philosophy it is submitted that all pre-nuptial agreements have an alternative dispute resolution clause. Upon the apparent breakdown of a marriage, divorce should not be an automatic step. Instead the parties ought to contract to utilise all means possible of salvaging their marriage. Marriage as an institution needs to be respected and valued; therefore, it ought not to be dissolved flippantly. As such, a pre-nuptial agreement ought to specify that upon the breakdown of a marriage, mediation is the first port of call.[120]

Invalid clauses

To conclude, it is thought pertinent to highlight some clauses that are typically deemed invalid in pre-nuptial agreements. A clause that stipulates the religion that a child, borne of the marriage, ought to practise has been deemed invalid.[121] Such a clause would likely be found to be an unconstitutional restriction on the free exercise of religion. Clauses that seek to limit[122] or set[123] child support in advance have been deemed invalid on the basis of protecting the welfare of the child. It is speculated that such an approach would be adopted in this jurisdiction so as to ensure "proper provision" for dependant children.[124]

A clause stating that the parties can never divorce has been deemed invalid in America. It was deemed unenforceable on public policy grounds as an illegitimate restriction of access to the courts.[125] It is questionable whether such a decision would be reached in this jurisdiction. In *Dalton v Dalton*[126] the High Court refused to enforce a separation agreement whereby the parties agreed to obtain a divorce abroad. O'Hanlon J. held

---

[120] It is accepted that throughout this book, rights such as privacy and autonomy have been celebrated. The natural flow of such moral argument is to conclude that parties to a pre-nuptial agreement ought to be able to contract to an alternative dispute resolution clause only if they choose. In light of this, the above submission is merely a recommendation. Nonetheless, it is posited that it ought to be adopted so as to preserve the unique concept of marriage.

[121] *Zummo v Zummo* 574 A.2d 1130 (Pa. Super. Ct. 1990).

[122] *Monmouth County Div. Of Soc. Servs. v GDM* 705 A.2d 408 (N.J. Super. Ct. Ch. Div. 1997).

[123] *Re Littlefield* 940 P.2d 1362 (Wash. 1997).

[124] See in general Shannon, "Pre-Nuptial Agreements in Ireland" (2003) I.J.F.L. 132.

[125] *Coggins v Coggins* 601 So.2d 109 (Ala. Civ. App. 1992).

[126] [1982] I.L.R.M. 418.

that to enforce such an agreement would be contrary to public policy. It is clear that, with the introduction of divorce in this jurisdiction, this case would no longer be binding. Nonetheless, the same principle may be applied; as divorce is now a constitutional right to all people, would it be contrary to public policy to enter an agreement to never divorce?

To answer this question in the affirmative would be to adhere to the traditional definitional approach to recognising marriage. The 1995 amendment to the Constitution introducing divorce had the effect of replacing one arbitrary definition of marriage with another, thus failing to address the need for reform. With marriage now being defined as a qualified commitment, capable of being extinguished, the law remains oblivious to the wishes of those seeking to enter marriage. To follow the traditional definitional approach to marriage, a couple wishing to enter a lifelong marriage, without the possibility of divorce, cannot do so. The retention of a definitional model of marriage, despite permitting parties to terminate the marriage, continues to neglect the autonomy, privacy and dignity of those wishing to enter marriage as it does not defer to their judgment as to the level of commitment they foresee their marriage to represent. The continuing role of the State in the formation and termination of marriage remains in conflict with the call for a cessation of such state activity. For the reasons postulated in Chapter 3, parties wishing to enter a perpetual marital union, without recourse to divorce, ought to be permitted to contract to such. The question remains as to the basis upon which this can be achieved.

The conundrum asserted by this argument requires one to address the issues of constitutional interpretation[127] and waiver of constitutional rights.[128] Essentially there are three modes of constitutional interpretation: literal, broad and harmonious. The harmonious method of interpretation lends itself to situations where two or more provisions of the Constitution appear to conflict one another. The premise upon which the harmonious method of interpretation is based is that the drafters of the Constitution ascribed values to each provision so as to permit it to be interpreted as a synchronised document free of inherent discord. Henchy J., dissenting in *People (DPP) v O'Shea*,[129] provided an engaging insight into this mode of interpretation:

---

[127]   See Kelly, *The Irish Constitution* (4th ed., Butterworths, 2003), paras [1.1.02]–[1.1.70].
[128]   *ibid.,* paras [7.1.68]–[7.1.78].
[129]   [1982] I.R. 384.

"Any single constitutional right or power is but a component in an ensemble of interconnected and interacting provisions which must be brought into play as part of a larger composition, and which must be given such an integrated interpretation as will fit harmoniously into the general constitutional order and modulation. It may be said of a constitution, more than any other legal instrument, that "the letter killeth, but the spirit giveth life". No single constitutional provision (particularly one designed to safeguard personal liberty and social order) may be isolated and construed with undeviating literalness."[130]

With this mode of interpretation developed the corollary theory of there being a hierarchy of constitutional rights. Naturally, if one seeks to interpret the Constitution in a harmonious manner, certain articles that appear to conflict each other are required to be interpreted in such a manner so as to cause one to prevail over the other, thereby preserving the internal consistency of the Constitution. The Supreme Court adopted this rationale in *People v Shaw*,[131] where Kenny J. stated:

"There is a hierarchy of constitutional rights and, when a conflict arises between them, that which ranks higher must prevail. … When a conflict of constitutional rights arises, it must be resolved by having regard to (a) the terms of the Constitution, (b) the ethical values which all Christians living in the State acknowledge and accept and (c) the main tenets of our system of constitutional parliamentary democracy."[132]

The present challenge posed by the theory concerning the ability of a couple to contract to a marriage without recourse to divorce gives rise to a potential conflict of constitutional provisions. In Ireland there is now a constitutional right to divorce,[133] yet there is also a clear constitutional obligation to protect the family based on marriage.[134] Following the reasoning of O'Hanlon J. in *Dalton v Dalton*, covenanting never to divorce would be contrary to public policy. On the other hand, covenanting never to divorce so as to preserve the family unit, as recognised by the Constitution, could be said to be in accordance with Art.41 of the Constitution.

---

[130]   *ibid.* at 426.
[131]   [1982] I.R. 1.
[132]   *ibid.* at 63.
[133]   Art.41.3.2°.
[134]   Art.41.1.2°.

It is suggested that in order to resolve this conflict there is a need to determine the constitutional origins of the right to marry. It has been mooted that there are two possibilities as to this.

First, one might argue that the right to marry is a derivative of the right to protect the family as enunciated in Art.41. As this right is a derivative of Art.41, it must also be proscribed by the stipulations of the said article. Therefore, the right to marry would be limited by the right to obtain a divorce. If that is the case, then it is asserted that parties to a marriage seeking to discard the divorce element of marriage would be unsuccessful in any subsequent legal challenge. Nonetheless, it may be argued that parties to such a marriage can waive their constitutional right to a divorce. The ability to waive one's constitutional rights was first alluded to by the Supreme Court in the context of personal rights under Art.40 in the case of *State (Nicolau) v An Bord Uchtála* where Walsh J. held:

> "there [is] no provision in Article 40 which prohibits or restricts the surrender, abdication, or transfer of any of the rights guaranteed in that Article by the person entitled to them."[135]

Later, in *G v An Bord Uchtála,* Walsh J. provided stronger support for this concept, stating:

> "Natural rights may be waived or surrendered by the persons who enjoy them provided such waiver is not prohibited either by the natural law or by positive law."[136]

Nonetheless, it is noted that the ability to waive one's constitutional rights is subject to one important caveat, that being, the need for full knowledge and consent.

Notwithstanding the apparent judicial support for the waiver of constitutional rights, it would appear that this concept does not stretch into the realm of the "family", as protected under Art.41. The rights set out in this constitutional provision are said to be "inalienable and imprescriptible". The interpretation of this by Kenny J. in *Ryan v Attorney-General* suggests such rights not being capable of waiver:

> "'Inalienable' means that which cannot be transferred or given away while 'imprescriptible' means that which cannot be lost by the passage of time or abandoned by non-exercise."[137]

---

[135]   [1966] I.R. 567 at 640.
[136]   [1980] I.R. 32 at 71.
[137]   *Ryan v Attorney-General* [1965] I.R. 294 at 308.

As such, the argument that parties can waive their right to marry, as founded in Art.41, would appear to fail. Yet hope is not lost, as there may be an alternative argument more capable of attaining support should this scenario come before the courts.

There is significant judicial support for the proposition that the right to marry is not a derivative right found in Art.41, but instead finds its basis in Art.40.3 of the Constitution as a personal right.[138] The significance of this proposition becomes apparent when one considers the qualifications imposed on the right to marry. Instead of being "inalienable and imprescriptible", a right to marry under Art.40.3 would be protected "as far as practicable" from "unjust attack". Evidently it would appear somewhat easier to justify a restriction on the right to marry if it was founded under Art.40.3 and not Art.41, and such restrictions are manifest in the Irish legal system, for example, laws concerning consanguinity and marriage, and age limits on marriage. Also, in *Foy v An t-Ard Chlaraitheoir,*[139] McKechnie J. held it not to be a violation of the right to marry to prohibit persons of the same sex from marrying, even if one party has undergone gender re-assignment. As such, the right to marry is not absolute, thereby providing further support for the assertion that it is a personal right founded in Art.40.3 and not Art.41.

Consequently, the right to marry, as interpreted by the Constitution, can be waived by the parties to such a marriage, the result being the ability to enter into a traditional marriage, without possible recourse to divorce. Thus, such a clause in a pre-nuptial agreement may indeed attract judicial recognition in the Irish courts, despite findings to the contrary in other jurisdictions.

THE REGULATION OF PRE-NUPTIAL CONTRACTS

The standard of review for pre-nuptial contracts must be capable of considering the various aspects of this unique form of contract. It is necessary to incorporate contract principles, as well as family law principles. Atwood reflects on the enormity of the task, commenting:

---

[138] See Costello J. in *Murray v Ireland* [1985] I.R. 532; also Fitzgerald C.J. dissenting in *McGee v Attorney General* [1974] I.R. 284. Furthermore, counsel for the respondents in *Foy v An t-Ard Chlaraitheoir*, unreported, High Court, McKechnie J., July 9, 2002 conceded that the right to marry was founded in Art.40.3. Notwithstanding this, it is noted that the Constitutional Review Group in its report on the Constitution recommended that the right to marry be expressly promulgated under Art.41 of the Constitution; see Constitution Review Group, *Report of the Constitution Review Group* (Government Publications, 1996), pp.332–333.

[139] *Foy v An t-Ard Chlaraitheoir*, unreported, High Court, McKechnie J., July 9, 2002.

"The features of antenuptial contracts that justify greater state supervision than is ordinarily exerted over commercial contracts include the special legal status of the marriage relationship in our society, the trust and confidence the law expects of marriage partners, the emotional intensity surrounding the decision to marry, the common belief that the marriage will last forever, and the potential lack of understanding of the economic rights that are being waived. This coalescence of factors, when viewed against the backdrop of persistent gender inequality in the marketplace, warrants a relaxation of the rules of contract to accommodate other social values."[140]

In examining different modes of review it is useful to reflect on developments in American case law, as it represents the most developed jurisdiction in this area. Interestingly, the law has moved from a substantive form of review, to one concentrating on procedural fairness, thereby reflecting the growth in popularity of contractual principles.

The substantive "fairness" approach

The decision in *Posner* represented a significant shift in this area of law within the United States. The courts would no longer adopt a rigid "public policy" approach in refusing to acknowledge pre-nuptial agreements made in contemplation of divorce. Instead the courts were now prepared to engage in such contracts, and determine their validity as a matter of law.

The first test to receive general approval was enunciated in the case of *Scherer v Scherer*,[141] where the court set out a three-step approach to analysing such contracts[142]:

1. Was the agreement obtained through fraud, duress, mistake or misrepresentation or non-disclosure of material facts?
2. Was the agreement unconscionable?
3. Have the facts and circumstances changed since the execution of the agreement to such an extent that to enforce it would be unfair or unreasonable?

---

[140] Atwood, "Ten Years Later: Lingering Concerns About the Uniform Premarital Agreement Act" (1993) 19 *Journal of Legislation* 127 at 135.

[141] 292 S.E.2d 662 (Ga. 1982).

[142] See Nasheri, "Prenuptial Agreements in the United States: A Need for Closer Control?" (1998) 12 I.J.L.P.F. 307.

As is evident, this test adopted both a procedural and substantive form of review fundamentally based on the concept of "fairness". This nebulous concept of "fairness" essentially permitted the court to impose a stealth form of "public policy" in the regulation of such agreements.

It was in 1990 that the "fairness" criteria of the *Scherer* test was jettisoned on the basis that it represented a "paternalistic and unwarranted interference with the parties' freedom to enter contracts".[143] In *Simeone v Simeone*[144] the court held that the "fairness" test was based on an attitude toward the weak bargaining power of women that no longer accorded with social reality.[145] As a result of this, and with the support of the UPAA, courts began to adopt standard contract principles to examine the procedural validity of such contracts in order to determine their enforceability.

A contractual form of review

Having determined that "the reasonableness of a pre-nuptial bargain is not a proper subject for judicial review",[146] courts began to analyse such agreements solely on a procedural basis of review. The terms of the UPAA accommodated such a development. The approach taken by the courts to applying ordinary contract principles, such as misrepresentation and duress, to pre-nuptial contracts, is stricter than might be expected if one was dealing with a standard contract. The reason for this is an appreciation of the unique nature of such contracts and the substantial effects they may have on society.

The dominance of contractarian principles in this field is illustrated in the provisions of the UPAA. As noted, the UPAA is mainly concerned with procedural fairness when it comes to regulating pre-nuptial agreements. Provisions concerning procedural matters such as voluntariness, full disclosure and financial obligations occupy prominent positions throughout the Act. In fact, the only provision concerning "substantive fairness" is that permitting courts to invalidate a pre-nuptial agreement on the basis that it may result in a former spouse requiring state financial assistance in order to support him/herself.[147]

---

[143] *Simeone v Simeone* 581 A.2d 162, at 166 (Pa. 1990).

[144] *ibid.*

[145] It was stated that previous decisions were based on the misguided assumption that "spouses are of unequal status and that women are not knowledgeable enough to understand the nature of contracts that they enter." *ibid.* at 165.

[146] *ibid.* at 166.

[147] UPAA § 6(b), 9B U.L.A. 369 (1987).

Similarly, the Australian Family Law Act 1975, as amended, appears to restrict the scope for judicial review of such contracts to procedural matters. As well as the standard procedural clauses concerning signature requirements, copies of the agreement, etc., the legislation divests the determination of the substantive fairness of the agreement in the parties themselves. Section 90G of the Act mandates that, having received independent legal advice, the fairness of the agreement be certified by the parties in the presence of a lawyer, who in turn further certifies that the agreement represents the parties' wishes and subsequently attaches this to the contract. Having fulfilled these procedural requirements in accordance with s.90G the agreement becomes binding. Significantly, "[i]f an agreement is binding, a court will not be able to deal with the matters with which the agreement deals."[148] Consequently, it seems clear that the intention of the Australian legislature was to restrict judicial review of prenuptial contracts to procedural matters only, thereby prohibiting any form of a "substantive fairness" test to be adopted.

Room for improvement?

It has been argued that the confusion caused between some courts adopting substantive modes of review and others procedural, has led to ambiguities as to the form pre-nuptial agreements can take.[149] Such a conflict has cast doubt on the validity of certain types of clauses.[150] There is a need to clarify the situation and provide a point of reference whereby lawyers advising clients can do so with more certainty. This was attempted in the English High Court case of *K v K (Ancillary Relief: Prenuptial Agreements)*[151] where Rodger Hayward Smith Q.C., sitting as deputy High Court judge, set out the following points of analysis necessary to determine whether a court should have regard to a pre-nuptial agreement[152]:

1. "Did [the parties] understand the agreement?
2. [Were the parties] properly advised as to its terms?

---

[148] Clause 129, Explanatory Memorandum on the Family Law Amendment Bill 1999.

[149] Silbaugh, "Marriage Contracts and the Family Economy" (1993) 93 N.W.U.L. Rev. 65.

[150] This is notable in relation to the validity of non-monetary contribution clauses as any review of such clauses necessitates a substantive review as to fairness. In a jurisdiction adopting a procedural mode of review it would be difficult to achieve this, thus eliminating the potential for these important clauses to be recognised.

[151] [2003] 1 F.L.R. 120.

[152] At present pre-nuptial agreements are not binding in England. Nevertheless, a court can take a pre-nuptial contract into account where it would be inequitable to disregard it, pursuant to s.25(2)(g) of the Matrimonial Causes Act 1973. This shall be discussed in greater detail below.

3. [Did one party's conduct cause the other party to be put] under any pressure to sign it?
4. Was there full disclosure?
5. [Was either party] under any other pressure?
6. [Did both parties] willingly sign the agreement?
7. [Did either party] exploit a dominant position, either financially or otherwise?
8. Was the agreement entered into in the knowledge that there would be a child?
9. Has any unforeseen circumstance arisen since the agreement was made that would make it unjust to hold the parties to it?
10. What does the agreement mean?
11. Does the agreement preclude an order for periodical payments for [either party]?
12. Are there any grounds for concluding that an injustice would be done by holding the parties to the terms of the agreement?
13. Is the agreement one of the circumstances of the case to be considered under s.25?
14. Does the entry into this agreement constitute conduct which it would be inequitable to disregard under s.25(2)(g)?
15. [Would the Court be] breaking new ground by holding [either party] to the capital terms of the agreement?
16. Insofar as maintenance for [either party] is concerned, if [the Court] is wrong in [its] interpretation of the agreement as above, and if the agreement precludes a maintenance claim, would it be unjust to hold the parties to that aspect of the agreement?"[153]

This approach represents an amalgamation of the procedural fairness and substantive fairness approaches that have featured independently in other jurisdictions.

---

[153] *K v K (Ancillary Relief: Prenuptial Agreement)* [2003] 1 F.L.R. 120, at 131–132. The answers to these questions, as concerning the case in hand, have been deleted so as to provide a succinct list of the factors deemed relevant by the court to consider.

The stage of judicial involvement

Upon litigation, the validity of a pre-nuptial contract can be analysed at two different points in time. First, the date of execution, and second, the date of performance. Examination at the date of performance incorporates elements extrinsic to the agreement that may render the agreement "unfair". Therefore, although an agreement may be fair at the time of contracting, it can be set aside at the time of enforcement.[154] Such a mode of analysis tends to reflect the traditional paternalistic attitudes of the courts to such agreements; most notably the need to protect the inferior bargaining position of women.

It is submitted, based on the moral arguments expounded in Chapter 3, that the pertinent time of review is that of the date of execution. Privacy, autonomy and ultimately the freedom to contract are not hollow philosophies upon which one can claim the right to contract to one's own marriage. On the contrary, these concepts carry with them obligations that must be fulfilled. If a person entering a pre-nuptial contract does not feel comfortable with its terms then he/she need not sign it and instead can seek to rely on state rules concerning ancillary relief. By exercising one's rights to enter into such a contract there is an inherent duty to honour it. If not, the basis for such a right becomes meaningless.

Furthermore, it has been argued that analysis at the date of execution promotes gender equality in such matters. The traditional paternalistic examination at the date of performance sought to ensure that women would not be unfairly treated by virtue of their inferior economic bargaining position in such contracts. Despite this it has been argued that in the long run it would be more beneficial to women to analyse these contracts at the date of execution.[155] It is thought that by ensuring fairness at the bargaining stage, women will be able to be actively involved in negotiations and determine aspects of the agreement for themselves.

In addition to this, it has been argued that due to the prospective context within which a pre-nuptial agreement is formulated, the standard of review ought to reflect this.[156] Appreciation of this reasoning is evident in various jurisdictions. As noted, the UPAA is predominantly concerned with procedural review, thus reflecting a mode of analysis at the

---

[154]   See *Button v Button* 388 N.W.2d 546 (Wis. 1986).

[155]   See in general Guggenheimer, "A Modest Proposal: The Feminomics of Drafting Premarital Agreements" (1996) 17 Women's Rts. L. Rep. 147.

[156]   Dnes, "An Economic Analysis of a Proposal to Reform the Discretionary Approach to the Division of Marital Assets in England and Wales" (Lord Chancellor's Department, Research Series, No.6/98, September 1998).

date of execution.[157] Also, in Australia it would appear that the supervision of the fairness of an agreement is finalised at the date of execution, thereby limiting any scope for future judicial review. As stated above, s.90G of the Family Law Act 1975 requires a solicitor to certify the procedural correctness of a pre-nuptial agreement. Despite a lack of case law on this point, it would appear that the presence of such a certificate satisfies any judicial inquiry into the fairness of a pre-nuptial contract, thus eliminating any significant form of judicial review at the performance stage.[158] A somewhat similar approach is taken in the Canadian provinces of Quebec and Alberta. Both provinces require the procedural aspects of such a contract to be verified before it is signed off as complete. In Quebec all marital contracts must be notarised,[159] and in Alberta parties to such a contract must consult a lawyer.[160]

The "cooling off" period

Briefly, in relation to a contractual form of review at the execution stage, it is submitted that there ought to be a period of time between the execution of the contract and the marriage ceremony. There have been cases where women have been given pre-nuptial agreements to sign and failure to do so has been threatened with cancellation of the wedding[161]; or even cases whereby the agreement was signed only hours before the ceremony.[162] Evidently there is a concern surrounding the presence of duress and undue influence in such cases. It is postulated that this fear can be quelled by enunciating a clear rule whereby a pre-nuptial agreement will only be recognised by a court if it is signed "X" number of days before the marriage ceremony. The British Government, in a Green Paper concerning this and other issues, suggested a period of 21 days[163]; it is submitted that this be a minimum.

---

[157] UPAA § 6.
[158] See in general Fehlberg and Smyth, "Binding Prenuptial Agreements in Australia: The First Year" (2002) 16 I.J.L.P.F. 127. Also as noted above, Clause 129 of the Explanatory Memorandum on the Family Law Amendment Bill 1999, stating: "If an agreement is binding, a court will not be able to deal with the matters which the agreement deals."
[159] Art.440 C.C.Q. (Civil Code of Quebec).
[160] *Alberta Matrimonial Property Act*, R.S.A. 1980, c. M-9, s.38(2).
[161] *Liebelt v Liebelt* 118 Idaho 845; 801 P.2d 52 (1990). This case concerned an agreement signed by the wife two days before the ceremony due to the husband threatening to cancel everything if she refused to do so.
[162] *Fechtel v Fechtel* 556 So. 2d 520; (Fla. 1990). This case concerned a pre-nuptial agreement signed by a wife only hours before the ceremony.
[163] The Home Office, "Green Paper: *Supporting Families: A Consultation Document*" (TSO, 1998).

Bix notes a potential problem with enforcing such a rule. He hypothesises that a couple may come before a court having signed a pre-nuptial agreement within the "cooling off" period, but having discussed its content outside of the period.[164] Such a scenario arose in the case of *K v K (Ancillary Relief: Prenuptial Agreement)*.[165] Although not strictly enforceable in England, the court in this case analysed the agreement as a circumstance to be taken into account in determining ancillary relief pursuant to s.25(2)(g) of the Matrimonial Causes Act 1973. The agreement was signed by the parties one day before the ceremony; nonetheless, due to the substantial negotiations in the preceding months concerning its formulation, the court deemed it admissible. Such a prudent decision would seem to negate the concerns of Bix; notwithstanding this, it is posited that such an approach ought not to be promoted, and a fixed time limit be adhered to.

THE ADVANTAGES AND DISADVANTAGES TO HAVING A PRE-NUPTIAL AGREEMENT

Advantages of a pre-nuptial agreement

A pre-nuptial agreement by its very nature reflects the construction marriage ought to take; that being an institution reflecting the committed relationship of two autonomous individuals.[166] It would allow a couple to escape the shackles of the traditional marriage and to enter a committed relationship on their own terms. The planning inherent in a pre-nuptial agreement can:

> "promote an egalitarian relationship, allow for privacy and freedom in relationships, clarify expectations, preclude potentially disastrous mismatches, and lay down mechanisms for solving problems."[167]

The four main advantages of a pre-nuptial agreement can be set out as the "Four C's"[168]:

---

[164] Bix, "Bargaining in the Shadow of Love: The Enforcement of Premarital Agreements and How We Think About Marriage" (1999) 40 Wm. & Mary L. Rev. 145 at 188.

[165] [2003] 1 F.L.R. 120.

[166] See Chaps 2 and 3.

[167] Barton, "Pre-Marital Contracts and Equal Shares on Divorce" (1998) 28 Fam. L. J. 423.

[168] The "Four C's" is an adaptation of a list of advantages as set out by Fehlberg and Smyth, "Binding Prenuptial Agreements in Australia: The First Year" (2002) 16 I.J.L.P.F. 127.

- Control over the course and conduct of the relationship.
- Choice as to the nature of the relationship.
- Conflict in the future can be reduced.
- Cost of any future dissolution of the marriage can be reduced.

The Lord Chancellor's Department noted similar advantages to the recognition and enforcement of pre-nuptial agreements, including[169]:

- A framework, upon which parties to a marriage could proceed so as to realise their expectations.
- It would promote the resolution of conflicts within a marriage without recourse to the legal system. It is thought that parties to such an agreement would be more likely to abide by its terms so as to avoid failing at something they formulated themselves.
- The negotiations involved in a pre-nuptial agreement would foster and promote a spirit of openness and communication within the relationship that would be expected to carry through to marriage and beyond.[170]

Notwithstanding these advantages, there are several concerns surrounding the enforcement of pre-nuptial contracts that need to be addressed.

Disadvantages of a pre-nuptial agreement

The traditionally perceived economically inferior bargaining position of women has occupied a prominent role in discourse surrounding pre-nuptial agreements. Its support, within this debate, is nonetheless ambiguous. Feminists are split as to whether pre-nuptial agreements exacerbate this traditional disparity or eliminate it. Neave argues that a pre-nuptial contract merely privatises the inequalities, as they currently exist, between men and women.[171] Whereas Guggenheimer argues that a pre-nuptial contract enhances the self-determination and bargaining power of women, by refusing to accord them any "'special protection" that might

---

[169] Mansfield, Reynolds and Arai (One Plus One Marriage and Partnership Research), "What Policy Developments Would Be Most Likely to Secure an Improvement in Marital Stability" (Lord Chancellor's Department, Research Series No.2/99).

[170] See in general Weitzman, *The Marriage Contract: Spouses, Lovers and the Law* (The Free Press, 1981), pp.227–229.

[171] Neave, "Resolving the Dilemma of Difference: A Critique of 'The Role of Private Ordering in Family Law'" (1994) 44 U. Toronto L. J. 97.

insulate them to such an extent that their perceived inferior status would be further bolstered.[172] Both aspects of this debate will be examined presently.

Those who claim that pre-nuptial contracts endorse the gender divide base their argument on a rationale comprised of social and psychological factors. There is a fear that a woman in love may not adequately protect her rights in contract negotiations:

> "What person [is] so exposed to imposition as a woman, contracting personally, with her intended husband, just on the eve of marriage, at a time when all providential considerations are likely to be merged into a confiding attachment or suppressed from an honourable instinct and sentiment of delicacy…?"[173]

The perceived advantage of pre-nuptial contracts as providing an element of "choice" to those entering marriage has been criticised by some as being no more than fiction.[174] Such an opinion is substantiated by the research of Atwood, who, from an overview of the 39 reported cases in 1992, challenging the validity of pre-nuptial contracts, found that 33 were initiated by women.[175] These statistics were said to highlight the question that if women were in fact free to choose the form of pre-nuptial contract governing their marriage, then why would such a high percentage of women party to such marriages initiate challenges to its formation?

Feminists who argue that pre-nuptial agreements enhance the economic bargaining position of women claim that a standard of review steeped in paternalism only aggravates the perceived inequality. Guggenheimer states:

> "This preference of emphasising women's inferior status and bargaining power over women's autonomous right to structure their relations as they see fit reifies the perception that women are the weaker sex and justifies the view that the law—and men— need to protect women from themselves."[176]

---

[172]   Guggenheimer, "A Modest Proposal: The Feminomics of Drafting Premarital Agreements" (1996) 17 Women's Rts. L. Rep. 147.

[173]   *Stilley v Folger*, 14 Ohio 610, 614 (1846), quoted with approval in *Osborn v Osborn* 10 Ohio Misc. 171, 226 N.E. 2d 814 (1966) and in *Rocher v Rocher* 13 Ohio Misc. 199, 232 N.E. 2d 445 (1967).

[174]   Fehlberg and Smyth, "Pre-Nuptial Agreements for Australia: Why Not?" (2000) 14 A.J.F.L. 6.

[175]   Atwood, "Ten Years Later: Lingering Concerns About the Uniform Premarital Agreement Act" (1993) 19 *Journal of Legislation* 127 at 133, n.29.

[176]   Guggenheimer, "A Modest Proposal: The Feminomics of Drafting Premarital Agreements" (1996) 17 Women's Rts. L. Rep. 147 at 155–156 (footnotes omitted).

It is thought that the formulisation of women's rights concerning marriage, in a contract, actually benefits them.[177] Furthermore, it is submitted that two of the proposals made above can help alleviate the fears of those who believe pre-nuptial contracts impose a negative impact on women's rights:

1. By attaching a tangible economic value to the work of women within the home it is asserted that they will be accorded a stronger economic position within any bargaining process with men. In addition to this, the recognition of non-monetary contribution clauses within pre-nuptial agreements would result in women being compensated for the opportunity cost of sacrificing potential careers so as to work at home and care for any children.

2. The assessment of pre-nuptial agreements, in a litigious context, ought to be focused on the execution stage of the agreement and not the performance date. At performance, a judge may exercise his/her power to determine whether a contract is unfair to women; essentially this represents a paternal viewpoint as to the position of women. Instead, analysis of an agreement at the execution stage forces procedural correctness, thereby benefiting women in the long run. Such an approach would permit women to set out standards upon which they wish an agreement to be based, rather than settling for a paternalistic conclusion of such.

Although the status of women, within the formulation of pre-nuptial contracts, is a legitimate concern, it is submitted that it need not be. By incorporating the two points above in a system where pre-nuptial contracts are enforceable, it is hoped that these concerns would be extinguished, thereby ensuring a level playing-field upon which parties to a marriage can formulate a pre-nuptial agreement.

A further concern involving pre-nuptial agreements and the interaction with women is that of the "Black Widow"[178] phenomenon. This con-

---

[177] Weitzman, *The Marriage Contract: Spouses, Lovers and the Law* (The Free Press, 1981), at 241.

[178] This concept originated in Dnes, *The Division of Marital Assets Following Divorce With Particular Reference to Pensions* (Lord Chancellor's Department, Research Series No. 7/97, 1997). It was developed further in Dnes, "An Economic Analysis of a Proposal to Reform the Discretionary Approach to the Division of Marital Assets in England and Wales" (Lord Chancellor's Department, Research Series, No.6/98, September 1998).

cept relates to pre-nuptial agreements that make unusually generous provision for wives upon the dissolution of a marriage; so much so that it may in fact induce dissolution on the part of the wife. This is a very real concern in America and has been confronted by the courts.[179] This problem is confounded with the presence of a "sunset" provision in a pre-nuptial contract. The effect of such a clause is to terminate the contract, or certain terms of the contract, after a specified period of time, or upon the occurrence of a certain event. To counter such a problem, it has been argued that a "good faith" clause be inserted within a "sunset" provision, thereby requiring any decision to terminate a marriage before the expiration of the pre-nuptial agreement to be made in good faith.[180] By causing the court to determine the bona fides of an application to dissolve a marriage it would help attenuate the growth of the "Black Widow" phenomenon.

Throughout this thesis the point has been made that state interference within marriage is not justified on grounds of equality, privacy, autonomy and dignity. It would appear that permitting a court to determine the bona fides of an application for divorce runs contrary to this. This point is conceded, but only on a limited basis. Marriage ought not be treated as a commercial enterprise, which would be the effect of the "Black Widow" phenomenon. Such a development would ultimately devalue the institution of marriage. Therefore, it is felt that permitting the courts to conduct an investigation into the merits of a divorce application in such a case is the lesser of two evils. Furthermore, such an investigation would only be permitted in cases where a question might arise as to the bona fides of a claim. Consequently, the onus would be on the claiming party to refute any suggestions of mala fides. It is thought that this would only affect a very small number of cases and therefore does not run contrary to the philosophies running through this thesis.

Finally, one of the main selling points concerning the enforceability of pre-nuptial agreements is the reduction in costs of any future divorce litigation. Irrespective of this, recent developments might suggest otherwise. With an increase in the popularity of pre-nuptial agreements comes

---

[179] See Atwood, "Ten Years Later: Lingering Concerns About the Uniform Premarital Agreement Act" (1993) 19 *Journal of Legislation* 127 at 137, n.43 referring to the cases of *Neilson v Neilson* 780 P.2d 1264 (Utah App. 1989); *Re Marriage of Noghrey* 169 Cal. App.3d 326 (Cal. Ct. App. 1985); *Matthews v Matthews* 162 S.E.2d 697 (N.C. Ct. App. 1968); *Gross v Gross* 464 N.E.2d 500 (Ohio 1984).

[180] Bix, "Bargaining in the Shadow of Love: The Enforcement of Premarital Agreements and How We Think About Marriage" (1999) 40 Wm. & Mary L. Rev. 145.

a concomitant increase in litigation as to their validity. It was thought that the presence of a pre-nuptial agreement would resolve all potential points of contention upon divorce; instead "binding ante-nuptial agreements are likely to introduce new opportunities for legal dispute on marriage break-down".[181] It has been argued that pre-nuptial contracts have become the focal point of legal ingenuity in seeking to have them declared invalid in individual cases.[182]

This would appear to be of genuine concern. One would find it difficult to curb the enthusiasm of lawyers in partaking in such litigation resulting in the prevention of mistakes and loopholes. Such contracts are the only viable option in seeking to eliminate any additional costs. It would appear that the best means of achieving this is to require such contracts to be verified before execution. Other jurisdictions have adopted such an approach. As noted, Australia requires a pre-nuptial agreement to be certified by a solicitor[183]; other jurisdictions require the agreement to be notarised,[184] or alternatively, registered.[185] The general purpose of such a provision is to prevent procedural improprieties in the execution of the pre-nuptial contract, thereby diminishing the possibilities of future litigation as to its validity. It is submitted that this approach be adopted so as to curb any escalation in costs due to future litigation that ultimately is avoidable.

DEVELOPMENTS IN ENGLAND

The above analysis of pre-nuptial contracts was conducted mainly with reference to jurisdictions in which such contracts are binding. Nonetheless, it is our neighbouring jurisdiction, England, which is of most interest to any possible developments in Ireland. In England, pre-nuptial contracts are not strictly enforceable, but their introduction would seem imminent.[186] Developments in English law provide somewhat of a portal within which it is possible to foresee potential future occurrences in our own jurisdiction. This is due to a number of factors, both social and legal;

---

[181] Eekelaar, "Should Section 25 Be Reformed?" (1998) 28 Fam. L. J. 469 at 471.

[182] Katz, "Marriage as Partnership" (1998) 73 *Notre Dame Law Review* 101.

[183] Family Law Act 1975, s.90G. The Canadian province of Alberta also requires a lawyer to verify the correctness of the agreement.

[184] Germany, Italy, The Netherlands, Norway, Spain, Sweden, Switzerland and Quebec.

[185] Denmark, Italy, Spain and Sweden.

[186] Frean, "Pre-nuptials will gain in popularity" *The Times* (Irish edition), May 25, 2006. This article comments on the fallout from the House of Lords judgments in *McFarlane v McFarlane; Miller v Miller* [2006] 3 All E.R. 1.

but mainly due to the uncanny similarities between English legislation concerning ancillary relief[187] and corresponding Irish legislation.[188]

The political climate in England suggests a social acceptance of the need to introduce pre-nuptial agreements as binding legal instruments. In 1991 the English Law Society recommended that pre-nuptial agreements be made enforceable, subject to a number of safeguards.[189] It was not until 1998 that the British Government hinted at reform in this area,[190] then expressly supporting such a move later that year.[191] Yet no legislation has been enacted, despite unwavering support.[192] Social developments suggest the need for such reform, with rising levels of divorce and a reduction in the length of marriages.[193] As a result it has been the judiciary that has attempted to interpret the law so as to reflect the needs of society.

Section 25 of the Matrimonial Causes Act 1973 provides the basis upon which the English courts can determine ancillary relief issues in any given case. In *Dart v Dart,* Thorpe J. reflected on the objective of s.25, stating:

> "The design of the 1973 statutory provisions was to give the judge exercising the power of equitable distribution the widest discretion to do fairness between the parties, reflecting the considerations and criteria laid out within the section...[which] would produce a bespoke solution to fit the infinite variety of individual cases."[194]

It is the need to accommodate this "infinite variety of individual cases" that has given rise to the consideration of pre-nuptial agreements in the English courts. As these agreements began to appear before the courts, the initial opinion of judges was one of contempt. In *F v F (Ancillary Relief: Substantial Assets)* Thorpe J. stated: "I do not attach any signifi-

---

[187] Matrimonial Causes Act 1973, s.25.
[188] Family Law (Divorce) Act 1996, s.20.
[189] The Law Society's Family Law Committee, *Maintenance and Capital Provision on Divorce* (May 1991), at para.3.56.
[190] Speech delivered by the Parliamentary Secretary, Mr Hoon, at the Solicitors Family Law Association's National Conference at Blackpool, delivered on February 21, 1998.
[191] The Home Office, "Green Paper: *Supporting Families: A Consultation Document*" (TSO, 1998), in particular para.4.49.
[192] See Rohan and Hoult, "Make Pre-Nuptial Agreements Legally Binding, says SFLA" *Law Society Gazette (UK)*, November 25, 2004.
[193] Thorpe, "The English System of Ancillary Relief" in Bailey-Harris ed., *Dividing the Assets on Family Breakdown* (Jordan Publishing, 1998), p.1.
[194] [1996] 2 F.L.R. 286 at 295.

cant weight to those contracts". [195] Later in *N v N (Foreign Divorce: Financial Relief)* Cazalet J. said such agreements "would be a relevant circumstance in determining an application for financial relief in England but ... would not conclude the matter." [196]

It was in *S v S (Divorce: Staying Proceedings)*[197] that Wilson J. reconciled these two opinions. This case concerned a husband and wife who lived in both New York and London. The wife issued divorce proceedings in England, but the husband sought a stay on proceedings on the basis that a New York court was the proper forum for the case. An important consequence of a decision in favour of the husband was that it would be likely to result in a pre-nuptial agreement between the parties being enforced, thereby significantly depriving the wife of the potential amount she could receive under English law. In finding for the husband, Wilson J. stated:

> "Under s 25(1), regard must be had to all the circumstances of the case. In *F v F* itself, the result of a strict application of the effect of the pre-nuptial agreements would have been, as the judge said, 'ridiculous'. In those circumstances [the agreements] inevitably constituted circumstances of negligible significance. But there will come a case...where the circumstances surrounding the pre-nuptial agreement and the provision therein contained might, when viewed in the context of the other circumstances of the case, prove influential or even crucial...I can find nothing in section 25 to compel a conclusion, so much at odds with personal freedoms to make arrangements for ourselves, that escape from solemn bargains, carefully struck by informed adults, is readily available here."[198]

In a similar vein, the court in *N v N (Jurisdiction: Pre-nuptial Agreement)*[199] reiterated the point that although a pre-nuptial agreement is not specifically enforceable, its existence is a factor to be taken into account having regard to the circumstances of the case as mandated by s.25 of the

---

[195]   [1995] 2 F.L.R. 45 at 66.

[196]   [1997] 1 F.L.R. 900 at 912.

[197]   [1997] 1 W.L.R. 1200.

[198]   *ibid.* at 1203–1204. The "ridiculous" effect that enforcement of the pre-nuptial agreement would have had in *F v F* was to cause the wife to be awarded the equivalent to a Federal German Judge's pension each year, despite the husband's estimated worth of between £150-£200 million. For an analysis of the potential effect of foreign pre-nuptial agreements in Ireland see p.171below.

[199]   [1999] 2 F.L.R. 745.

Matrimonial Causes Act 1973. The case of *G v G (Financial Provision)*[200] illustrates the potential significance of a pre-nuptial agreement. In this case the parties were married for four years and had a pre-nuptial contract. Upon separation they varied the terms of the pre-nuptial contract and converted it into a separation deed. The court found the conduct of the parties in abiding by the pre-nuptial agreement and formulating it in terms of a separation deed to almost provide complete resolution to the case.

The case of *M v M (Pre-nuptial Agreement)*[201] concerned a husband and wife, both Canadian, who entered marriage on foot of the wife's pregnancy. A pre-nuptial agreement was entered into prior to the marriage at the behest of the husband. Following a five-year marriage, divorce proceedings were instituted, within which the wife claimed to have been pressurised into signing the agreement whilst in a vulnerable state. If the agreement was held binding, then the wife, personally, would receive a lump sum of £275,000. If, however, the wife was successful in her claim, then she stood to receive a lump sum of £1,300,000. In reference to the debate as to whether a pre-nuptial contract should be classified as a circumstance to be taken into account,[202] or as a feature of the parties' conduct,[203] O' Connell J. stated:

> "In my view it matters not whether the court bears such an agreement in mind as part of the circumstances of the case (a very important factor) or as an aspect of the parties' conduct. Under either approach the court should look at any such agreement and decide in the particular circumstances what weight should, in justice, be attached to it."[204]

In determining the relief to be granted, O'Connell J. adopted a somewhat half-way house approach in relation to the pre-nuptial agreement in this case, commenting:"[i]n my view it would be as unjust to the husband to ignore the existence of the agreement and its terms as it would be to the wife to hold her strictly to those terms." Therefore, considering the agreement as "one of the more relevant circumstances of this case",[205] he granted the wife a lump sum of £875,000.

The judgment of Rodger Heywood Smith Q.C., sitting as High Court

---

[200]   [2000] 2 F.L.R. 18.
[201]   [2002] 1 F.L.R. 654.
[202]   Matrimonial Causes Act 1973, s.25(1).
[203]   Matrimonial Causes Act 1973, s.25(2)(g).
[204]   [2002] 1 F.L.R. 654 at 661.
[205]   *ibid.* at 664.

Deputy Judge, in the case of *K v K (Ancillary Relief: Pre-nuptial Agreement)*[206] provides the most detailed analysis of the effects of a pre-nuptial agreement to date. This case concerned a marriage, entered into on foot of a pregnancy and subsequent family pressure, lasting only 10 months. The wife's assets were estimated at £1 million, most of which was in a trust. The husband's wealth was estimated at £25 million, although much larger figures were speculated throughout the case. The pre-nuptial agreement provided the wife with a lump sum payment of £100,000 upon dissolution of the marriage within five years, with a compound interest of 10 per cent for each year. Having analysed the pre-nuptial agreement in the manner set out above,[207] the court concluded that the wife should receive £120,000, thereby effectively enforcing the contract.

Other English cases concerning ancillary relief are of interest due to the noticeable absence of a pre-nuptial agreement, and subsequent speculation as to what effect such an agreement might have had. The recent House of Lords decision in the joined cases of *Miller v Miller* and *McFarlane v McFarlane*[208] has sparked huge debate over not just the enforceability of the pre-nuptial agreements in England, but the need for such agreements. The facts and circumstances surrounding the *McFarlane* case have been briefly summarised above.[209] In *Miller* the facts were rather unique. The parties were married for two years and nine months. At the time of marriage the husband was worth £17 million; at divorce he was worth £17.5 million. It was argued that his wealth was a factor altogether independent from the marriage, and therefore any award made to the wife should be minimal due to the brevity of the marriage.

The House of Lords refused to draw a distinction between short- and long-term marriages:

> "A short marriage is no less a partnership of equals than a long marriage… To confine the *White* approach to the 'fruits of a long marital partnership' would be to re-introduce precisely the sort of discrimination the *White* case…was intended to negate."[210]

---

[206] [2003] 1 F.L.R. 120.
[207] See pp.112–113 above.
[208] [2006] 3 All E.R. 1.
[209] See pp.88–90 above.
[210] [2006] 3 All E.R. 1 at para.17-19.

Furthermore, it was held that due to the investments the husband made in a new company during the marriage, he was actually worth an additional £12–£18 million. By virtue of this, and the expensive lifestyle that the wife had grown accustomed to, the House of Lords made an order granting the wife £5 million of the husband's fortune. It is the results of these judgments, one granting a lump sum of £5 million, the other indefinite annual payments of £250,000, that has caused a stir amongst those considering pre-nuptial agreements as an option before marriage.[211] Surely, following the growing acceptance of pre-nuptial agreements in recent times, this judgment will provide the impetus for legislative change in this area in England.

To conclude, the position in England at present can be summarised as one whereby having "regard to all the circumstances of the case"[212] judicial discretion permits pre-nuptial agreements to be considered as matters of "material consideration".[213] Furthermore, the courts are obliged to consider such contracts "if it would be inequitable to ignore [them]."[214] The trend seems to be that courts will recognise a pre-nuptial agreement provided the parties freely entered into it.[215]

Having embarked on a study of pre-nuptial agreements, with particular focus on developments in England, it is now time to analyse the current state of Irish law in this area. Despite the relative youthfulness of divorce within Irish law, ancillary relief represents a somewhat more mature legal concept, inaugurated under the Judicial Separation and Family Law Reform Act 1989. Recent developments in the area of divorce, ancillary relief and separation agreements demonstrate a possible shift in reasoning concerning these concepts. Analogies can be drawn with similar occurrences in England also, thereby giving rise to potential scope for the enforceability of pre-nuptial agreements in Irish law.

---

[211] See in general Frean, "Pre-nuptials will gain in popularity" *The Times* (Irish edition), May 25, 2006. Shannon, "UK Divorce Rulings to Spur Renewed Interest in Prenuptial Agreements", *The Irish Times*, May 30, 2006.

[212] Matrimonial Causes Act 1973, s.25(1).

[213] *N v N (Foreign Divorce: Financial Relief)* [1997] 1 F.L.R. 900 at 913.

[214] Matrimonial Causes Act 1973, s.25(2)(g).

[215] See The Law Society of England, "Protocols for Ancillary Relief" in *Family Law Protocol* (2nd ed., The Law Society of England, 2006).

5. Recent Developments in Irish Law

Having discussed the jurisprudential framework within which a pre-nuptial agreement must operate, and the practical effects of such agreements, it is pertinent to discuss the relevance and application of such agreements in Irish law. Although occupying no apparent standing in Irish law, several developments in recent years have formed a basis upon which an informed debate concerning pre-nuptial agreements can now take place. Most notably the introduction of divorce into Irish law, via the 1995 referendum, has diminished the persuasiveness of arguments against pre-nuptial agreements on the grounds that marriage is a life-long union that cannot be contracted away from. Furthermore, the effect of the Family Law (Divorce) Act 1996 in the area of property ownership and distribution has provided an incentive for seeking a pre-nuptial agreement amongst those who have something to "protect".

One must not be mistaken into thinking that divorce in Ireland opened the floodgates for the acceptance of pre-nuptial agreements. The fallacy of such an opinion is illustrated by the fact that a pre-nuptial agreement has yet to come before the courts in any substantive context. Instead, it is the general attitude of the Irish courts in the area of ancillary relief that provides a framework from which it is becoming increasingly apparent that pre-nuptial agreements ought to be recognised. The level of judicial discretion in Irish family law is unparalleled, causing parties to litigation to feel aggrieved as to the outcome. The response of the judiciary in such circumstances is to proclaim it to be the responsibility of the Oireachtas to enact legislation so as to minimise any potential injustice.[1] This broad level of discretion has also rendered the interpretation of Irish family law ambiguous. It is becoming increasingly hard for practitioners to advise their clients as to the likely outcome of a case concerning ancillary relief. This leads to frustration amongst the parties to such litigation, which further exacerbates an already tense situation. From this it is becoming clear that people involved in ancillary relief disputes view the role of the court in a negative manner. To counteract this trend it is clear that a judicial appreciation for the private ordering of such matters between parties be adopted. As shall be demonstrated, there is a growing body of case law supporting such a proposition.

---

[1]   See judgment of Keane J. in *PO'D v AO'D* [1998] 1 I.L.R.M. 543, in particular at 558.

The introduction of a "clean break" divorce, for better or for worse, has recognised the need to achieve finality and certainty where possible in marital breakdown litigation. These two objectives are readily attainable under a properly formulated pre-nuptial agreement. It is speculated that if such an agreement were to come before the courts, in circumstances that permitted finality to be achieved, then it would be difficult for the court to look past the agreement. Also, in seeking to determine the appropriate ancillary relief to be granted in a case, the courts tend to examine the role and contributions each party made to the marital relationship. From this there is an enhanced judicial awareness of marriage being a contract or partnership between two parties. As noted in Chapter 3, the natural progression of such an interpretation is to permit such parties to privately order their relationship without state interference.

The above matters will be examined and discussed so as to demonstrate the shift in direction of Irish family law towards private ordering, or indeed the need for private ordering. Notwithstanding this, the legislature has already acknowledged the existence of pre-nuptial agreements in Irish law. Section 113 of the Succession Act 1965 permits a future spouse to renounce his/her legal rights over his/her intended spouse by way of a pre-nuptial contract; it states:

> "The legal right of a spouse may be renounced in an ante-nuptial contract made in writing between the parties to an intended marriage or may be renounced in writing by the spouse after marriage and during the lifetime of the testator."

Although never tested, this section does enjoy the presumption of constitutionality.[2]

Furthermore, s.14 of the Family Law (Divorce) Act 1996 acknowledges such agreements in the context of property adjustment orders. It permits the court, in making any property adjustment order, to vary "for the benefit of either of the spouses and of any dependent member of the family or of any or all of those persons of any ante-nuptial or post-nuptial settlement (including such a settlement made by will or codicil) made on the spouses".[3] Although reference is made to "settlements" and not "agreements" in s.14, this section has been interpreted in such a manner so as to include pre-nuptial "agreements". In *N v N*,[4] McGuinness J. gave

---

[2]   Riordan, "Pre-Nuptial Contracts" (1997) 2 *Bar Review* 193.
[3]   Family Law (Divorce) Act 1996, s.14(c).
[4]   [1995] 1 Fam L.J. 14.

a broad interpretation to the meaning of "post-nuptial settlement", effectively causing it to mean a separation agreement.[5] It is arguable that the corollary to such reasoning is that an "ante-nuptial settlement" can be interpreted so as to include ante-nuptial agreements. Crowley makes the point that although s.14(c) only refers to the variation of such agreements, it does not suggest that this be done in all cases; therefore, it is foreseeable that a court may refuse to vary an ante-nuptial settlement, thereby implicitly adopting it.[6]

Despite this quasi-acknowledgment of pre-nuptial agreements in Irish law, a broader basis must be formed upon which a general acceptance of such agreements can be instituted. The following analysis endeavours to achieve just that.

JUDICIAL DISCRETION IN IRISH FAMILY LAW

Each family law case that comes before the courts tends to be unique. This raises the problem of seeking to formulate a set of guidelines to determine such cases. Such guidelines must appreciate the fact that not only is an element of certainty desirable in family law litigation, but so is flexibility so as to contend with the unique nature of each individual case. The inherent conflict involved in attempting to accommodate these two objectives was alluded to by Ormrod L.J., stating:

> "it is difficult for practitioners to advise clients in [family law] cases because the rules are not very firm... It is the essence of such a discretionary situation that the court should preserve, so far as it can, the utmost elasticity to deal with each case on its own facts... There is bound to be an element of uncertainty in the use of the wide discretionary powers given to the court under the [governing legislation] and no doubt there always will be, because as social circumstances change so the court will have to adapt the ways in which it exercises discretion."[7]

---

[5] In doing so, McGuinness J. relied on the English case of *Prinsep v Prinsep* [1929] P. 225 where Hill J. stated: "the particular form of it does not matter...what does matter is that it should provide for the financial benefit of one or other or both of the spouses...The term 'settlement' thus appears to include a separation agreement whether made orally or in writing."

[6] Crowley, "Pre-Nuptial Agreements—Have They Any Place in Irish Family Law?" [2002] 1 I.J.F.L. 3; Crowley, "Divorce Law in Ireland: Facilitating or Frustrating the Resolution Process?" (2004) 16 *Child & Family Law Quarterly* 49.

[7] *Martin v Martin* [1977] 3 All E.R. 762 at 768.

Nowhere is this conflict between certainty and flexibility more apparent than in the field of ancillary relief. Ancillary relief is available to parties following a judicial separation or divorce. The factors in determining such relief, in the context of judicial separation, are set out in s.16(2) of the Family Law Act 1995; and in the context of divorce, in s.20(2) of the Family Law (Divorce) Act 1996. Both sections replicate each other, therefore it is only necessary to set out s.20(2) of the 1996 Act for present purposes. Section 20(2) states:

> "Without prejudice to the generality of *subsection (1)*, in deciding whether to make such an order as aforesaid and in determining the provisions of such an order, the court shall, in particular, have regard to the following matters—
>
> (*a*) the income, earning capacity, property and other financial resources which each of the spouses concerned has or is likely to have in the foreseeable future,
>
> (*b*) the financial needs, obligations and responsibilities which each of the spouses has or is likely to have in the foreseeable future (whether in the case of the remarriage of the spouse or otherwise),
>
> (*c*) the standard of living enjoyed by the family concerned before the proceedings were instituted or before the spouses commenced to live apart from one another,[8] as the case may be,
>
> (*d*) the age of each of the spouses, the duration of their marriage[9] and the length of time during which the spouses lived with one another,
>
> (*e*) any physical or mental disability of either of the spouses,
>
> (*f*) the contributions which each of the spouses has made or is likely in the foreseeable future to make to the welfare of the family, including any contribution made by each of them to the income, earning capacity, property and financial resources of the other spouse and any contribution made by either of them by looking after the home or caring for the family,

---

[8] The phrase "commenced to live apart from one another" is not present in s.16(2) of the Family Law Act 1995. Instead it states, "or before the spouses *separated*" (emphasis added).

[9] The phrase "duration of their marriage" is not present in s.16(2) of the Family Law Act 1995. Also, instead of referring to the "length of time the spouses lived with one another", s.16(2) states when the spouses lived "together".

(*g*)   the effect on the earning capacity of each of the spouses of the marital responsibilities assumed by each during the period when they lived together and, in particular, the degree to which the future earning capacity of a spouse is impaired by reason of that spouse having relinquished or foregone the opportunity of remunerative activity in order to look after the home or care for the family,

(*h*)   any income or benefits to which either of the spouses is entitled by or under statute,

(*i*)   the conduct of each of the spouses, if that conduct is such that in the opinion of the court it would in all the circumstances of the case be unjust to disregard it,

(*j*)   the accommodation needs of either of the spouses,

(*k*)   the value to each of the spouses of any benefit (for example, a benefit under a pension scheme) which by reason of the decree of judicial separation concerned that spouse will forfeit the opportunity or possibility of acquiring,

(*l*)   the rights of any person other than the spouses but including a person to whom either spouse is remarried."

Despite these guidelines the determination of ancillary relief is still a "game of judicial roulette".[10] There is no apparent limitation on the exercise of judicial discretion in such cases, bar the vague and ambiguous objective of acting in the "interests of justice".[11] The *in camera* nature of the majority of family law disputes renders it difficult to determine any clear approach taken by the courts in such cases.[12] One must persevere with the limited amount of judgments available in an attempt to glean any sense of guidance as to the limits of judicial discretion in ancillary relief cases; if indeed there are any limits. The following is an analysis of the case law in this area, from which it is hoped that a picture can be drawn as to the present state of ancillary relief determination in this jurisdiction. From there it can be decided if there is a need for improvements in this field, and determined if pre-nuptial agreements might form a part of such improvements.

---

[10]   Shatter, "Open Sesame for Divorce" *The Irish Times*, February 18, 1997.

[11]   Family Law (Divorce) Act 1996, s.20(5).

[12]   For an analysis of this problem see Monaghan, "The Slicing of the Marital Cake—The Relevance of Separation Agreements to the Making of Property Adjustment Orders" [1999] 2 I.J.F.L. 8.

Prior to the growth in divorce litigation and the resultant ancillary relief, it was clear that the judiciary had "a wide area of discretion"[13] in this field. Nevertheless, recent decisions have illustrated just how wide this area of discretion really is. In *CO'R v MO'R*[14] the parties, although married for seven years, only cohabited as man and wife for three-and-a-half years. There were two children to the marriage, and in these proceedings the wife sought a judicial separation and ancillary relief. O'Donovan J., in the High Court, refused to grant a property adjustment order conveying the family home to the wife due to the relatively short period of the marriage and the lack of financial contribution provided by the wife. Instead he granted her a right to occupy the house, to the exclusion of the husband, until such time as the children completed their full-time education. The financial complexity of this case was not helped by the lack of cooperation by the husband in assisting the court to determine his assets; yet O'Donovan J. undertook a substantial reordering of the marital assets so as to provide for the maintenance of the wife and children in this case. It is apparent from this case that due to the comfortable lifestyle enjoyed by the parties by virtue of the husband's wealth, the discretion available to the court was exercised to its fullest extent so as to ensure that there was no considerable drop in the standard of living of either party, in particular the non-income spouse.

In *MK v JP (otherwise SK)*[15] the Supreme Court attempted to impose limitations and clarity to the level of discretion available to courts in ancillary relief proceedings. This case concerned an application for divorce between two parties who married in 1963 and had six children. They split in 1982 and entered into a separation agreement. The husband then obtained a divorce in the Republic of Haiti and remarried in the United States of America. Whilst the applicant wife cared for the children, with the menial assistance of the maintenance provided by the husband, his standard of living rose dramatically. Having previously worked in a non-descript position in a multi-national firm operating in Ireland, he went on to become the President of that firm in the United States. The initial hearing of this case was in the High Court before Lavan J. who granted the divorce application with an order for a lump sum of £1.5 million in favour

---

[13]   *JD v DD* [1997] 3 I.R. 64 at 91.

[14]   Unreported, High Court, O'Donovan J., September 19, 2000. For analysis see Power, "Case and Comment" [2001] 2 I.J.F.L. 24; and Byrne and Binchy, *Annual Review of Irish Law 2000* (Round Hall Sweet & Maxwell, 2001), pp.254–256.

[15]   [2001] 3 I.R. 371.

of the applicant wife, equating to approximately half of the husband's assets. He also increased the maintenance to be paid to the wife and granted a pension adjustment order of 80 per cent of the husband's pension entitlements in favour of the wife. The husband appealed this decision to the Supreme Court on two grounds. First, he claimed that the High Court judge failed to have regard to the provisions set out in s.20 of the Family Law (Divorce) Act 1996. Secondly, that the judge failed to consider the pre-existing separation agreement between the parties.[16]

McGuinness J. in the Supreme Court, with whom Murphy and Murray JJ. concurred, set out a number of principles, some of which shall be dealt with below. For present purposes, however, she noted the "considerable area of discretion"[17] available to judges under the provisions of the 1996 Act. Notwithstanding this, she stated that there are restrictions on the exercise of this discretion. In particular, regard must be had to the factors set out in s.20 of the 1996 Act; and in giving judgment it is imperative that the court set out the provisions of s.20 relied upon in reaching its conclusion. Not only would this provide a sense of clarity, but it would also allow an appellate court to review decisions in this field. The notable absence of this in the judgment of Lavan J. meant that the Supreme Court was not in a position to review his decision, thereby causing the matter to be sent back to the High Court for a retrial. Before analysing the subsequent High Court decision it is necessary to examine the intervening case law, as it would prove determinative to the High Court decision in this case.

As noted above in the case of *CO'R v MO'R* the standard of living enjoyed by the parties during their marriage is a factor taken into account by the courts in determining ancillary relief. This point was further developed in the case of *CF v JDF*[18] concerning an application for judicial separation. The parties married in 1989 and had two children together. They separated in 2000 with the wife receiving €2,000 per month maintenance. In these proceedings the applicant wife not only sought a judicial separation but also a lump sum of €500,000 and an increase in maintenance. O'Sullivan J. in the High Court granted the judicial separation with a lump sum of €408,000 (€28,000 of which was to cover the costs

---

16   This second ground shall be dealt with below in the context of the effect of pre-existing separation agreements; see pp.154–156.

17   *MK v JP (otherwise SK)* [2001] 3 I.R. 371 at 383.

18   Unreported, High Court, O'Sullivan J., May 16, 2002. For analysis see Power, "Case and Comment" [2002] 4 I.J.F.L. 22.

of the extra days of litigation due to the husband's lack of cooperation), and increased the maintenance to €2,100 per month. Importantly, he stated that, in providing for the dependant spouse in such cases the court does not stop at providing for his/her "reasonable requirements/needs". On the contrary, if there are sufficient resources available then the court can grant a party relief over and above their reasonable needs. This approach would appear to mirror recent developments in English jurisprudence.[19]

Perhaps the most comprehensive of all judgments in the area of ancillary relief is that of the Supreme Court in the case of *DT v CT*.[20] The facts of this case shall be set out below in the context of a "clean break" divorce,[21] but for present purposes several of the Supreme Court judges made pertinent comments as to the level and control of judicial discretion in these cases. The level of discretion afforded to the courts by the legislature under the 1996 Act was described as "ample"[22] and "extremely broad".[23] Furthermore, in "ample resources" cases, where the assets of the parties far outweigh their needs,[24] the courts are given "full reign"[25] as to the level of discretion they may exercise. It seemed to be accepted amongst the judges that the "relevance and weight of the factors [set out in s.20(2) of the 1996 Act] will depend on the circumstances of each case."[26] In addition, it was stated that there is no hierarchy amongst the factors set out in s.20(2).[27] It is clear from this judgment that the element of flexibility desired by the judiciary in determining cases concerning ancillary relief, far outweighs any concerns as to the lack of clarity in such cases. The only clarity brought to this area by this judgment and that of the Supreme Court in *MK v JP (otherwise SK)*[28] is that a judge, in deciding such a case, must set out the factors of s.20(2) of the 1996 Act and state their relevance to the case at bar.

---

[19] See Chap.4, pp.121–126.

[20] [2003] 1 I.L.R.M. 321.

[21] See p.144 below.

[22] [2003] 1 I.L.R.M. 321 at 359.

[23] *ibid.* at 371.

[24] Interestingly it appears to be commonly accepted that for a case to fall under the category of "ample resources", the marital assets must exceed €5 million; see judgment of McKechnie J. in *BD v JD*, unreported, High Court, May 4, 2005.

[25] *DT v CT* [2003] 1 I.L.R.M. 321 at 371.

[26] *ibid.* at 352.

[27] *ibid.* at 338.

[28] [2001] 3 I.R. 371.

A model example of this approach is that of the judgment of O'Neill J. in the retrial of *MK v JP (otherwise SK).*[29] One of the few guiding principles to be set out in this area was succinctly asserted by O'Neill J., stating:

> "…it is clear that what the Court of First Instance must do is go through the various factors set out in section 20(2) *seriatim* and deal with the circumstances of the case in the light of these factors insofar as they are relevant to the circumstances of the case, assessing in the light of the evidence, the weight to be attached to each factor."[30]

In considering these factors, O'Neill J. concluded that the wife should receive a lump sum of €450,000 so as to enable her to purchase suitable accommodation for herself. He also made an order for periodic maintenance amounting to €40,000 per annum and full benefit of the husband's Irish pension.

Byrne and Binchy commend the analysis of O'Neill J. as being both "masterful and comprehensive".[31] Following this approach of setting out the factors in s.20(2) and their relevance to individual cases, one would hope to discover some consistency in the judgments in this area. Nonetheless, it would appear that this assumption is unfounded. In *BD v JD,*[32] a case concerning judicial separation, McKechnie J. echoed the sentiments of the Supreme Court in *DT v CT* concerning the appropriate weight to be accorded to each of the factors set out in s.16 of the 1995 Act. Furthermore, he approached each and every factor in accordance with the dicta of O'Neill J. in *MK v JS (otherwise JK)*. Yet, in the opinion of McKechnie J., the determining factors in ensuring "proper provision" was made were those of fairness, justice and equity.[33] Needless to say, such factors give licence for a variety of conclusions to be reached in any one case.

One of the clearest points to arise from the judgment of the Supreme Court in *DT v CT* was that the date for assessing the value of assets in a case concerning ancillary relief was that of the trial itself. Notwithstanding this, O'Higgins J. in the case of *MP v AP*[34] took liberty to ques-

---

[29] [2003] 1 I.R. 326.

[30] *ibid.* at 350.

[31] Byrne and Binchy, *Annual Review of Irish Law 2003* (Thomson Round Hall, 2004), p.345.

[32] Unreported, High Court, McKechnie J., December 5, 2003.

[33] *ibid.* at para.74; p.56 of transcript.

[34] Unreported, High Court, O'Higgins J., March 2, 2005.

tion this under the rubric of exercising judicial discretion so as to ensure "proper provision". This case concerned an application for divorce and a further claim for ancillary relief. The parties were married in 1974, and adopted two children. They lived separately and apart from 1992, on foot of a separation agreement, the terms of which shall be dealt with in greater detail below.[35] Suffice to say, the applicant wife received the bulk of the assets under the agreement, with the husband starting afresh. The husband's wealth improved dramatically in the following years, predominantly due to his position as an equity partner in a Dublin law firm. Despite the clear principle enunciated by the Supreme Court concerning the appropriate stage for the assessment of marital assets being the date of trial, O'Higgins J. stated:

> "Although it is true that in many, if not most, cases there will be a division of the assets existing at the time of the hearing, there is no requirement that that be done in every case. What is required is that 'proper provision' be made and it is clear that the consequences of such provision is very often an appropriate division of the assets."

From this analysis it becomes increasingly clear that there are no clear principles governing this area of law. The guiding principle is that "proper provision" be made between the parties, and that any order made be done so in the "interests of justice".[36] On this basis it is clear that a variety of conclusions can be reached. The only sense of clarity injected in this area concerned the procedure to be adopted by the courts. In such cases a judge is now obliged to set out the factors enunciated in s.16(2) of the Family Law Act 1995 in judicial separation cases, and in s.20(2) of the Family Law (Divorce) Act 1996 in divorce cases. Nevertheless, this fails to provide any sense of substantive consistency in cases. It is clear that the need for flexibility has found favour in Irish family law jurisprudence to the almost extinction of clarity, certainty and consistency.[37] The level of discretion available to judges in determining ancillary relief has been criticised as causing them to assume a "patriarchal and authoritarian approach towards the regulation of the family, particularly in the context of

---

[35] See pp.159–160 below.

[36] Family Law (Divorce) Act 1996, s.20(5).

[37] For a discussion on this point see Martin, "Judicial Discretion in Family Law" (1998) 11 I.L.T. 168; Martin, "Distribution of Marital Assets on Divorce in the Republic of Ireland" [1999] *International Family Law* 109.

marriage breakdown."[38] It is submitted that this level of discretion and ambiguity in the division of property following marital breakdown illustrates the need for the recognition of pre-nuptial agreements, rather than being a basis for their recognition.[39]

Other trends that have emerged in recent case law in this area provide reasons as to why pre-nuptial agreements ought to be recognised, and shall be demonstrated presently.

THE EMERGENCE OF A "YARDSTICK" IN THE CALCULATION OF ANCILLARY RELIEF

In several of the judgments of the Supreme Court in *DT v CT*[40] detailed analysis was given to English jurisprudence on ancillary relief, in particular concerning cases of "ample resources". A concept that emerged, particularly in the judgments of Keane C.J. and Denham J., was that of a reference point or "yardstick" in the calculation of ancillary relief.[41] The "yardstick" analogy was set out by Lord Nicholls in the House of Lords judgment in *White v White*.[42] It refers to a marker against which any calculation of ancillary relief in a given case can be referred so as to ensure neither party is discriminated against. In *White* it was thought that to achieve "fairness" in the division of marital assets, equality ought to be the "yardstick".

In contemplating the effectiveness of such a concept in Irish law, Keane C.J. noted an important divergence in approaches adopted by the English and Irish courts in this field, that being, the English courts are more concerned with the *division* of assets, whereas the primary concern for Irish courts is the making of proper *provision*.[43] Notwithstanding this, Keane C.J. felt that:

> "the court might be justified in treating, in 'ample resources' cases, one third of the net assets as a yardstick at the lower end of the scale."[44]

---

38 Martin, "Judicial Discretion in Family Law" (1998) 11 I.L.T. 168 at 168.
39 Although one might speculate that the level of discretion afforded to judges in such cases might permit them to recognise a pre-nuptial agreement if the circumstances justified it.
40 [2003] 1 I.L.R.M. 321.
41 It is noted that this concept was previously referred to by McGuinness J. giving judgment for the Supreme Court in *MK v JP (otherwise SK)* [2001] 3 I.R. 371.
42 [2000] 2 F.L.R. 981.
43 *DT v CT* [2003] 1 I.L.R.M. 321 at 340.
44 *ibid.* at 341.

It is submitted that, although Keane C.J. made significant reference to the concept of a "yardstick" in Irish law, he did not specifically adopt it; whilst Denham J. appeared to be more adamant in her support for such a concept.[45] It is posited that *DT v CT* does not represent precedent in Irish law as to the concept of a "yardstick" in the calculation of ancillary relief; it is merely *obiter*. Nonetheless, its practicality in cases of "ample resources" is not to be dismissed lightly. In *MK v JP (otherwise JK)*[46] O'Neill J. appeared to have been in favour of adopting a "yardstick" in the determination of ancillary relief. He speculated that it ought to be alluded to following an examination of the factors set out under s.20(2) of the Family Law (Divorce) Act 1996, so as "to ensure that no bias or invidious discrimination has crept in because the wife has adopted the traditional role of homemaker."[47]

Nonetheless, judicial and academic opinion are divided on this point. *C v C*[48] concerned a judicial separation between a couple of "ample resources". The couple married in 1987 and had four children. They lived on a large farm adjacent to a manor house and estate. The husband's family owned the manor house and surrounding estate, as well as several other properties. The income of the parties derived from their work in a souvenir shop on the estate. The wife's contribution consisted of working in the shop and on the farmland, as well as giving £10,000 of her own money to service a debt of her husband's. The parties split in 2003 following the husband's refusal to go on holiday with the family, who upon return found him to be cohabiting with another woman. The total net value of the marital assets was £24.261 million, and the husband's net income was £725,000. The wife sought maintenance of €240,000 per year and €120,000 per year for the children. O'Higgins J. in the High Court felt that it would not be prudent to adopt a "yardstick" of one third of the husband's assets as recommended by members of the Supreme Court in *DT v CT*. He stated that the facts of this case did not justify such an approach as the marital assets were primarily belonging to the husband's family, without any meaningful contribution by the wife. It is submitted that this was the correct approach to take, and no injustice or discrimination was inflicted on the wife as she was amply provided for by the court with a lump sum order of €3.3 million, so as to purchase suitable accom-

---

[45] *ibid.* at 384–385.
[46] [2003] 1 I.R. 326.
[47] *ibid.* at 349.
[48] Unreported, High Court, O'Higgins J., July 25, 2005.

modation, and annual maintenance of €240,000. The judge made an order granting maintenance of €20,000 per annum for each child, but the husband was to provide for the school fees, amounting to €125,000 per year.

The problem with adopting a mathematical "yardstick" is that in some cases it can represent an arbitrary division of marital assets, unrepresentative of the reality of the marital contributions. Lord Denning in *Wachtel v Wachtel*[49] favoured such an approach. It has since, however, been rejected by the English courts.[50] Dismissing the introduction of mathematical formulae in the determination of ancillary relief, Scarman L.J. in *Calderbank v Calderbank* stated:

> "every case will be different and no case may be decided except upon its particular facts…the proportion of the division is dependent on the circumstances."[51]

This reasoning was previously referred to by McGuinness J. in *JD v DD*[52] as forming persuasive grounds for the rejection of any such approach. Trenchant opposition to any such approach was also evident in the Supreme Court judgment in *DT v CT*. Fennelly J. was opposed to the adoption of any set mathematical approach, whether it be a "yardstick" or "rule of thumb", stating:

> "Once more, it is important to note that [ss.20(2)(f) and (g) of the Family Law (Divorce) Act 1996 do] not erect any automatic or mechanical rule of equality. Nor [do they] institute any notice of family resources or property to be subjected to division. Several considerations militate against the adoption of such rules of thumb. The children of the marriage have to be considered and their provision by one spouse may mean that property should not be equally divided. One or both of the parties may have entered into a new relationship, possibly involving children. The supposed *'breadwinner'* or *'homemaker,'* as the case may be, may not, depending on the circumstances, deserve to be placed on an equal footing.
>
> It is only with the greatest care, therefore, that one should formulate any general propositions. The judge must always and in every case have regard to the particular circumstances of the case."[53]

---

49   [1973] 1 All E.R. 829.
50   *Preston v Preston* [1982] 2 F.L.R. 331.
51   *Calderbank v Calderbank* [1975] 3 All E.R. 333 at 340.
52   [1997] 3 I.R. 64.
53   *DT v CT* [2003] 1 I.L.R.M. 321 at 417–418 (emphasis in original).

It is therefore far from clear whether any mathematical "yardstick" forms a part of Irish law in the determination of ancillary relief. The only purpose for such a development would be to "guard against any unconscious or inadvertent discrimination."[54] The adoption of a "yardstick" has the advantage of bringing a much needed sense of certainty and clarity to this field of law. On the other hand, it dissipates the much cherished flexibility of the Irish judiciary in this field. It is fair to say that its advantages are nullified by its disadvantages, and vice versa. Nonetheless, it is submitted that such an approach ought to be adopted, subject to one important caveat. Parties to ancillary relief disputes ought to be allowed to contract away from any mathematical approach so as to accommodate their individual circumstances.[55] The basis for this proposition is that enunciated in Chapter 3, concerning privacy, autonomy, equality and dignity. The means of contracting away from such a set formula comes in the form of a pre- or post-nuptial agreement between the parties.

It is proposed that such an approach harmonises the advantages of certainty and clarity with that of flexibility. The certainty and clarity comes from the knowledge of there being a mathematical formula available to assist in determining such cases. The flexibility derives from the ability of parties to deviate from such a formula/yardstick so as to represent their own requirements. To date, discourse surrounding flexibility in the field of ancillary relief has been concerned with that of the judiciary. It is asserted that this is misguided. As postulated in Chapter 3, paternalism and state interference in the marital domain ought to be extinguished. It is for the parties to a marriage to determine its course, conduct and, if necessary, its termination. On foot of this, the only flexibility we ought to be concerned with in the forum of ancillary relief is that of the parties to the proceedings and not the judiciary. Pre-nuptial agreements are a means of providing for this and ought to be embraced under Irish law. It is conceded that such an agreement must first cross the Rubicon of ensuring "proper provision", a determination still within the area of judicial review, but upon successfully doing so, its terms ought to be recognised and enforced.

---

[54] *BD v JD*, unreported, High Court, McKechnie J., December 5, 2003, at para.71; p.54 of transcript.

[55] For an analysis of this theory see Dnes, "An Economic Analysis of a Proposal to Reform the Discretionary Approach to the Division of Marital Assets in England and Wales" (Lord Chancellor's Department, Research Series, No.6/98, September 1998).

The main function of a mathematical "yardstick" is to guard against discrimination between the parties in the determination of ancillary relief. The same can also be achieved under a pre-nuptial agreement contracting away from such a set approach. A valid pre-nuptial agreement, entered into voluntarily with the assistance of independent legal advice, does not facilitate discrimination. Moreover, if a party voluntarily agrees to enter such an agreement, which discriminates against him or her, contrary to legal advice, then so be it. Such an agreement should still be upheld, as one ought to be estopped from claiming such an agreement to be invalid further down the road. It is submitted that any introduction of a "yardstick" into the determination of ancillary relief in Irish law, ought to be accompanied by the option to contract away from it. Such a development gives weight to the need to recognise pre-nuptial agreements under Irish law.

THE INTRODUCTION OF A "CLEAN BREAK" DIVORCE

Having discussed the need for pre-nuptial agreements to bring certainty and clarity to the determination of ancillary relief in Irish law, it is now thought expedient to discuss the basis upon which this can be achieved. The first proposed ground in discussing this is the possibility of attaining a "clean break" divorce. A "clean break" divorce is one whereby the parties to a divorce are no longer dependant on each other by any means. Such a divorce brings finality to the relationship. Initially, it was widely accepted that there was no possibility of obtaining a "clean break" upon divorce under the Family Law (Divorce) Act 1996.[56] The reasoning behind this was alluded to by the then Attorney-General David Byrne S.C.:

> "The Irish people ascribe a very high value to the institution of marriage...generally the Irish people, although in favour of the introduction of divorce, did not regard divorce as an easy solution to the problem of marital breakdown. They do not see it as a neat, clean or painless process and recognise that it will have enduring consequences."[57]

---

[56] Indeed, no reference was made to the possibility of a "clean break" divorce in the White Paper on Divorce in the run up to the 1995 referendum, despite substantial international material on this topic. See in general Ward, *Divorce: Who Should Bear the Cost?* (Cork University Press, 1993).

[57] Shannon (ed.), *The Divorce Act in Practice* (Round Hall, 1999), p.viii.

It was thought that a "clean break" divorce would result in the "feminisation of poverty".[58] There was a genuine fear that wives who worked in the home would be discriminated against under such a system, as they would have sacrificed their earning capacity so as to benefit their husband and then upon a "clean break" divorce would be left financially desolate. It was considered that the structure of s.20 of the 1996 Act, permitting an infinite number of court applications for ancillary relief, precluded any possibility for a "clean break":

> "The reality is that financial certainty on divorce is not there for the asking, not facilitated on the face of things by the legislation and by judicial pronouncement, and not something for which there would necessarily be widespread approval."[59]

Early judicial pronouncements in this field seemed to approve of obtaining as much certainty and finality as possible in such litigation. In *F v F*, a case concerning the interaction of a divorce *a mensa et thoro* and judicial separation, Denham J. stated, *obiter*, that:

> "[c]ertainty and finality of litigation are important. Some issues in family law are not capable of a final order by law e.g. maintenance. However, the fact that some issues in family law courts are not capable of finality, does not deprive this area of the law of the important concepts of certainty and finality."[60]

Notwithstanding this, when the possibility of a "clean break" came before the courts in a substantive manner, it was categorically declared unattainable under Irish law. *JD v DD*[61] concerned a couple married in 1966 who had five children. The applicant worked in the home and was financially dependent on the respondent. The respondent was a wealthy business man, and from 1991 ran his own auctioneering business. In 1996 the applicant discovered that he was having an extra-marital affair. She instituted High Court proceedings for judicial separation and ancillary relief. At the time of the hearing the wife was 55 years old, and had no real desire to pursue a career outside the home. She sought a lump sum of

---

[58] Weitzman, *The Divorce Revolution: The Unexpected Consequences for Women and Children in America* (Free Press/MacMillan, 1985).

[59] Coggans, "Maintenance, Property and Discovery" in Shannon (ed.), *The Divorce Act in Practice* (Round Hall, 1999), p.26.

[60] *F v F* [1995] 2 I.R. 354 at 369.

[61] [1997] 3 I.R. 64.

£400,000 so as to provide her with an income for the remainder of her life, effectively seeking a "clean break". The husband offered to pay a lump sum of £200,000 and periodic maintenance of £20,000 per annum. McGuinness J., in the High Court, embarked on a comprehensive analysis of the possibility of a "clean break" under Irish law.

It was noted that s.15(2) of the Judicial Separation and Family Law Reform Act 1989 had permitted the court to grant a property adjustment order once and once only. However, this section was replaced by s.9 of the Family Law Act 1995 which permits a property adjustment order to be made at any stage during the lifetime of either spouse. In light of this amendment, McGuinness J. concluded:

> "It would therefore appear that there is no limit to the number of occasions on which a spouse can seek and the court can grant, if appropriate, a property adjustment order, save that such an order can only be granted during the lifetime of the other spouse and cannot be granted in favour of a spouse who has remarried."[62]

McGuinness J. then proceeded to distinguish the above dicta of Denham J. in *F v F* on the basis that it was enunciated within the context of the 1989 Act whereby finality and certainty were indeed possibilities. Nonetheless, the introduction of the 1995 Act brought an altogether different complexion on this area of law, causing McGuinness J. to state:

> "With all the respect which is due to the views of the learned Denham J., it appears to me that by the subsequent enactment of the Family Law Act, 1995 and the Family Law (Divorce) Act, 1996, the Oireachtas had made it clear that a 'clean break' situation is not to be sought and that, if anything, financial finality is virtually to be prevented…The court, in making virtually any order in regard to finance and property on the breakdown of a marriage, is faced with the situation where finality is not and never can be achieved…The statutory policy is, therefore, totally opposed to the concept of the 'clean break'. This policy is not only clear on the face of the statutes but was most widely discussed, referred to and advocated in the considerable debate that surrounded the enactment of divorce legislation…Given that the whole tenor of the Act of 1995 (and indeed the Act of

---

62   *ibid.* at 68.

1996) is against the concept of finality, I do not consider that in
making financial orders in this case I should fly in the face of
the clear policy of the legislature and endeavour to create a
'clean break' which cannot, in any event, be achieved."[63]

McGuinness J. would go on to reiterate this view in her position as Supreme Court judge in the case of *MK v JP (otherwise SK)* stating:

"The concept of a single capital payment to the wife to meet
her 'reasonable requirements' for the remainder of her life has
never in fact formed a part of Irish law...In this jurisdiction the
legislature has, in the Family Law (Divorce) Act, 1996, laid down
a system of law where a 'clean break' solution is neither permissible nor possible."[64]

In light of such persuasive reasoning, one would have been permitted to
conclude that any debate surrounding the possibility of a "clean break" in
Irish law was well and truly extinguished. Nonetheless, the subsequent
case of *DT v CT*[65] resurrected this debate once more. This case concerned
a couple married in 1980, who had three children. The husband was a
solicitor and the wife a doctor; however, she sacrificed her career to help
establish the husband's practice by means of acting as his secretary and
cleaning the office, as well as caring for their children. At the date of trial
the husband's wealth was estimated at £14 million, £11 million of which
was generated following the separation; and the wife's was £1 million.
Keane C.J. noted that:

"[i]t is, of course, beyond argument that the Irish legislation
precludes the courts from giving the same effect as does the
English legislation to the 'clean break' principle."[66]

But he continued:

"It seems to me, that, unless the courts are precluded from so
holding by the express terms of the Constitution and the relevant statutes, Irish law should be capable of accommodating
those aspects of the 'clean break' approach which are clearly
beneficial. As Denham J. observed in *F v F* [1995] 2 IR 354,

---

[63]   *ibid.* at 89–90.
[64]   *MK v JP (otherwise SK)* [2001] 3 I.R. 371 at 383.
[65]   [2003] 1 I.L.R.M. 321.
[66]   *ibid.* at 336.

certainty and finality can be as important in this as in other areas of the law. Undoubtedly, in some cases finality is not possible and thus the legislation expressly provides for the variation of custody and access orders and of the level of maintenance payments. I do not believe that the Oireachtas, in declining to adopt the 'clean break' approach to the extent favoured in England, intended that the Courts should be obliged to abandon any possibility of achieving certainty and finality and of encouraging the avoidance of future litigation between the parties."[67]

In a similar vein Denham J. noted that there is no constitutional or legislative provision expressly mandating a "clean break"; instead the only objective to be achieved is that of "proper provision". The facts of a case may warrant the issuing of a "clean break" so as to make "proper provision". She was of the opinion that:

"[t]he principles of certainty apply to family law as to other areas of the law. Certainty is important in all litigation. Certainty and consistency are at the core of the legal system."[68]

Similarly Murray J. (as he then was) stated:

"I also agree that when making proper provision for the spouses a court may in the appropriate circumstances seek to achieve certainty and finality in the continuing obligations of the divorced spouses to one another."[69]

Fennelly J., in direct agreement with Keane C.J., stated:

"In the present case, where the amplitude of resources makes it possible, the desire of the parties for financial finality should not be frustrated. The Act expressly empowers the court to make orders at any time after the divorce, but that fact does not preclude the court from taking note of a provision already made in the form of a lump sum intended to facilitate a clean break."[70]

Although there appears to be general support for the consideration of achieving finality and certainty in ancillary relief matters, the judgment

---

[67] *ibid.* at 337.
[68] *ibid.* at 353.
[69] *ibid.* at 380.
[70] *ibid.* at 387.

itself in *DT v CT* has been subject to intense criticism. Crowley equates this decision to one of unwarranted judicial activism, stating:

> "While legislation is perpetually subject to interpretation by the judiciary, in this instance it is suggested that the judiciary has deliberately chosen to ignore a policy decision taken by the legislature and has effectively re-invented the aims of the legislation."[71]

Although in favour of the result and the principles set out in the decision, she feels that the means adopted has resulted in the end being based on an unjustified exercise of judicial power. Crowley calls on the legislature to amend this area of law so as to provide legitimate authority to the introduction of "clean break" divorce in Irish law, similar to that in England.[72] Shannon is concerned that the introduction of a "clean break" divorce into Irish law may lead to a two-tier divorce system whereby those who can afford a "clean break" can avail of one, whilst others must content themselves with the possibility of perpetual financial ties.[73]

Despite these concerns, it would appear that where possible the courts will seek to achieve a "clean break". Mindful that a "clean break" is not possible under a judicial separation, McKechnie J. in *BD v JD*[74] sought to achieve as much finality and certainty to the proceedings as possible. The main asset in this case was the husband's business, estimated to be worth £10 million, thereby classifying this case as one of "ample resources". In light of this, McKechnie J. stated:

> "Furthermore, whilst I am conscious that no clean break can be achieved between Mr. and Mrs. D. and that these ancillary orders issue under section 16 of the Act of 1995, nevertheless I should say that it is my intention to bring as much finality and certainty to the situation as the law permits me to so do."[75]

---

[71] Crowley, "Divorce Law in Ireland: Facilitating or Frustrating The Resolution Process?" (2004) 16 *Child & Family Law Quarterly* 49.

[72] Section 3 of the Matrimonial and Family Proceedings Act 1984 introduced s.25A into the Matrimonial Causes Act 1973 so as to expressly provide for a "clean break" option.

[73] Shannon, "What Price a 'Clean Break' Divorce Now?" (2002) 96 (10) *Law Society Gazette* 20.

[74] Unreported, High Court, December 5, 2003, McKechnie J. For analysis see Byrne and Binchy, *Annual Review of Irish Law 2003* (Thomson Round Hall, 2004) at p.345.

[75] *ibid.* at para.75; p.56 of transcript.

The court ordered the husband to pay the wife a lump sum of £4 million over a scheduled period of three years, thereby effectively enabling the parties to enjoy a clean break.[76]

In *WA v MA*, Hardiman J. on circuit in the High Court, referring to *DT v CT* commented:

> "It appears, therefore, that the *desideratum* of certainty and finality, where that is attainable, has been fully recognised by the Courts."[77]

Furthermore, in *RG v CG*, Finlay Geoghegan J., alluding to *DT v CT*, also stated:

> "It appears that in accordance with the [dicta of Keane C.J. in *DT v CT*], save as precluded from doing so by the Constitution and the relevant statutes that the court should in family proceedings seek to uphold the principle of certainty and finality of litigation and the avoidance of further litigation."[78]

Although the bedrock upon which the existence of a "clean break" in Irish law currently stands may not represent compelling judicial interpretation, it is fair to say that a "clean break", where achievable, is now a dis-

---

[76] This was successfully appealed to the Supreme Court on the basis that the trial judge should have taken into account the realisation costs of making assets available so as to honour the lump sum order. Despite granting the wife a lump sum of £4 million, the High Court order would result in the husband paying out between £4.8 and £5.68 million. Nonetheless, for present purposes the Supreme Court did not dispute the intention to bring as much certainty and finality to this case as possible. See *BD v JD*, unreported, Supreme Court, December 8, 2004; [2005] (Autumn) Fam. L.J. 11. For analysis see Power, "Practice and Procedure—Tax and Costs in Family Law Cases" [2005] 1 I.J.F.L. 22; Power, "Practice and Procedure—Tax and Costs in Family Law Cases Part 2" [2005] 3 I.J.F.L. 28. This case appeared before McKechnie J. once again in the form of a Notice of Motion on behalf of the wife seeking directions as to the mode and manner the court would adopt in hearing this case following the Supreme Court ruling; see *BD v JD*, unreported, High Court, McKechnie J., May 4, 2005. Effectively McKechnie J. held that there would only be a partial retrial concerning the means by which a lump sum would be payable without burdening the husband with exorbitant tax and realisation expenses. Therefore, one can assume that the principles enunciated by McKechnie J. at first instance still stand. Although set to appear before McKechnie J. once more for hearing, the author has been unable to locate any transcript of such a hearing.

[77] *WA v MA* [2005] 1 I.R. 1 at 15, also reported in [2005] 1 I.L.R.M. 517. The facts of this case shall be set out in detail below in relation to the effect of pre-existing separation agreements; see p.156 below. For analysis and comment see Power, "Practice and Procedure—Clean Break Settlements" [2005] 2 I.J.F.L. 28.

[78] *RG v CG* [2005] 2 I.R. 418, at 425–426. The facts of this case shall be set out in detail below in relation to the effect of pre-existing separation agreements; see p.158 below.

tinct possibility under Irish law. There are a number of positive connotations surrounding such a development. Eekelaar asserts that "[t]he idea of the 'clean break' incorporates three elements: self-determination, self-sufficiency, and finality."[79] By accepting the possibility of a "clean break" the Irish courts have lent their support to these elements. It is submitted that the next step in promoting these concepts is the recognition and enforcement of pre-nuptial agreements. As discussed in Chapter 3, the private ordering of family law is centred around concepts such as privacy, autonomy, equality and dignity. The adoption of a "clean break" divorce system represents a partial shift toward embracing these concepts. It only represents a "partial" shift in that it embraces these concepts at the termination stage of marriage, whereas for a complete appreciation of these concepts recognition is also required at the formation stage of marriage. It is argued that the means of doing so would be to recognise and enforce pre-nuptial agreements. The recent mantra of the courts concerning finality and certainty is meaningless unless it represents finality and certainty on terms agreed, where possible, by the parties themselves. Therefore, the introduction of "clean break" divorce represents a basis upon which it can be argued that pre-nuptial agreements ought also to be recognised.

It is thought that this point would also find favour with those opposed to "clean break" divorce because the autonomy it promotes can also provide people with a basis upon which to agree, in a pre-nuptial agreement, not to give effect to a "clean break" in the event of a breakdown in the marriage. In concluding this section it is noted that "clean break" divorce incorporates elements of privacy, autonomy, equality and dignity that have been implicitly accepted by the courts; and it is such moral argument that causes one to conclude that marriage, in both its termination and formation stage, ought to be determined by the parties to it, thereby representing a basis for one to argue that pre-nuptial agreements ought to become part of Irish law.

---

[79] Eekelaar, "Post-Divorce Financial Obligations" in Katz, Eekelaar and Maclean (eds), *Cross Currents: Family Law and Policy in the US and England* (OUP, 2000), p.413.

THE INCREASING TREND TOWARDS THE PRIVATE ORDERING OF FAMILY LAW MATTERS

The argument postulated in Chapter 3 concerning the desire for matrimonial matters to be privately organised by the parties to such matters without state interference is moving from an aspirational viewpoint to one of increasing necessity. The judicial system is simply unable to cope with the magnitude of diversity coming before it in the form of matrimonial disputes. The levels of tension and emotion surrounding such disputes are not conducive to a court atmosphere. The legislature attempted to regulate this area in the form of the Acts of 1995 and 1996. Nonetheless, it is submitted that the legislature has failed in doing so, thus causing the alternative of private ordering to represent an attractive option.

Crowley has commented that the interpretation and implementation of the 1996 Act has neglected the objective of seeking resolution to disputes, and instead has resulted in an unnecessary adversarial nature to divorce cases:

> "[T]he parties to the marriage become opposing factions in court proceedings that do not lend themselves to the incorporation or adoption of existing agreements, made by the parties typically with the aid of independent legal advice... The fault for such a contentious system lies with both the legislature and the courts. The Divorce Act 1996 fails to embrace properly the value and importance of existing agreements previously believed to constitute a full and final settlement between the parties. In turn, the courts have compounded this shortcoming by refusing to incorporate any element of finality in the current system."[80]

Cretney has argued that because of the negative connotations surrounding the word "court", generally in relation to crime and punishment, family law ought to be disentangled from such a forum. The crux of Cretney's argument is that there is a general perception that the "court" is a necessary component in the divorce process. He claims that there is a need to question this assumption. Not being so radical as to eliminate the role of the judiciary from divorce proceedings altogether, he simply argues that it should not play an automatic role in such proceedings. Instead, the private ordering of such matters ought to be promoted:

---

[80] Crowley, "Divorce Law in Ireland: Facilitating or Frustrating the Resolution Process?" (2004) 16 *Child & Family Law Quarterly* 49.

> "The more the courts distance themselves from unnecessary
> intervention in family life the better."[81]

It is submitted that the Irish legislature has aggravated this problem by
failing to define key aspects of ancillary relief, thus leading to contentious litigation. A demonstrative illustration of this concerns the definition of what constitutes a marital asset. Where two parties equally contribute to the marriage, whether in an economic or non-economic sense,
this tends not to cause dispute. Alternatively, in cases involving inheritance, assets gained post-separation, and "career assets"—to name but a
few—significant points of contention tend to arise. It is submitted that
this problem will intensify further in coming years as it is now common
case that, due to economic pressures, parties are marrying later in life
and bringing individual assets to the marriage that traditionally were regarded as marital assets, *e.g.* property. An obvious, yet effective, resolution to this problem is the promotion of private ordering of matrimonial
matters, including the recognition and enforcement of pre-nuptial agreements. If parties to a marriage can decide before the marriage what is and
is not to constitute marital property, then future disputes will be significantly reduced.

There is a modicum of appreciation for the private resolution of
marital disputes in Irish family law as it stands. Sections 5 and 6 of the
Judicial Separation and Family Law Reform Act 1989 and ss.6 and 7 of
the Family Law (Divorce) Act 1996 require parties to such proceedings
to consider alternative forms of dispute resolution, such as mediation,
before embarking on judicial litigation. It has been argued that privately
agreed upon resolutions to marital disputes are more likely to survive the
test of time in comparison to a court order.[82] This is apparent in other
jurisdictions. In 1997 a study was carried out in Scotland which concluded
that the ratio of private agreements to divorces was one to four,[83] whereas
in Australia the figure was higher, at 38 per cent.[84] It is submitted that ss.5
and 6, and ss.6 and 7 of the 1989 and 1996 Acts respectively, represent a

---

[81]   Cretney, "Private Ordering and Divorce—How Far Can We Go?" (2003) 33 Fam Law 399 at
       405.

[82]   See in general Wasoff, "Mutual Consent: Separation Agreements and the Outcomes of
       Private Ordering in Divorce" (2005) 27 *Journal of Social Welfare and Family Law* 237.

[83]   Wasoff, McGuckin and Edwards, *Mutual Consent: Written Agreements in Family Law*
       (Central Research Unit, The Scottish Office, Edinburgh, 1997).

[84]   Sheehan, "Financial Aspects of the Divorce Transition in Australia: Recent Empirical
       Findings" (2002) 16 *International Journal of Law, Policy and the Family* 95.

small step toward appreciating the advantages of parties to a marriage privately organising its course, conduct and, if necessary, its termination. Nonetheless, further steps need to be taken to reduce the level of acrimony and conflict commonly associated with marital disputes. Upon the basis of the present partial legislative intention to achieve this, it is posited that pre-nuptial agreements ought to play a role in this area of Irish law.

Recent pronouncements by the Irish courts suggest that improvements in this field would be welcomed. O'Neill J. in the case of *MK v JP (otherwise SK)* commented:

> "I should add that the approach adopted by the parties in setting out at the start of the trial what they considered to be a proper provision is of great assistance to the court."[85]

Furthermore, in *BD v JD*,[86] McKechnie J. noted that many people see the courts as a forum to vent their anger and frustration at their former spouse. He questions this perceived role of the courts, and believes it to be a misguided assumption. Such activities, he felt, would be better suited elsewhere.

Perhaps the most express form of approval for the private ordering of marital disputes can be seen in the dicta of Keane J., in the Supreme Court case of *PO'D v AO'D*.[87] This case raised the question of whether a party to a separation agreement was estopped from seeking a judicial separation. In answering this question in the positive Keane J., with whom Lynch and Barron JJ. concurred, stated:

> "[W]here parties have entered into a binding contract to dispose of differences that have arisen between them as husband and wife, it would be unjust to allow one party unilaterally to repudiate that agreement, irrespective of whether it took the form of a compromise of proceedings actually instituted."[88]

This represents clear authority for the proposition that the courts will uphold a privately ordered resolution of a marital dispute, provided it would be in the interests of justice to do so. On this basis, one could argue that the private ordering of marital matters in a voluntary, just and

---

[85] *MK v JP (otherwise SK)* [2003] 1 I.R. 326, at 344.
[86] Unreported, High Court, McKechnie J., May 4, 2005.
[87] [1998] 1 I.L.R.M. 543.
[88] *ibid.* at 558.

equitable manner ought to be enforced in the Irish courts. A pre-nuptial agreement embracing these factors should then be recognised. This argument takes a further twist when one considers the effect of pre-existing separation agreements, and in particular "full and final settlement" clauses.

THE EFFECT OF PRE-EXISTING SEPARATION AGREEMENTS

Many separation agreements executed between parties to a broken-down marriage contain "full and final settlement" clauses. Such clauses are designed to achieve a clean break between the parties. There is precedent stating that, in judicial separation proceedings, separation agreements are given significant consideration. In *PO'D v AO'D*[89] it was held that a party to a separation agreement cannot unilaterally seek a judicial separation so as to obtain additional ancillary relief. It is only in recent times that separation agreements, in the context of divorce proceedings, have been considered by the Irish courts. It has been argued that the decision of the Supreme Court in *DT v CT* has strengthened the validity of such clauses.[90] Nonetheless, as shall be seen, the extent of judicial deference to such agreements in divorce cases has been varied.

The decision of Buckley J. in the Circuit Court case of *MG v MG*[91] reflects a considered and reasoned opinion as to when it is permissible for a court to disregard the terms of a separation agreement in subsequent ancillary relief proceedings. The parties to this case entered into a separation agreement in 1995, following 20 years of marriage in which they reared three children. In the agreement the applicant husband transferred his interest in the family home to the wife in return for £20,000 to be paid at some future date. At the time of entering into the agreement the family home was worth £200,000. In 1996 the applicant husband sought the wife's consent so as to enable him to obtain a divorce in the Dominican Republic, in consideration for him waiving the £20,000 owed. On foot of this foreign divorce the husband remarried; but in 1998 he lost his job and found it difficult to maintain any long-term employment. As a

---

[89]   [1998] 1 I.L.R.M. 543.

[90]   See Shannon, "What Price a 'Clean Break' Divorce Now?" (2002) 96(10) *Law Society Gazette* 20.

[91]   Unreported, Circuit Family Court Dublin, Buckley J., July 25, 2000. For a case note see Reid, "Court Slow to Interfere with Separation Terms Agreed by Intelligent Parties Legally Advised" *The Irish Times*, October 2, 2000. Also see Power, "Case & Comment" [2000] 4 I.J.F.L. 29; Shannon, *Divorce: The Changing Landscape of Divorce in Ireland*, (Round Hall, Dublin, 2001).

result he found it difficult to meet his maintenance requirements under the agreement, therefore seeking a court order to reduce such payments.

In deciding the case, Buckley J. noted that the separation agreement had been drafted in light of the ancillary relief provisions of the Family Law Act 1995, which mirror those of the Family Law (Divorce) Act 1996. As such, it was fair to assume that the parties were aware of their corresponding legal entitlements and obligations, and sought to honour these within the agreement. He noted that s.20(3) of the 1996 Act required the court to "have regard" to any pre-existing separation agreements in cases seeking ancillary relief. With little Irish authority on the nature and extent of this obligation he referred to Canadian jurisprudence, as Canada has a similar legislative requirement.[92] Of concern to the court in this case was the extent to which the circumstances had changed between the parties in the time following the execution of the separation agreement, and whether these changes rendered the agreement unenforceable. Following the decision of the Canadian Supreme Court in *Willick v Willick*,[93] Buckley J. held that, just because a change in circumstances may have been objectively foreseeable, it does not necessarily mean that it was one contemplated by the parties. For a change in circumstances to render a prior existing separation agreement unenforceable, it must be a "sufficient change", as defined by L'Heureux Dubé J. in *Willick*:

> "In deciding whether the conditions for variation exist, it is common ground that the change must be a material change of circumstances. This means a change such that, if known at the time, would likely have resulted in different terms."[94]

Buckley J. acknowledged the dicta emerging from the Irish courts encouraging the ascertainment of certainty and finality to family litigation. He stated that where the parties were well-educated, intelligent persons, who received independent legal advice before entering a separation agreement, and the agreement was of recent date, then the courts should be slow to make any radical changes to such an agreement. Applying this principle to the facts of the case he concluded that the husband's foreign divorce and subsequent loss of employment were foreseeable at the time of entering the agreement.[95] Despite this, the substantial increase in value

---

[92] Canadian Divorce Act 1985, s.17.
[93] 119 DLR (4th) 405; [1994] 3 S.C.R. 670.
[94] [1994] 3 S.C.R. 670, at 688.
[95] The husband had lost his job on previous occasions during the marriage, causing his recent unemployment to come as no great shock.

of the family home, from £200,000 to £800,000 since the execution of
the agreement was unforeseeable; causing Buckley J. to doubt that the
husband would have so easily surrendered his share in the property had he
foreseen this. Therefore, the separation agreement was upheld, but with
one minor variation. An order was made that, if the family home was ever
sold, the husband would receive 10 per cent of its net sale price.

This decision is important as it not only displays judicial deference
to the private ordering of matrimonial matters, but does so in a comprehensive and reasoned opinion. A validly executed agreement between two
parties of sound mind, fully aware of the effect of the agreement they are
signing, should not be unilaterally cast aside by one party merely because
circumstances have changed. From the judgment in *MG* it is clear that if
a party feels aggrieved due to the effect of changing circumstances on a
separation agreement, then that person is required to prove that there has
been a "sufficient change" in circumstances.

A detailed analysis of the effect of a prior existing separation agreement in divorce proceedings is evident in the judgment of O'Neill J. in
the High Court decision of *MK v JP (otherwise SK).*[96] This case concerned a couple married in 1963 who had six children. The parties split in
1982, and in the following years the husband prospered, eventually becoming President of a multi-national company based in America. Importantly, the parties entered into a separation agreement in 1982 which,
according to a Supreme Court decision of an appeal on the initial decision granted in this case,[97] ought to be considered by the trial judge in
determining the appropriate level of ancillary relief, in accordance with
s.20(3) of the Family Law (Divorce) Act 1996. O'Neill J. held that, in
considering the ancillary relief in a case in which there is a prior existing
separation agreement, the agreement must be included in the analysis with
the other factors set out in s.20(2) of the 1996 Act. Notwithstanding this,
it is at the discretion of the judge, depending on the circumstances of the
case, as to the order in which each of these factors is considered. The
ultimate concern in considering the relevance of a prior existing separation agreement is to ensure that it satisfies the "proper provision" requirement:

> "Undoubtedly in a case where the separation deed is of recent
> date it would be likely that a court would consider the terms of

---

[96]   [2003] 1 I.R. 326.
[97]   *MK v JK (otherwise SK)* [2001] 3 I.R. 371.

the deed of separation at an initial stage and unless there was manifest a change of circumstance such that a different provision would have been likely to have been made when the separation agreement was entered into, the inquiry might well proceed on the basis that in the absence of any material change of circumstance, that the separation deed having been entered into at a recent date and with the benefit of appropriate advice, *prima facie* contained 'proper provision'. It would appear to me that the wording of section 20(1) not only permits but indeed could be said to contemplate such an approach where it says as follows:

> '... the court shall ensure that such provision as the court considers proper having regard to the circumstances exists ...'
>
> A recent separation deed in force in circumstances where there is no manifest changes in circumstance could be said to fulfil the requirements of section 20(1) ."[98]

On the other hand, if a separation deed was of a "more distant origin in time"[99] then a different form of review would be required. In such circumstances it would be more likely that material changes in circumstances would give cause for a fresh inquiry as to whether "proper provision" was made between the parties. Consequently, such an examination would take place first, ahead of any review of the separation deed.[100]

> "Construing section 20(1) with section 20(3), gives rise in my view to the unavoidable conclusion that in complying with section 20(3) that the court, required to 'have regard' to the terms of a separation agreement must examine that agreement to ensure that at the time of the application, the agreement, in the light of the circumstances of the party, either at that time 'makes a proper provision' or that it contains obligations which will ensure that such provision will be made."[101]

In light of the 20-year passage of time between the execution of the separation agreement and the divorce proceedings, O'Neill J. concluded that

---

[98]   *MK v JK (otherwise SK)* [2003] 1 I.R. 326 at 345.
[99]   *ibid.* at 345.
[100] *ibid.* at 345.
[101] *ibid.* at 346.

the agreement in this case failed to provide "proper provision" due to the material change of circumstances between the parties.[102] The reasoning of O'Neill J. in this case has been praised for its appreciation of the interaction between s.20(2) and s.20(3) of the 1996 Act[103] and, as shall be seen, has provided subsequent courts with the means by which the effect of a prior existing separation agreement in divorce litigation can be determined.

A notable case in this line of authority is that of *WA v MA*[104] decided by Hardiman J., on circuit for the High Court. This case concerned a couple who married in 1978, but whose relationship broke down in 1988. With no children to be provided for the parties entered into a deed of separation in 1993 following intensive negotiations during the previous year. Both parties obtained independent legal advice, and the wife was supported by her father and brother throughout the negotiations. Of particular importance to the facts of this case was a "side agreement" entered into by the parties coinciding with the execution of the deed of separation. This "side agreement" provided that the deed of separation was to be a "full and final settlement" between the parties and was to constitute the terms for ancillary relief in the event of a future divorce. The separation agreement effectively divided the marital assets in half amongst the parties, causing Hardiman J. to comment "that the separation agreement was a fair one and provided ample and approximately equal opportunities for the parties to thrive in its aftermath"[105] and "undoubtedly represented proper provision for both parties."[106] Following the separation, the husband prospered significantly due to several land purchases, aided by his mother, and at the date of trial had an estimated wealth of €7 million. In contrast, the wife's fortunes declined dramatically following the separation. She maintained her farmland in an inefficient manner by employing the services of an agricultural labour company. Also, money was squandered on the construction of a "fabulous" house well in excess of her needs. At the time of hearing her estimated worth was €1.25 million.

---

[102] *ibid.* at 362.

[103] Byrne and Binchy, *Annual Review of Irish Law 2003* (Thomson Round Hall, 2004) at 345.

[104] [2005] 1 I.R. 1; [2005] 1 I.L.R.M. 517. For analysis see Byrne and Binchy, *Annual Review of Irish Law 2004* (Thomson Round Hall, 2005) at 306; Power, "Practice and Procedure—Clean Break Settlements" [2005] 2 I.J.F.L. 28.

[105] *WA v MA* [2005] 1 I.R. 1 at 8.

[106] *ibid.* at 10.

In examining the terms and effect of the separation agreement, Hardiman J. noted a number of influential factors, including the following:

- Both parties had obtained legal and accountancy advice as to the nature of the agreement.
- The wife was supported by her father and brother, both skilled in agricultural matters, throughout the negotiations, thereby vitiating any possibility of undue influence or misrepresentation on behalf of the husband.
- The agreement sought to achieve as close to an equal division as was possible in the circumstances. Both parties were left financially independent following the agreement.

Hardiman J. referred to the judgment of O'Neill J. in *MK v JP (otherwise SK)* and in particular to his analysis of the interaction of s.20(2) and s.20(3) of the 1996 Act. He noted the distinction drawn by O'Neill J. between separation agreements of recent vintage and those more distant in origin, and in the context of this case commented:

"In my view, the significance of the date of the separation agreement depends entirely on the general circumstances of the case, at least in the case of an agreement made after the enactment of the Judicial Separation and Family Law Reform Act, 1989."[107]

For this reason, and the fact that, following *DT v CT*, finality and certainty, where achievable, are desirable objectives in ancillary relief litigation, Hardiman J. held the separation agreement in this case to be binding. He concluded that the difficulties experienced by the wife were wholly of her own doing without any input from the husband. Equally, the same can be said of the husband's prosperity. In light of such circumstances he stated:

"Particularly having regard to the terms of s.20(3) of the Act of 1996, I cannot approach the question of what is 'proper' in the circumstances of this case without giving very significant weight to the terms of the separation agreement…Still more fundamentally, I do not consider it just to [make an order against the husband in the circumstances of this case] and therefore I am precluded from doing so by the terms of s.20(5)."[108]

---

[107] *ibid.* at 13.
[108] *ibid.* at 20.

In distinguishing this case from that of *MK v JP (otherwise SK)*, Hardiman J. thought it compelling that the separation agreement had been drafted in light of the Judicial Separation and Family Law Reform Act 1989. The existence of the 1989 Act at the time of drafting the agreement provided a jurisprudential framework upon which a separation agreement, seeking to provide "proper provision", could be formulated.[109]

This issue was to come before the High Court again shortly after the decision in *WA v MA*. The case of *RG v CG*[110] concerned a couple married in 1982, who had three children but separated in 1998. In 2000 the High Court granted a judicial separation; in light of this the parties came to an agreement as to ancillary relief, to which the court made an order on consent. In the agreement was a provision declaring it to constitute a "full and final settlement of all matters arising pursuant to the Judicial Separation and Family Law Reform Act 1989, the Family Law Act 1995 and any amending legislation".[111] Furthermore, the agreement proclaimed to make "proper provision" within the meaning of the Family Law (Divorce) Act 1996. In 2003 the husband filed for divorce, arguing that there was no need to make additional ancillary relief orders as the order of consent adequately provided for the wife and children.

Finlay Geoghegan J. rejected the husband's argument that the determination of ancillary relief was outside the competence of the court by virtue of the 2000 order of consent. She felt that such a principle would run contrary to public policy. Finlay Geoghegan J. stated that "proper provision" must be valid at the time of divorce proceedings. She held that the acknowledgment of "proper provision" in the 2000 order of consent was made merely in the contemplation of a future divorce, rather than an imminent divorce, thus suggesting a need to fully consider all foreseeable circumstances between parties to a separation agreement before executing it:

> "The acknowledgment included in the Consent of 7th November, 2000 if it is to relate to a proper construction of the Act of 1996 must be considered to be an acknowledgment of potential proper provision at a future unknown date. What if divorce proceedings had not been brought for a period of 10 years? When so properly construed it appears too uncertain to be a matter which this Court should take into account."[112]

---

[109]   *ibid.* at 19–20.
[110]   [2005] 2 I.R. 418.
[111]   *ibid.* at 421.
[112]   *ibid.* at 428.

Finlay Geoghegan J. held that, due to the fact that the husband had acquired wealth in excess of what was contemplated by the parties when reaching an agreement in 2000, it was necessary to make further ancillary relief orders so as to ensure "proper provision" between the parties.

As is clear, there is a divergence in opinion between Hardiman J. and Finlay Geoghegan J., as to the effect of prior existing agreements between parties as to ancillary relief. Nonetheless, these judgments are not completely irreconcilable. Both cases can be distinguished from each other on a number of grounds. First, *WA v MA* concerned a separation agreement, whereas *RG v CG* concerned a consent order following a judicial separation. Secondly, in *WA v MA* there was a complete division of the marital assets seeking to achieve equality between the parties and subsequently leaving them both financially independent. Also, there were no children to the marriage. In contrast, the wife was left financially dependant on the husband in *RG v CG* and also had to care and provide for their three children. In light of these differences, it is submitted that the judgment of Hardiman J., in *WA v MA,* is authorative for the proposition that, where "proper provision" has been satisfied, a private agreement between two parties to the breakdown of a marriage should be enforced by a court in subsequent divorce proceedings.

In *MP v AP,*[113] O'Higgins J. had the benefit of the judgments in *WA v MA* and *RG v CG* in deciding the effect of a prior separation agreement in subsequent divorce proceedings. In this case the parties married in 1974 and had adopted two children. From 1992 they lived separate and apart, and in that year settled judicial separation proceedings by means of agreement. Under the agreement the family home was to be sold and the proceeds split between the parties. The wife was to receive a lump sum of £175,000 and £1,800 maintenance per month.[114]

In considering the effect of s.20(3) of the 1996 Act, O'Higgins J. reiterated the sentiments expressed by O'Neill J. in *MK v JP (otherwise SK)*, as endorsed by Hardiman J. in *WA v MA*, stating:

> "The weight to be attached to a prior settlement will vary from case to case depending on many factors including the length of time since it was reached, the financial background against which such settlement was reached, when compared with the present circumstances, and the reasonable expectations of the parties

---

[113] Unreported, High Court, O'Higgins J., March 2, 2005.
[114] £1,400 of which was for the wife, and £200 per child.

at the time of the settlement. The relative importance of these factors themselves will vary according to the circumstances of a case."[115]

Taking into account the factors of this case he stated:

"The agreement is an important document and the background against which the present proceedings must be considered."[116]

One of the motives behind the wife's claim for additional ancillary relief was the diminution of her wealth as a result of her "failure to manage resources". Due to the fairness of the separation agreement, O'Higgins J. was reluctant to make any considerable orders that might radically alter it. Notwithstanding this, he did feel that the maintenance ought to be increased to €38,000 per year after tax, mainly because of the huge disparity in the income levels of the parties. Importantly, however, he was not willing to make a property adjustment order, despite the husband owning several properties both in Ireland and abroad. Also, due to the increase in maintenance, he absolved the husband's obligation to pay for the wife's VHI and other medical expenses.

To conclude, it is clear that the judgment of O'Neill J. in *MK v JP (otherwise SK)* provided a sound jurisprudential platform upon which prior existing separation agreements can be considered in subsequent divorce litigation. The judgments in *WA v MA* and *MP v AP* represent pragmatic consideration and appreciation for the private ordering of marital affairs. From this growth in judicial deference to separation agreements, it is submitted that such reasoning permits the recognition of pre-nuptial agreements in Irish law, as a "circumstance"[117] to be taken into account in subsequent divorce litigation.

Shannon highlights the counter-argument to this, based on legislative interpretation grounds. He notes that the specific reference by the legislature to "separation agreements" in s.20(3) of the 1996 Act precludes, on a literal interpretation, the consideration of any other form of agreement.[118] Notwithstanding this, it is submitted that there are three further provisions within s.20 of the 1996 Act that might permit the consideration of a pre-nuptial agreement. Section 20(1) requires the court

---

[115] *MP v AP*, unreported, High Court, O'Higgins J., March 2, 2005 at 34.

[116] *ibid.* at 3.

[117] Family Law (Divorce) Act 1996, s.20(1).

[118] Shannon, "Pre-Nuptial Agreements: Hedging Your Bets" (2000) 94(3) *Law Society Gazette* 16 at 19.

to have regard to the "circumstances" that exist between parties to a claim for ancillary relief. Furthermore, s.20(5) requires the court to make orders "in the interests of justice". It is foreseeable that a case might come before the courts in which a pre-nuptial agreement constitutes a "circumstance" to be taken into account, without which an order could be made "in the interests of justice". In addition, the Irish courts may adopt an approach similar to that in England[119] and deem a pre-nuptial contract entered into between the parties as conduct which "in all the circumstances of the case would be unjust to disregard".[120]

As has been illustrated thus far in this section, there is not only a need but a basis upon which pre-nuptial agreements might be recognised in Irish law. The overarching level of judicial discretion in ancillary relief matters is in need of limitation. Such discretion connotes paternalism entering the private realm of marriage. It is necessary to realign the balance between the need for flexibility in ancillary relief matters and certainty and finality. The unrestricted exercise of judicial discretion will lead to the devaluation of private ordering in everyday life. Attempts to provide certainty and clarity, in the guise of a "yardstick", are misguided as they fail to accommodate the unique nature of all cases. It is submitted that pre-nuptial agreements represent a suitable remedy within which these countervailing needs can be balanced. Such agreements accommodate flexibility in the sense that they are formulated by couples themselves. Clarity is provided from the outset, and the parties have a sense of certainty as to where they stand in the relationship.

MARRIAGE AS A CONTRACT/PARTNERSHIP IN IRISH LAW

In Chapter 3 it was postulated that marriage was a partnership between two people and should be interpreted as a relational contract. There has been international support for such a proposition, most notably in jurisdictions permitting same-sex marriage. Nonetheless, Irish attitudes towards marriage tend to reflect a traditional, Roman Catholic perception of marriage. Gender roles are accorded to both parties, with the husband deemed to be the "breadwinner" and the wife the "homemaker". This approach has led to discrimination amongst women in society, preventing them from achieving careers outside the family home. Furthermore, the non-economic contributions made by women to marriage are deemed inferior to the economic contributions made by men. Throughout this

---

[119] *M v M (Pre-nuptial Agreement)* [2002] 1 F.L.R. 654, in particular at 661.
[120] Family Law Divorce Act 1996, s.20(2)(i).

book it has been argued that equality should reign supreme in any interpretation of marriage. It is thought that the best means of achieving this is to relate marriage to a partnership governed by a relational contract.

There have been recent judicial pronouncements suggesting that such a development may be imminent. Notwithstanding this, it is pertinent to note that Irish courts have displayed an appreciation of this for some time. In *N (otherwise K) v K,* McCarthy J. commented:

> "Marriage is a civil *contract* which creates reciprocating rights and duties between the parties but, further, establishes a status which affects both the parties to the *contract* and the community as a whole."[121]

Also, Finlay C.J., in *Re Article 26 and the Matrimonial Home Bill 1993,*[122] referred to the partnership model of marriage in relation to the commendable objective of seeking to achieve joint ownership of matrimonial homes. Although the objective was ideal, the manner in doing so was deemed an unconstitutional interference into family autonomy.[123] Nonetheless, Finlay C.J. did comment on the fundamentals of marriage, stating:

> "The Court accepts, as it has indicated, the advantages of encouraging, by any appropriate means, joint ownership in family homes as being conducive to the dignity, reassurance and independence of each of the spouses and to the *partnership* concept of marriage which is fundamental to it."[124]

Keane J. (as he then was), in the Supreme Court case of *PO'D v AO'D,*[125] referred to early dicta interpreting marriage as a contract. He quoted[126] Lord Westbury L.C. who in *Hunt v Hunt* stated:

> "Before the Reformation, as we all know, marriage was regarded by the church, and therefore regarded by the law, as a sacrament. It was a *contract* of the highest possible religious obligation."[127]

---

[121]   *N (Otherwise K) v K* [1985] I.R. 733 at 754 (emphasis added).

[122]   [1994] 1 I.R. 305.

[123]   This point shall be dealt with in greater detail below; see p.167.

[124]   *Re Article 26 and the Matrimonial Home Bill 1993* [1994] 1 I.R. 305 at 326 (emphasis added).

[125]   [1998] 1 I.L.R.M. 543.

[126]   *ibid.* at 553–5.

[127]   *Hunt v Hunt* (1861) 4 De G F & J 221 (emphasis added).

In addition he noted that early decisions recognised marriage as involving "obligations which both [parties] have *contracted* in the sight of God", with the law providing the courts with "the right of adjudicating upon the nature of the matrimonial *contract*" in light of "the principles of the matrimonial *contract*."[128]

In recent decisions concerning ancillary relief, the role and contributions of both parties to a marriage has come to the forefront, and with it a fresh interpretation of marriage. In seeking to determine appropriate ancillary relief in the judicial separation case of *JD v DD,* McGuinness J. noted:

> "On a practical level this marriage was a lengthy *partnership* of complementary roles and it seems to me that it should result in a reasonably equal division of the accumulated assets."[129]

Reflecting this partnership analogy, O'Donovan J. in *CO'R v MO'R* stated:

> "Moreover, in so far as the parties, themselves, are concerned, it seems to me that such ancillary orders as I choose to make in association with the decree of Judicial separation which I have already granted must be tailored to reflect the contribution which each of the parties made to the marriage, the current income and worth of each of the parties and their current responsibilities."[130]

Perhaps the most explicit rejection of the traditional conception of marital roles is evident in the judgment of the Supreme Court in *DT v CT*, with Keane C.J. stating:

> "In Irish society today, it can no longer be assumed that the husband and wife will occupy their traditional roles in which the husband has been the breadwinner and the wife the home builder and carer."[131]

From this, the Supreme Court concluded that it was impermissible to discriminate against the homemaker, merely because he/she did not contribute economically to the family income. The majority of the court

---

[128] *Mortimer v Mortimer* (1820) 2 Hagg Con 310, (emphasis added).

[129] *JD v DD* [1997] 3 I.R. 64 at 95 (emphasis added).

[130] *CO'R v MO'R,* unreported, High Court, O'Donovan J., September 19, 2000 at 30. For analysis see Power, "Case and Comment" [2001] 2 I.J.F.L. 24; Byrne and Binchy, *Annual Review of Irish Law 2000* (Round Hall Sweet & Maxwell, 2001) at 254–256.

[131] *DT v CT* [2003] 1 I.L.R.M. 321 at 338.

held that, where the marital assets exceed the "reasonable requirements" of the parties, it would not be just to limit the wife's award to her "reasonable requirements", thereby allowing the husband to enjoy the surplus.[132] Instead, the wife should also be permitted to have the benefit of some of the surplus.[133] It was this topic of marital contributions that proved to be the catalyst for the reappraisal of marriage and its formation.

The judgment of Murray J. (as he then was) in *DT v CT* proved to represent the strongest commendation for this enlightened interpretation of marriage. He makes several references throughout his judgment to the marriage contract being a partnership contract.[134] He acknowledges the ability of parties to a marriage to alter its terms throughout the relationship:

> "Husband and wife having mutual duties and responsibilities for the welfare of each other and the marriage, will throughout the marriage, make private decisions as to the role each of them will play in the support of the marriage, the achievement of their goals and their lifestyle."[135]

With the developments in Irish society in the last 20 years,[136] there is a need to adopt a fresh and contemporary analysis of marriage within the constitutional context, so as to do justice to the contemporary nature of the Irish Constitution.[137] In determining ancillary relief, Murray J. states:

> "Proper provision should seek to reflect the equal *partnership* of the spouses."[138]

In light of such opinions in *DT v CT*, O'Neill J., in *MK v JP (otherwise SK)*[139] held that in order to protect the applicant wife from discrimination she was entitled to a share of the husband's wealth acquired in the 20 years following their separation. The rationale for such an opinion was based on the fact that, by caring for the six children following the separation, the wife had enabled the husband to pursue career opportunities without being "tied down" to a family. As a result, the wife's contribution to the family home deserved recognition, and compensation so to speak, from the husband's resultant wealth:

---

[132] In reaching this conclusion the majority relied on the decision of Lord Nicholls in the House of Lords decision in *White v White* [2000] 2 F.L.R. 981.

[133] Murphy J. dissented on this point.

[134] See in particular *DT v CT* [2003] 1 I.L.R.M. 321 at 374–377.

[135] *ibid.* at 375.

[136] See Chap.1.

[137] *DT v CT* [2003] 1 I.L.R.M. 321 at 376.

[138] *ibid.* at 377 (emphasis added).

[139] [2003] 1 I.R. 326.

"[T]he role of the dependant homemaker and child carer, usually the wife is not to be disadvantaged in the distribution of assets by reason of having a non economic role."[140]

From this, it is apparent that O'Neill J. viewed the marriage as a partnership, thereby entitling the wife to a significant share of her estranged husband's wealth.

In *BD v JD,* McKechnie J. reiterated the need to ensure that neither party is discriminated against in determining ancillary relief due to their roles in the marriage.[141] Abbott J. expressed similar sentiments in *N v N* stating:

"The applicant's continuous work in the farm and in the home means that it would be unjust to deal with her on any basis less than the equivalent of the equality notwithstanding that in terms of the physical assets of the family they were inherited by the respondent and provided entirely insofar as the land was concerned by the respondent."[142]

The above case law demonstrates a new found appreciation for the role of the non-economic contributing spouse to a marriage. It represents a welcome appreciation for the role of the homemaker in Irish society. The Californian Supreme Court colourfully alluded to a similar development in that jurisdiction stating:

"A woman is not a breeding cow to be nurtured during the years of fecundity, then conveniently and economically converted into cheap steaks when past her prime…[T]he husband simply has to face up to the fact that his support responsibilities are going to be of extended duration—perhaps for life. This has nothing to do with feminism, sexism, male chauvinism, or any other trendy social ideology. It is ordinary common sense, basic decency, and simple justice."[143]

The comparisons between partnership law and marriage are self-evident, causing Morris to recommend that principles of partnership law be introduced into the marital structure, especially in cases involving family busi-

---

[140]   *ibid.* at 349.
[141]   unreported, High Court, McKechnie J., December 5, 2003 at para.54.
[142]   unreported, High Court, Abbot J., December 18, 2003 at 13.
[143]   *Re Marriage of Brantner* (1977) 67 Cal. App. 3d 416, at 419–20.

nesses.[144] He acknowledges the role that a pre-nuptial contract might play in such a context, stating:

> "Pre-nuptial agreements could operate as a private ordering of marital property much in the same way as a partnership agreement regulates a firm's private business affairs, and statute could impose a default regime."[145]

The realisation of marriage constituting the partnership of two individuals represents a milestone in this area of law. On this basis, one can persuasively argue that parties to a marriage ought to be entitled to order their marital affairs in a private manner. A pre-nuptial agreement would provide a means of doing so; in addition it would prove instrumental in resolving future points of contention, especially concerning the determination of "marital assets". At present, Irish law appears to be ebbing toward such a stance. It is hoped that on this basis further cause will be given to the argument in favour of introducing pre-nuptial agreements into Irish law.

FAMILY AUTONOMY—THE RIGHT OF MARRIED COUPLES TO MAKE DECISIONS

The individual right of autonomy was examined in Chapter 3, as a means of constructing a persuasive moral argument for the expansion of the meaning of marriage. Another form of autonomy exists in Irish jurisprudence in the context of the family. It has long been recognised that there is a right to family autonomy. The substantive effect of this right has been to declare the family domain free from state interference and to respect the decisions taken by the family unit. At present the family under Irish law is one based on the institution of marriage. Despite general assertions for widespread reform as to the legal interpretation of marriage, it may be possible to introduce pre-nuptial agreements into Irish law within the current constitutional context. The current interpretation of family autonomy, which comes into effect upon marriage, may provide a basis upon which a pre-nuptial agreement between a married couple ought to be respected and, subject to the caveat of providing "proper provision", enforced.

---

[144]   Morris, "Putting a Value on 'Human Capital' in Resolving Matrimonial Disputes" [2005] 2 I.J.F.L. 9.
[145]   *ibid.* at 17.

Family autonomy has been interpreted as meaning the right of a family unit, *i.e.* a married couple, to make decisions concerning that unit, without unjust state interference. The nature of this right was discussed in detail by the Supreme Court in the case of *Re Article 26 and the Matrimonial Home Bill 1993*.[146] The concern surrounding this Bill, justifying an Art.26 reference, was that its effect was to automatically accord joint ownership of the matrimonial home to the parties to the marriage, irrespective of any agreement they had reached themselves. It was argued that this was an unjust interference with the right to family autonomy, in that it arbitrarily interfered with the decision-making authority of the family unit. Illustrating the peremptory nature of this Bill, Finlay C.J. commented:

"In some instances the net effect of these legislative proposals would be automatically to cancel a joint decision freely made by both spouses as part of the authority of the family and substitute therefore a wholly different decision".[147]

In holding the Bill to be unconstitutional on the basis that it violated Art.41, Finlay C.J. stated that:

"the rights which attach to the family including its right to make decisions within its authority are inalienable and imprescriptible and antecedent and superior to all positive law".[148]

The right of family autonomy, and its nature and scope, came before the Supreme Court once again in *North Western Health Board v HW*.[149] This case concerned the carrying out of a PKU[150] test on a child. The test was designed to detect a metabolic condition that could lead to brain damage. It involved taking a tiny blood sample, by way of a pinprick to the heel. The applicant health board contended that it was in the best interests of the child to carry out the test. The respondent parents objected, on grounds of the belief that it was wrong to inflict pain on another person. They argued that it would be an unconstitutional infringement on the family domain if the test was to be carried out against their wishes. It was accepted that the chances of the child having contracted any brain abnor-

---

[146] [1994] 1 I.R. 305.
[147] *ibid.* at 326.
[148] *ibid.*
[149] [2001] 3 I.R. 622.
[150] Phenylketonuria.

malities were highly unlikely[151]; yet it was thought prudent to conduct the test.

Although this case concerned the interaction of the rights of the parents to make a decision concerning their child, and the vindication of the child's rights, it is also relevant to the decision-making authority of the family unit.

The five Supreme Court judges delivered separate judgments and by a majority held that the health board was not entitled to interfere with the authority of the parents to make a decision concerning their child.[152] The judgments of Hardiman J. and Keane C.J., dissenting, represent a substantive examination of the constitutional issues surrounding family autonomy.[153] Keane C.J., favouring the paramount position of the child in these circumstances, analysed the constitutional context in which family rights operate, and their background.[154] Byrne and Binchy, commenting on this discourse, note:

> "His words were elegant and humane, but were noteworthy for what they failed to include."[155]

The fatal flaw to the analysis of Keane C.J., according to Byrne and Binchy, is his failure to contend with the notion of the family being an autonomous decision-making body, capable of deciding matters contrary to the views of the State.

Hardiman J., on the other hand, views the rights of the child in these circumstances as falling under the overall umbrella of the rights belonging to the family. Parents are entitled to exercise these rights on behalf of their children without state interference, unless "in exceptional circumstances" the parents "for physical or moral reasons fail in their duty towards their children",[156] in which case the State is entitled to interfere. Pertinent to the decision-making authority of the family, Denham J. stated:

---

[151]	The possibility of contracting any of the suspected conditions surrounding non-administration of the test ranged from one in every 3,500, to one in every 49,000.

[152]	Denham, Hardiman, Murphy and Murray JJ. for the majority; Keane C.J. dissenting.

[153]	For a criticism of the Supreme Court judgments see Mills, "Constitutional Law–PKU: Please Keep Unclear" (2001) 23 D.U.L.J. 180. Essentially, Mills argues that the Supreme Court failed to clearly balance the rights of the parents to decide what is best for their child, and the rights of the child itself in such circumstances.

[154]	*North Western Health Board v HW* [2001] 3 I.R. 622, at 686–687.

[155]	Byrne and Binchy, *Annual Review of Irish Law 2001* (Thomson Round Hall, 2002), at 323.

[156]	Art.42.5 of the Constitution.

"The family is the decision maker for family matters—both for the unit and for the individuals in the family. Responsibility rests fundamentally with the family."[157]

Byrne and Binchy comment that this statement of Denham J. represents "a philosophy of considerable restraint on the parts of the courts in exercising the power to intervene in the process of decision-making in the family."[158]

In a similar vein, Murray J. (as he then was) strongly defended the autonomy of the family unit, stating:

"One of the inherent objects of the Constitution is the protection of liberties. Article 41.2, in providing that 'The State, therefore guarantees to protect the Family in its Constitution and authority...' provides a guarantee for the liberty of the family to function as an autonomous moral institution within society and, in the context of this case, protects its authority from being compromised in a manner which would arbitrarily undermine the liberty so guaranteed."[159]

As is apparent from the judgments of the Supreme Court both in *Re Article 26 and the Matrimonial Home Bill 1993*[160] and *North Western Health Board v HW*,[161] the right to family autonomy is heavily protected and can only be lost in exceptional circumstances. It is submitted that the constitutional protection afforded to this right ought to ensure the enforceability of a pre-nuptial agreement. The logic behind this argument is as follows. A family unit, *i.e.* a married couple, has a constitutional right to make decisions concerning that unit, without unjust interference from the State. A pre-nuptial agreement is such a decision. It is submitted that marriage, and the subsequent formation of a family for Irish constitutional law purposes, is a condition precedent to the execution of a pre-nuptial agreement. A pre-nuptial agreement, although by its very nature is drafted before marriage, cannot come into effect until after a marriage; otherwise there would be nothing for it to regulate. As a result, the execution of the pre-nuptial agreement occurs simultaneously with the

---

157   *North Western Health Board v HW* [2001] 3 I.R. 622 at 722.
158   Byrne and Binchy, *Annual Review of Irish Law 2001* (Thomson Round Hall, 2002) at 327.
159   *North Western Health Board v HW* [2001] 3 I.R. 622 at 737.
160   [1994] 1 I.R. 305.
161   [2001] 3 I.R. 622.

marriage and the attainment of the rights and privileges surrounding marriage under Irish law, including the right to family autonomy. This right, "inalienable and imprescriptible and antecedent and superior to all positive law",[162] protects the validity of the decision to enter the pre-nuptial agreement and the agreement itself.

The obvious counter-argument to this is the protection of the institution of marriage, also arguably constitutionally protected by virtue of it being the basis upon which a family is formulated. Typically this argument is one based on public policy, whereby it is thought that pre-nuptial agreements run contrary to the philosophies commonly attached to marriage. It is asserted that such an argument does not hold much weight for the reasons posited in Chapter 3 of this book, and for a further reason in light of the Supreme Court decision in *North Western Health Board v HW*.[163] In that case there was a risk to the life of the child in not detecting possible abnormalities. Although it is conceded that this risk was minimal, there was still a risk to the life of the child, a point Keane C.J. seemed to deem pertinent. In deferring to the judgment of the parents in this case, the majority effectively held that the right to family autonomy was superior to that of the protection of life. Based on the theory of there being a hierarchy of constitutional rights,[164] the right to family autonomy ranks above that of the protection of life. In turn, surely the right to the protection of life ranks above the institution of marriage. If so, then family autonomy ought to prevail over the protection of the institution of marriage, which it has done by way of the introduction of divorce into Irish law.

This analysis displays an apparent basis available under Irish law for the recognition of pre-nuptial agreements, without the need for reform as has been argued throughout this book. Nonetheless, it is argued that the reforms postulated throughout ought to be given effect so as to fully appreciate the true meaning of marriage.

---

[162]   *Re Article 26 and the Matrimonial Home Bill 1993* [1994] 1 I.R. 305 at 326.
[163]   [2001] 3 I.R. 622.
[164]   *People v Shaw* [1982] I.R. 1.

COULD A FOREIGN PRE-NUPTIAL AGREEMENT BE RECOGNISED IN IRELAND?

A point of interest in this discussion is the potential for the recognition of foreign judgments and instruments concerning matrimonial matters. It is clear that Irish courts recognise foreign divorces.[165] The question must be asked as to why other matrimonial matters can not be similarly recognised *e.g.* a pre-nuptial agreement.

Under Pt III of the Family Law Act 1995 it is possible for a party to a divorce in another jurisdiction to come before the Irish courts in search of additional ancillary relief, provided they meet the jurisdictional requirements.[166] Such a case came before Quirke J. in the High Court recently, where he sought to shed some light on this discrete area of law.[167] The case concerned a couple married in Ireland in 1976, but subsequently divorced in Spain in 1996. So as to satisfy the maintenance requirements of the wife, the husband paid her a sum of £50,000, intended to be full and final provision. Nevertheless, the wife subsequently discovered that the husband was the beneficiary of a trust valued at €2,900,000. She therefore claimed that the husband failed to make full disclosure of his assets at the time of the divorce hearing, and therefore failed to make proper provision. As she had no recourse under Spanish law, the applicant wife came before the Irish courts seeking relief. Having previously held that the jurisdictional requirements had been satisfied,[168] Quirke J. continued to contend with the substantive issues of the case. He sought to legitimise the ability of an Irish court to amend the effect of a judgment of a foreign court. In doing so he relied on English authority,[169] and held it

---

[165] Family Law Act 1995, Pt III. Indeed Ireland is now required to recognise the jurisdiction of courts in other Member States of the European Union in matters that fall under the scope of the Brussels II Convention (Council Regulation (E.C.) No. 1347/2000, O.J. 2000 L160/ 19). The Brussels II Regulation covers matters concerning annulment, judicial separation and divorce (Art.1(1)(a)). A case comes under the scope of the Regulation provided there is a "real link" between the applicant and the Member State exercising jurisdiction (Recital 12 to Council Regulation (E.C.) No. 1347/2000; see Chapter II of the Regulation for the grounds permitting the exercise of jurisdiction). The effect of this Regulation is to provide a uniform set of jurisdictional rules concerning the above matrimonial matters; the rationale being the aspiration to create an integrated and common judicial area throughout the European Union. A consequence of this Regulation is the extinction of "limping marriages", *i.e.* a marriage recognised as valid in one or more jurisdictions despite being terminated in another jurisdiction; typically this is caused by one country failing to recognise the divorce laws of another country.

[166] Family Law Act 1995, s.27.

[167] *MR v PR (Relief after Foreign Divorce)* [2005] 2 I.R. 618.

[168] *MR v PR*, unreported, High Court, Quirke J., August 8, 2003.

[169] *Holmes v Holmes* [1989] Fam. 47.

permissible for an Irish court to merely "fill the gap" left by a foreign court in such a matter as before the court in this case, and not to go so far as to review the correctness or rectify the decision of that court.[170]

That being the context in permitting an Irish court to exercise its judgment in such a case, Quirke J. followed by asserting the grounds for doing so. He held it "appropriate" for an Irish court to intervene in such matters as contemplated under Pt III of the 1995 Act only if there were "exceptional circumstances" whereby the result of the foreign proceedings had rendered an "unfair or unjust" state of affairs, with no further remedy available to the applicant in that foreign jurisdiction.[171] The facts of the present case satisfied the above grounds due to the fact that the respondent failed to disclose all his assets,[172] the reduced standard of living suffered by the applicant, and the fact that there was no means of redress under Spanish law. The case was decided in favour of the applicant wife; nonetheless, the parties subsequently came to an agreement between themselves as to the appropriate relief.

This case raises interesting questions concerning the ability and indeed justification for Irish courts to interfere in matrimonial matters previously governed by the law of another jurisdiction. Whilst the effect of Pt III of the 1995 Act and the Brussels II Regulation is to embrace the concept of pluralism, it would appear that it is in danger of doing so in an arbitrary manner. How can one permit the uniformity of jurisdiction concerning divorce but not pre-nuptial agreements? The distinction seems tentative at best. How can it be said that Ireland is qualified to adopt a universal attitude to deciding matters concerning annulment, divorce, judicial separation and the resultant ancillary relief, but not pre-nuptial agreements?[173]

---

[170] *MR v PR* [2005] 2 I.R. 618 at 629–30.

[171] *ibid.* at 631–32. Importantly Quirke J. placed a caveat on the exercise of this power later in his judgment, stating at 639:

   "The statutory relief granted [under Pt III of the 1995 Act] is not intended to compensate the applicant for the past financial or other hardship or inequity. It is intended to alleviate present inequitable financial or other hardship or reduced circumstances caused by a seemingly unjust outcome resulting from divorce proceedings in another jurisdiction where no comparable remedy is now available to the applicant. It is intended to do so in a just and equitable fashion."

[172] Although it was generally accepted that neither party was aware of the true value of the trust fund at the time of divorce.

[173] This question previously arose in the context of guardianship and adoption. In *Northampton County Council v ABF and MBF* [1982] I.L.R.M. 164, Hamilton J. examined the merits of a case already subject to the jurisdiction of the English courts on the basis that the respondent in this case, an English citizen, sought to rely on Art.41 of the

Just because there is a connection between one of the parties to a case and Ireland, why should the Irish courts be permitted to impose their own moral judgment as to the support obligations of a man to his former wife,[174] despite a foreign court, with manifestly stronger connections with the parties, holding otherwise? Traditionally, private international law adopts a neutral attitude toward the substantive content of foreign laws, subject only to the public policy proviso. Although Quirke J. sought to justify his intervention in this case on the basis that he was not reviewing the correctness of the foreign judgment, but instead could only "fill the gap" created, it simply does not prove compelling. The presence of a "gap" is a purely subjective assertion; taking a rational approach one would expect a court delivering judgment in a case to consider all relevant matters and leave no gaps. Yet a court of another jurisdiction with different moral tendencies can subsequently deem there to be a "gap", thereby permitting it to impose its opinions.

There is significant potential for this problem to be further exacerbated with the recent publication of the European Commission's Green Paper titled *Conflict of Laws in Matters Concerning Matrimonial Property Regimes, including the Question of Jurisdiction and Mutual Rec-*

Constitution. Although having no connection with Ireland, Hamilton J. permitted the respondent to make such a claim. His reasoning was based on principles of natural law, whereby Art.41, and indeed other fundamental rights under the Constitution, have their origin in the natural law, thereby giving it universal application, regardless of citizenship issues.

Since this decision, the Irish courts have adopted a much more pragmatic approach to such cases, analysing the bases for any claims seeking to establish a connection with Ireland so as to have a case heard here, despite proceedings in another jurisdiction.

See *Kent County Council v CS* [1984] I.L.R.M. 292 (distinguishing the judgment of Hamilton J. in *Northampton County Council v ABF and MBF* [1982] I.L.R.M. 164); *Oxfordshire County Council v JH and VH*, unreported, High Court, Costello J., May 1988.

[174] Part III of the Family Law Act 1995 can be traced back to previous English legislation in this area, the Matrimonial and Family Proceedings Act 1984. The Irish Law Reform Commission addressed this area of law prior to the enactment of the 1995 Act, and expressed the stance Irish law ought to take in relation to ancillary relief for foreign divorces. Its comments suggest it to be permissible for an Irish court to impose its own views as to the appropriate level of maintenance for a spouse following a foreign divorce, despite divorce not being available in Ireland at that time:

"In cases where a divorce is recognised…the [Irish] Court should have a discretionary power, acting on the principles of our domestic legislation, to protect the rights of a spouse with respect to maintenance, occupation and beneficial ownership of the family home and barring orders."

See Law Reform Commission, *Report on the Recognition of Foreign Divorces and Legal Separations* (LRC 10-1985), p.27.

ognition.[175] The potential of such a reform would be to permit citizens of different Member States, living in another Member State, to choose the law of divorce they wish. This could result in Irish courts granting a divorce between a Swedish couple living in Ireland on the basis of Swedish law. Whilst the Commission asserts that such a reform would not be the harmonisation of divorce law throughout the European Union, but instead the rules governing the choice of law in this field, there are real fears that it will undermine the Irish divorce system.[176]

If a court can act in such a manner in matters concerning divorce, then why not include pre-nuptial agreements? If parties come before an Irish court seeking a divorce, and there is a pre-nuptial agreement executed in another jurisdiction, can it be applied? Initially it would seem that this would depend on there being a choice of law clause in the pre-nuptial agreement. Traditional choice of law rules would dictate that the validity of such an agreement is to be determined by the laws of the place of contracting.[177] Nonetheless, modern developments within this field of law tend to focus on the level of interest both jurisdictions have with the proceedings.[178] As such, one can imagine the situation where an Irish court faced with such a predicament would have to consider the validity of a pre-nuptial agreement. The general approach to such a scenario in the United States of America is to apply the law of the State where the contract was executed, unless that law is contrary to the public policy of the

---

[175]   COM(2006) 400 Final (SEC(2006) 952), 17 July 2006, available at http://eur-lex.europa.eu/ LexUriServ/site/en/com/2006/com2006_0400en01.pdf

   The catalyst for this report was the substantial increase in couples of diverse nationality living together in other Member States. Five million people in the European Union live in a country other than their country of birth. It is further estimated that there are some 2.5 million items of real property owned by married couples in Member States different from that of their residence. Also, 170,000 divorces each year, equating to 16 per cent of all divorces, concern couples of diverse nationality (p.3 of Green Paper). The Commission claims that the subsequent legal difficulties involved in such disputes has given rise to the need to unify this area of law.

[176]   See Smyth, "EU split likely on commission's divorce plan" *The Irish Times*, July 15, 2006; "Irish law on divorce defended" *The Irish Times*, July 15, 2006.

[177]   Such an approach was initially adopted in the United States of America; see Restatement of Conflict of Laws 332.

[178]   This is evident in the United States of America where in *Lewis v Lewis* 748 P.2d 1362, 1365 (Hawaii 1988) the parties were residents in New York when they executed a pre-nuptial agreement and married. They then moved to Hawaii, and subsequently divorced. The court applied Hawaiian law so as to test the validity of the pre-nuptial agreement because Hawaii had a greater interest in the matter than New York due to a number of factors, including, the parties had been living there for several years, and their most expensive piece of property was located in Hawaii.

State where performance was sought.[179] As argued throughout this book, public policy ought to accord with the autonomy and privacy of individuals entering marriage, therefore recognising a foreign pre-nuptial agreement in such circumstances.

It is submitted that such a scenario ought to be actionable under Irish law, because if Irish courts can act with a sense of universal wisdom in relation to divorce and ancillary relief, then why not in relation to pre-nuptial agreements. There is no substantive argument supporting a distinction to be drawn between the two.

CONCLUSION

The level of judicial discretion in the field of ancillary relief, as highlighted in this chapter, weighs too heavily in favour of flexibility, to the detriment of clarity and certainty. This illustrates the need to amend this area of law. It is submitted that a pre-nuptial agreement would be a welcome development in Irish law. There are several grounds upon which this can be achieved.

If the Irish courts are to adopt a "yardstick" in the calculation of ancillary relief, then it should only represent a presumption, accompanied by a means of rebutting it. The best means of rebutting such a presumption comes in the form of a pre-nuptial agreement. It is submitted that failure to accommodate the rebuttable nature of such a "yardstick" would result in arbitrary decisions in ancillary relief cases, to the detriment of those concerned in such cases. Although the future of a "yardstick" in Irish law is far from clear, any future judicial consideration needs to be accompanied by an analysis of the alternatives to any such rule, thereby paving the way for the acceptance of pre-nuptial agreements.

The Irish judiciary is beginning to find favour with the need to attain certainty and finality in family law matters. The introduction of "clean break" divorce is representative of this. This has resulted in a greater deference to pre-existing separation agreements in ancillary relief cases. Respect for the private ordering of family law matters is growing amongst the Irish judiciary, resulting in the acceptance of the ability for parties to "bargain in the shadow of love".[180] It is asserted that the natural progression of this phenomenon is the acceptance and enforcement of pre-nup-

---

[179] See *Black v Powers* Record No. 1544-05-1, Court of Appeals Virginia, April 25, 2006, Humphreys J.

[180] This phrase is an adaptation taken from the title of Bix, "Bargaining in the Shadow of Love: The Enforcement of Premarital Agreements and How We Think About Marriage" (1999) 40 Wm. & Mary L. Rev. 145.

tial agreements. In addition to this, the recent acknowledgment of marriage as representing a partnership/contract eliminates traditional barriers to the private ordering of matrimonial matters. From this it is clear that a fresh approach is being taken to interpreting Art.41 of the Constitution. Marriage no longer represents a public status, formed on the basis of a perpetual union in the eyes of the State. Instead, it reflects the reasoned decision of two parties to enter into a committed relationship. Increasingly the judiciary are deferring to the judgment of the parties to a marriage as to its course, conduct and termination, and subsequent distribution of assets. With this fresh perspective, the path is now clear for the introduction of pre-nuptial agreements. The legal instruments are already in place, in the form of contract law, to regulate these agreements, thus causing one to believe that it is only a matter of time before such agreements are enforceable in Ireland.

A pre-nuptial agreement, although formulated before marriage, takes effect simultaneously with the marriage. In short, marriage is a condition precedent to the execution of pre-nuptial agreements. Consequently, such agreements ought to come under the protection of family autonomy. With society ready for the acceptance of such agreements, and the legal structure being available to regulate them, it is submitted that pre-nuptial agreements ought to become part of Irish law.

6. Conclusion

With over 30,000 millionaires now living in Ireland,[1] it is no longer a question of *if* a pre-nuptial agreement will present itself before an Irish court, but *when*. Irish society has changed dramatically in the last 20 years. People now enter marriage having already joined the property ladder, or attained lucrative employment, thus causing them to consider the need to protect personal acquirements, due to the possibility of divorce. The means of accommodating this new-found philosophy in Irish society, whilst protecting the institution of marriage, is to introduce enforceable pre-nuptial agreements. This would rectify a small, but growing, short-coming concerning marriage in Ireland; but there is also need for greater reform in this area.

With the introduction of divorce into Irish law the fundamental rationale supporting traditional notions of marriage was extinguished. Marriage no longer automatically represents an irrevocable union between a man and a woman for life; instead it is a revocable union, akin to a partnership. The perpetual nature of marriage was deemed its most fundamental characteristic and rendered such a relationship unique, and with its eradication there is a need to examine the concept of marriage as a whole.

Traditionally, marriage has been deemed a public institution, thereby justifying state regulation. With sociological developments, however, support for the State's role in marriage is in rapid decline. Family diversity is an ever-increasing phenomenon in Irish society. There is a need for the law to appreciate this. The constitutional family, based on marriage, fails to recognise a substantial proportion of what society regards as families. The Constitution can no longer stigmatise non-marital couples who have children, or those in permanent committed relationships who are not willing to enter marriage, when society freely accepts them. The Constitution is said to be a "living"[2] document, capable of keeping pace with social developments. If this is true then there is a need for urgent reform of its perception of the family, and consequently marriage.

The narrow prescriptive approach adopted by Irish courts in cases concerning family formation is no longer tenable. The *form* a family is supposed to take can no longer be indicative of there being a family; instead, the *function* ought to represent the defining characteristic. The

---

[1] Slattery, "Republic now second wealthiest nation" *The Irish Times,* July 11, 2006.
[2] *Sinnott v Minister for Education* [2001] 2 I.R. 545 at 680 *per* Murray J. (as he then was).

European Court of Human Rights has embraced this philosophy and protected it by adopting a broad functional approach to interpreting the constituent elements of a family. The introduction of such a mode of interpretation would result in the constitutional family being redefined in a manner independent of marriage. Consequently, marriage would no longer enjoy the quasi-constitutional protection currently extolled, thereby facilitating reform of this institution.

A constant stumbling-block to the reformation of marriage is the failure to address the issue of the perceived need to define marriage. Definitions, although concise and clear, have one major downfall, that is, by defining what something is, one also defines what it is not. In a social context, such as marriage, this invariably leads to discrimination. Marriage itself ought not to be defined. If there is a need to illustrate its existence and meaning, then we ought to establish a conceptual framework setting out the factors and elements typically associated with marriage.

Furthermore, the State definition of marriage ought to be discarded. With marriage comes a plethora of rights and privileges, and by limiting access to this institution the State is manifestly discriminating against those currently unable to enter marriage. The State uses marriage as a proxy through which it can regulate society. There is, however, no justification for using marriage in this manner. Such state interference is a violation of the privacy, autonomy and dignity of those who are party to a marriage.

Generally marriage is deemed to be a public institution. In order to undertake reform in this area it is necessary to postulate a moral argument capable of contending with such a public phenomenon, before asserting what marriage ought to represent. Therefore, although the core argument concerning the state regulation of marriage is the conflict between individual autonomy and paternalism, there is a need to defer to egalitarian philosophies also, so as to appreciate the perceived public element of marriage. Principles of equality demonstrate the discrimination apparent in the state regulation of marriage by virtue of its under-inclusive definition of marriage. On this basis the argument for reform attracts public support. Central to any reform is the need to respect individual autonomy and privacy, and other related concepts flowing from the concept of "dignity". The decision to marry is one of life's most important and defining moments; as such, the aspirations and objectives of those seeking to marry ought to be recognised and protected.

By according those wishing to enter marriage the privacy they desire as to the form of marriage they seek to enter, the "common good" is enhanced by virtue of the inherent respect for autonomy and dignity this would involve. So as to accommodate such an interpretation of marriage, it is submitted that a contractual model of marriage should be adopted. The law of contract, through regulation of a relational contract, would be capable of governing the formation of marriage in a rational manner whilst deferring to the decision-making process of the individuals to the marriage. The introduction of a contractual model of marriage is conducive to recent developments in Irish law in this area. No-fault divorce injects an amoral termination of marriage into Irish society, thus removing the uniqueness once characteristic of marriage, resulting in a rationality typically associated with contractual matters. Moreover, by perceiving marriage as a form of committed partnership, the element of negotiation present in forming business partnerships becomes a possibility in the context of marriage. By setting the terms to their marital contract, individuals can enter the form of marriage that best suits their own needs and expectations. The forum for such negotiation is a pre-nuptial agreement.

With the transposition of marriage from status to contract, the recognition and enforcement of pre-nuptial agreements has become more popular. Traditionally, pre-nuptial contracts in contemplation of future separation were deemed contrary to public policy. Nonetheless, such a view was cast aside as courts began to recognise the ability of pre-nuptial agreements to bring certainty, stability and clarity to marital relations. With "no-fault" divorce and the ability to obtain a "clean break" resulting in the termination of marriage becoming more prevalent, there is a need to balance the law concerning marriage with a reassessment of the formation of marriage. It has been asserted throughout this book that the optimum means of doing so is to recognise pre-nuptial agreements as being enforceable. It is hoped that this will alleviate some of the perceived "risk" in getting married, thereby restoring popularity in the institution of marriage.

Traditionally, the unique nature of marriage was thought to derive from its perpetual nature. With the advent of divorce it is clear that this is no longer the case; in fact one must question its validity as a proposition even before the introduction of divorce. It is submitted that the unique nature of marriage is the formation of a committed relationship personal to the parties to it. Each and every marriage is unique and individual. It ought to reflect the wishes and intentions of the parties to it. Gradually the law in Ireland is beginning to appreciate this as marriage is being recognised as a partnership. On foot of this, there is no moral basis for the failure to recognise pre-nuptial agreements. If parties to a marriage deem a pre-nuptial agreement to be necessary to their marriage then this autonomous decision ought to be respected. The only role of the law is to maintain the procedural correctness of such contracts and the preceding negotiations. Philosophies expounding individual rights such as privacy, autonomy and equality are not meaningless propositions. These rights cannot be exercised in one context and arbitrarily cast aside in another. The right of people to enter marriage on their own terms is manifest and ought to be protected and promoted. It is hoped that the enforcement of pre-nuptial agreements in this jurisdiction will foster such ideals.

The regulation of pre-nuptial agreements is necessary so as not to devalue the institution of marriage. Experience from other jurisdictions where pre-nuptial contracts are enforceable demonstrates the utility of insisting on independent legal advice prior to entering such an agreement, the full disclosure of assets, a clause stipulating periodic review of the contract, and dispute resolution clauses. In deference to the autonomy of individuals and their ability to make rational decisions, the standard of review for pre-nuptial contracts ought to concentrate on procedural rather than substantive issues. Furthermore, such review should only be conducted at the execution stage and not the performance stage, thereby eliminating a paternalistic form of review. A number of advantages would attach to such a proposal, including the fostering of the rights to autonomy and privacy, and also it would promote gender equality in the long run as women, generally considered to be the economically weaker spouses, would be on an equal footing with men at the time of execution. In addition, it is thought prudent to enforce a "cooling-off" period between the date of execution and the day of the marriage ceremony; 21 days would appear sufficient.

The willingness of the Irish judiciary to achieve a "clean break" where possible, and the recent judicial deference to separation agreements and "full and final settlement clauses" in subsequent ancillary relief disputes, represent an appreciation of factors such as self-determination, independence, self-sufficiency and finality. In turn, it has been posited that these elements represent the foundations upon which pre-nuptial agreements ought to be recognised and enforced. Consequently, it is submitted that, in keeping with the tide of Irish family law, the private ordering of marital matters ought to be fostered, with the enforcement of pre-nuptial agreements being accommodated.

At present the framework is in place under which a pre-nuptial agreement can be recognised in Irish law. Section 20 of the Family Law (Divorce) Act 1996, which sets out factors to be accounted for in the determination of ancillary relief, requires the court to consider all the circumstances of a case so as to declare an order in the interests of justice. It is foreseeable that a case may come before an Irish court, in which this objective can only be achieved by recognising a pre-nuptial agreement.

Recent judicial pronouncements as to the structure of marriage representing a partnership, favour the fostering and appreciation of the autonomy and privacy of parties to such a marriage. By recognising marriage as a partnership, regulated by contract, the courts are almost required to have regard to the decision-making prowess of the parties to a marriage. Resultantly, the private ordering of matrimonial matters becomes more amenable to Irish jurisprudence, thus providing a means whereby pre-nuptial agreements may become enforceable.

It has been argued throughout this book that there is a need for widespread reform as to the legal interpretation of marriage, and consequently the family, which in turn would pave the way for pre-nuptial agreements. Yet this may not be necessary for pre-nuptial agreements to become enforceable. Under the rubric of Art.41, it ought to be permissible for the parties to a marriage to decide to enter a pre-nuptial agreement which would enjoy the subsequent constitutional protection of family autonomy. As marriage is essentially a condition precedent to the execution of a pre-nuptial agreement, such an agreement becomes effective simultaneously with marriage, and under Irish law the formation of a "family". As such the decision to enter a pre-nuptial agreement ought to be respected as one exercised in the realm of family autonomy.

Furthermore, the Irish courts may have to contend with the application of such agreements in the context of foreign marriages. If the Irish courts are deemed qualified to impose their moral judgment on the provision of ancillary relief following a divorce granted by a foreign court, then why not extend this logic to the recognition of foreign pre-nuptial agreements? Moreover, there is a strong basis upon which one can foresee the Irish courts being forced to contend with a pre-nuptial agreement in the context of a foreign marriage. At present Irish courts can give judgment on matters subsequent to a foreign divorce, such as ancillary relief. It is thought that the ability to consider matters prior to the marriage and its formation is a natural progression from this point, thereby giving rise to the potential for pre-nuptial agreements to a foreign marriage to come under the scope of Irish law.

To conclude, the legal interpretation of marriage in Ireland is in drastic need of reform. At present the State is permitted to impose its paternal viewpoint on one of the most private realms of life. The decision to marry is a life-defining moment, personal to those party to it. The autonomy and privacy of such individuals ought to be respected, thereby permitting them to enter the form of marriage they choose. A natural consequence of such reform would be the entitlement of parties to enter pre-nuptial agreements. It is asserted that such a development in Irish law would bring some much needed clarity and certainty to the all too ambiguous concept of ancillary relief. It is noted, however, that reform of the law concerning marriage may not be necessary for pre-nuptial agreements to be recognised as enforceable in Ireland. There is compelling argument to suggest that the framework is already present. Nonetheless, it is concluded that broad reform is needed in this area of Irish law, so as to properly promote and protect the fundamental rights of the citizens of the State.

Index

The letter "n" indicates a footnote, for example, 105n120 indicates footnote 120 on page 105.

Abbreviations used in index
PNAs—Pre-nuptial agreements
ECtHR—European Court of Human Rights